Raves for
Jen Lancaster
Bright Lights, Big Ass

"Lessons we've learned from Jen Lancaster: Bitter is the new black; Target is the new Neiman's; pit bulls and surly neighbors are the new Samanthas, Charlottes and Mirandas; and midday whiskey is always a good idea. *Bright Lights, Big Ass* is a bittersweet treat for anyone who's ever survived the big city."　　　　　　　　　—Jennifer Weiner

"Refreshing, hysterical, illuminating! From the title on, *Bright Lights, Big Ass* is an anti-haute hoot. In a voice that's charming and snarky, hilarious and human, Jen Lancaster tells the ultraglamorous truth about real big-city living. And it's better than anything on TV. Jen Lancaster does not teeter around on Manolo Blahniks or have lobster for breakfast. She eats pork chops and Lucky Charms. She dreams of shopping sprees at Target. She works temp jobs and spends too much time Googling things online. She wears footie pajamas. In other words, she's a lot like the rest of us. Thank God! And this wonderful, sweet, funny book proves once and for all that Carrie Bradshaw and her *Sex and the City* cronies are big, fat liars. Of course. Of course they are."
　　　　　—Lori Jakiela, author of *Miss New York Has Everything*

"*Bright Lights, Big Ass* is brightly crafted and big on laughs. Jen Lancaster is wickedly funny, refreshingly honest and totally unapologetic."
　　　　　—Caprice Crane, author of *Stupid and Contagious*
　　　　　and *Forget About It*

"Jen Lancaster may be one of the few authors around capable of writing her own sitcom; she's smart, wry, and never afraid to point out her own shortcomings while letting us into her uniquely funny world."
　　　　　—Melanie Lynne Hauser, author of *Super Mom Saves the World*

"Jen Lancaster is the Holy Trinity of funny."
　　　　　—Nicole Del Sesto, author of *All Encompassing Trip*

continued...

"After reading *Bright Lights, Big Ass*, I'm convinced Jen Lancaster is the illegitimate love child of Nora Ephron and David Sedaris. She's simply that great—a genetic hybrid of two of America's most loved writers. In *Bright Lights, Big Ass*, Jen Lancaster gives the proverbial 'finger' to the Carrie Bradshaw lifestyle trading Barneys, Manolo Blahnik, and Bergdorf's for her very own shopping Holy Trinity: Target, Trader Joe's and Ikea, allowing women everywhere to rejoice in their $60 Issac Mizrahi Target coats."

—Robert Rave, author of *Conversations & Cosmopolitans:
How to Give Your Mother a Hangover*

"Jen Lancaster is like David Sedaris with pearls and a supercute handbag."   —Jennifer Coburn

"Part *Seinfeld*, part antidote to *Sex and the City*, *Bright Lights, Big Ass* is the must read for anyone who has ever suffered through a regretfully torturous workout with her trainer, a run-in with irrational, perhaps psychotic neighbors, a long-winded, insipid telemarketer or the black hole known as Ikea. (And really, isn't this everyone?) Nothing and no one is spared from Jen Lancaster's acerbically sharp wit, as she gives voice to all of the things we wish we could say, but don't. I defy you not to laugh out loud on nearly every page. Someone give this girl her own show, already! *That* would be must-see TV."

— Allison Winn Scotch, author of
The Department of Lost and Found

Bitter Is the New Black

···

"The funniest new author from the blogosphere. A must read."
—Jessica Cutler, Author of *The Washingtonienne*

"A wry account of job seeking peppered with scathing one-liners."
—*The Washington Post*

"An irreverent, abrasive, and funny self-portrait."
—*Chattanooga Times–Free Press*

New American Library
Published by New American Library, a division of
Penguin Group (USA) Inc., 375 Hudson Street,
New York, New York 10014, USA
Penguin Group (Canada), 90 Eglinton Avenue East, Suite 700, Toronto,
Ontario M4P 2Y3, Canada (a division of Pearson Penguin Canada Inc.)
Penguin Books Ltd., 80 Strand, London WC2R 0RL, England
Penguin Ireland, 25 St. Stephen's Green, Dublin 2,
Ireland (a division of Penguin Books Ltd.)
Penguin Group (Australia), 250 Camberwell Road, Camberwell, Victoria 3124,
Australia (a division of Pearson Australia Group Pty. Ltd.)
Penguin Books India Pvt. Ltd., 11 Community Centre, Panchsheel Park,
New Delhi - 110 017, India
Penguin Group (NZ), 67 Apollo Drive, Rosedale, North Shore,
Auckland 1311, New Zealand (a division of Pearson New Zealand Ltd.)
Penguin Books (South Africa) (Pty.) Ltd., 24 Sturdee Avenue,
Rosebank, Johannesburg 2196, South Africa

Penguin Books Ltd., Registered Offices:
80 Strand, London WC2R 0RL, England

First published by New American Library,
a division of Penguin Group (USA) Inc.

First Printing, May 2007
10   9   8   7   6   5   4   3

Copyright © Jen Lancaster, 2007
All rights reserved

N
A   REGISTERED TRADEMARK—MARCA REGISTRADA
L

LIBRARY OF CONGRESS CATALOGING-IN-PUBLICATION DATA:

Lancaster, Jen, 1967–
    Bright lights, big ass / Jen Lancaster.
        p.   cm.
    ISBN: 978-0-451-22125-4
    1. Lancaster, Jen, 1967–   2. Authors, American—21st century—Biography.   3.
Chicago (Ill.)—Social life and customs.   I. Title.
    PS3612.A54748Z466   2007
    813'.6—dc22
    [B]   2006032863

Set in Bulmer MT
Designed by Elke Sigal

Printed in the United States of America

PUBLISHER'S NOTE
While the author has made every effort to provide accurate telephone numbers and Internet
addresses at the time of publication, neither the publisher nor the author assumes any responsibility for errors, or for changes that occur after publication. Further, publisher does not have
any control over and does not assume any responsibility for author or third-party Web sites or
their content.

Bright Lights, Big Ass

A Self-Indulgent, Surly Ex-Sorority Girl's Guide
to Why It Often Sucks in the City,
or Who Are These Idiots and
Why Do They All Live Next Door to Me?

Jen Lancaster

 NEW AMERICAN LIBRARY

For Angie, Carol, Jennifer, and Wendy,

who were there from the very first word

and who promise to host an intervention

(complete with umbrella drinks)

should the need arise

Contents

These stories are true, and the characters are real, as are the events. However, I've changed names and descriptions to protect the innocent and to keep my stupid neighbors from egging my house.

Where skin-deep is the mode, your traditional
domestic values are not going to take root and flourish.

—JAY MCINERNEY, *BRIGHT LIGHTS, BIG CITY*

....

You're moving to Chicago? Ha!
You'll come crawling home the first time
you bounce a rent check.

—TODD LANCASTER, MAY 6, 1996

Bright Lights, Big Ass

Dear Carrie Bradshaw,

You are a fucking liar.

And for that matter, so are Jay McInerney, Bret Easton Ellis, and everyone else who's ever claimed city life to be nothing but a magical, mythical, all-around transcendent experience chock-full of beautiful, morally ambiguous people lounging around at fabulous parties, clad in stilettos, and offering up free piles of blow.

Because, seriously?

No one's ever offered me anything more provocative than a cough drop or a hug in my ten years here in Chicago. Which is fine. I mean, I really don't *want* cocaine or a threesome. Frankly, I'm too busy trying to scrape up rent money to engage in that kind of stuff, anyway. (But it might be nice to be *asked*, for crying out loud.)

My point is you and the rest of your ilk on *Sex and the City* painted an inaccurate portrait of city life. Most of us don't spend our days getting buffed and polished at the city's finest spas and then ripped at the most au courant watering holes. And we don't hunker down in trendy bistros over $40 breakfasts while discussing spanking an investment banker with Samantha, Miranda, and Charlotte, either.

Real urbanites are way more likely to have a collection of shopping bags from Target than Prada. The majority are never going to know what it's like to get a chemical peel by a meaty-armed Swede named Inga.

And they're okay with that.

And you know what?

I am, too.

The thing is, although metropolitan living can be fabulous at times, more often than not it's just me watching reality TV with my husband, Fletch, seeing rats so often I've named my favorites "Bitey" and "Señor Skinnytail," and accidentally reporting the guy next door to Homeland Security.

In no way, shape, or form does your fictional existence mirror my real urban life and I thought you should know.

And if you don't like it, you can kiss my big, fat, pink, puffy down parka.

Best,

Jen

Dear Alderman,

I'm writing you regarding the condition of my block on Racine Ave. In the past four months, the amount of garbage littering the street has increased dramatically.

I'm particularly concerned about the sidewalk area bordering the empty lot on the west side of the road. Last year the area was neatly maintained with gravel covering most of it. Recently it has become a dumping ground for take-out food containers, empty beer bottles, condom wrappers, and this morning, the pièce de résistance, a single woman's slipper and *an old pair of men's pants*.

I have no idea what's happening on my block while I sleep, but if it involves someone losing their pants, it can't be good and I would like you to make it stop.

Thanks in advance,

Jen Lancaster

Dear Yellow Pages Customer Care,

I'm writing to inform you of the Leaning Tower of Phone Books you saw fit to station outside the gate of my condo complex last week.

There are sixteen townhomes in this development. Most of the residents here are single professionals (read fat girls), although a few of us are married or, um, partnered. But in total, approximately twenty-two people live here.

So, can you please explain the math that led you to believe that sixteen units/twenty-two people require *forty-eight sets of White Pages* and *forty-eight sets of Yellow Pages*? Although I understand the rationale of dropping off a few extra books, leaving *sixty-four* extra is not only patently ridiculous but also incredibly wasteful.

Should you care to salvage any of the phone books that have not yet been peed on by my dog, I suggest you do so quickly before something unfortunate happens to them, which may or may not involve a book of matches and a bonfire. (And possibly a pair of pants, although I do not hold you responsible for their presence.)

Looking forward to a speedy resolution,

Jen Lancaster

To: angie_at_home, carol_at_home, wendy_at_home,
jen_at_work
From: jen@jenlancaster.com
Subject: *party over, oops, out of time*

Howdy,

I wasn't yet close to most of you guys during my fabulous old
life, so you'll have to take my word for it when I say back in the
dot-com era Fletch and I were true social butterflies—not a
weekend went by that we didn't see friends. Our calendars
were filled with dates for dinners, drinks, parties, mixers, gather-
ings, brunches, etc. We were Paris Hilton (minus the skank).

Of course, now we're old, fat, and far less liquid, so those days
are long gone . . . which brings me to my present dilemma.

A nice couple is coming over tonight. It's the first time we've
had anyone here since we got our lives back and I don't really
remember how to entertain anymore. Sure, I can still handle the
physical aspects of having guests—thorough cleaning, fresh flowers on the mantel, cookie-scented candles, proper lighting, delicious snacks, etc.

But the interaction aspect?

Not so much.

I'm afraid since I've used proper conversation skills so infrequently in the past couple of years, I've become socially retarded. I fear when our guests get here I'll blurt something Peter Griffin–like from *The Family Guy*, e.g., "Bob Crane of *Hogan's Heroes* had his skull bashed in by his friend who liked to videotape him having rough sex."

Then Fletch will play a Helmet album while demonstrating our awesome new vacuum, a cat will jump on the buffet and lick the cheese, Maisy will crap on the floor, and we'll call it a night.

But I'm probably just being paranoid, right?

Jen

To: angie_at_home, carol_at_home, wendy_at_home, jen_at_work
From: jen@jenlancaster.com
Subject: *party over, oops, out of time, part 2*

10:03 p.m.—Fletch whips out the Dyson.

10:05 p.m.—Guests remember a previous engagement and leave.

And you all thought I was kidding.

Sucks and the City

I'm clad in my favorite power suit, crafted from the wool of cosseted Australian sheep (of course) and lovingly pieced together by the finest tailors ever to lay thread to silk. My portfolio gleams in an equally polished and manicured hand and my Chanel sunglasses hold back a perfectly arranged coif. Poised on the edge of my seat in the senior vice president of Operations' office, I'm crushing my interview, or at least I am until he asks the one thing I'm not sure how to answer:

"If you're a former vice president, why exactly do y'all want a job gittin' my coffee?"

An excellent question.

For which I have no response.

I take a deep breath and surreptitiously glance at my surroundings in order to buy a minute. The senior vice president's office is mostly chrome and glass and skyline, yet it's not cold or impersonal. Likely it's because Mr. James, the man behind the title, radiates such warmth. First, his accent is incredibly disarming. How do you *not* love anyone who says "y'all" without a trace of irony? Perhaps it's an inaccurate prejudice, but it seems like almost everyone with a Southern accent is nice. With their slow, long consonants, I bet they have a really hard time yelling at anyone effectively. By the time they'd get out the appropriate epithet about goin' straight to Hades for cutting them off in traffic, the offending driver would already be halfway down the off-ramp.

This office really speaks to Mr. James's personality. A couple of deeply green rubber trees soften the light from the window and lush, variegated ivies trail down from the top of his credenza. I read an article once about the effects of plants in the workplace—supposedly they not only clean the air but also reduce employee stress.[1]

All the surfaces in his office are littered items that speak volumes about his personality. There's a two-foot-long paper-clip chain draped over the corner of his computer monitor, likely constructed during a boring conference call. There's something oddly appealing about someone who's not too professional to fidget on occasion. Under a pile of paperwork I see the end of a familiar pink wrapper, telling me he was probably eating Almond Roca before our interview. (I sort of love anyone who thinks there's nothing wrong with candy for breakfast.)

Handsome sterling-framed photographs line the other end of his L-shaped desk. Posed on a sailboat is a pretty young

---

[1] Of course, not laying employees off without giving them a reason also reduces stress, but that's another story.

blonde girl and an identical older blonde woman, both with big, flashy white teeth, the sun setting in the background. Another photo shows a white German shepherd and a yellow Lab, covered with leaves and mud, smiling those big openmouthed doggie grins, ankle-deep in a creek. A dozen more pictures of happy people are scattered in the corner, with State of Texas and rainbow flags forming an ad hoc backdrop for them all.

Okay, honestly? I didn't know you could be both gay *and* Texan. I mean, come on, *Bush Country*? It's a president! It's a euphemism! It's heterosexuality on a stick! The joy of realizing my two favorite characteristics could be combined must be a lot like what the guy who invented Reese's Peanut Butter Cups felt.[2]

With his sweet drawl and easy laugh, I desperately want to land this assignment. It's only supposed to last a couple of months, which is perfect because this will neatly bridge the gap between selling my first book and receiving a check for it. (The book sold based on a proposal, outline, and a few sample chapters, so I actually have to finish writing it by June 1. But I also have to generate enough income in the interim to keep my lights on, so here I am.)

I envision him and me gossiping like sorority girls after the oddly clad chief executive officer stops by his office. Seriously, I've seen this man on CNBC and, *damn*. I don't care what Marc Jacobs says, there's no good way to pair windowpane plaid, vests, and stripes together[3] without appearing to

---

[2] Harry Burnett Reese. Because I? Am all about the Trivial Pursuit answers.

[3] Gentlemen, a bit of advice, if I may? The fine staff at Brooks Brothers will never allow you to leave the store looking like a well-tailored rodeo clown. Just so you know.

have stepped straight off the set of *Newsies*. "*He's* the CEO?" I'd ask. "Pfft, not in *those* pants he's not," Mr. James would reply. Then we'd explode into a fit of giggles before tottering off for a lunch that included a lot of wine.

Not only do I want this man for my boss, I yearn for him to be my boy-friend. Which, for those of us happily married, should never be confused with "boyfriend." The former includes having slushy fruit drinks while singing show tunes at Sidetracks and a penchant for J-Lo movies, the latter a vow-violating touching of one another's goodies. But the thing is, I'm afraid if I can't answer this question properly, it's never going to happen.

Even without the boss, this is a choice assignment on its own merits. My recruiter told me the assistant is essentially there to answer the CEO's call if Mr. James is on another line. Otherwise, he's almost entirely self-sufficient. He does need someone to get his coffee, but only because he's got arthritis in his ankles. The last girl who worked here managed to arrange her whole wedding from the desk, with the boss's blessing.[4] I practically salivated when she described all the uninterrupted time I'd have to write.

I shift uncomfortably in my chair while beaming the glazed, terrified smile of a Miss America contestant who's completely forgotten her platform after having dropped her flaming baton. *Was it AIDS? Animals? Animals with AIDS? And do you think the judge will hold his second-degree burns against me? Shit!*

At this point I should mention that the portfolio's

---

[4] And he even bought her a toaster off her Williams-Sonoma registry!

pleather, that my fake Chanel sunglasses are strategically placed to cover up my overblown roots, and that the outfit's an ill-fitting reminder of the brief period in the dot-com days when I was rich. What used to be an Italian power suit is now a lethal weapon—one wrong inhale and hand-tooled ivory buttons will blast off my chest like buckshot. As my chances of working with this darling man will greatly diminish should a wayward endangered toggle accidentally blind him, I breathe in rapid, shallow gasps and mull over an appropriate answer.

Naturally, I can't fault him for asking. I mean, why *would* a former associate vice president be interviewing for a temporary assistant's position? Especially since back in the day I was a Prada-toting, insult-hurling, penthouse-dwelling smart-ass with *my own* pack of assistants ready to procure my hot beverages on demand.[5] I made important decisions, closed huge deals, and single-handedly kept the Nordstrom shoe department in business. However, after a particularly virulent (and not undeserved) bout of unemployment my world was forever altered. Due to my own arrogance[6] I didn't realize until far too late it was a bad idea to tell potential employers, "I don't get out of bed for less than $10,000 a month." Particularly since (a) we were in a recession at the time, and (b) with a bachelor's degree in political science, my only real skill was ordering people to bring me those lattes.

Eventually, the economy turned around and I was given a

---

[5] Vanilla latte, full fat, extra foamy, two Equals, and make it snappy. Ooh, and get me a maple scone, too!
[6] Read stupidity.

choice: go back to the business world or pursue a writing career. I went with the option that included working in polar-bear-print pajamas.

Mr. James senses my discomfort and smiles at me in encouragement. He leans forward and raises his eyebrows, the same way he would if we were having lunch and he simply couldn't wait to hear what juicy detail I might dish next. His sensitivity and geniality prove too much and I feel the word-vomit bubbling up in the back of my throat. Much as I try to stop the sound from spurting out of my mouth, I am wholly unsuccessful.

"Mr. James," I bleat, "I've got to be honest—"

"Aw, Jen, please call me Skip," he interjects.

"Okay, um, *Skip*." After temping and being in a subordinate position for so long, it feels strange to be allowed to call someone by their given name again. "Do you know Carrie Bradshaw?"

"Personally, or do you mean the character from *Sex and the City*?"

"The character."

"Well, I guess so, yes." His accent is so twee and cute it makes me want to put him in corduroy overalls and place him on a shelf. Yaa-iss.

"Here's the thing—Carrie Bradshaw is a fu—, I mean, a damn"—I cough—"*ahem*, a *dang* liar. Seriously, she lives in a chichi part of town in a great apartment and has forty thousand dollars' worth of shoes. She's forever out having drinks with her friends and she's *not* the kind of girl who goes to Dollar Beer Night at a seedy sports bar. She's all 'top shelf or don't bother, please.' Plus, every time a trendy restaurant opens? She's there, and you know they're the twenty-five-dollars-and-that's-just-the-dollop-of-goat-cheese-appetizer kind of places. She doesn't cook and buys all her meals out. She keeps sweaters in her oven, you know." I pause and catch a breath before another wave of verbal diarrhea hits.

"I watch the show on occasion, but I'm afraid I don't follow."

"Think about it—what does she do for a living?"

"She, um, has that column, right? About datin' and sex?" Say-ekks.

"Ding, ding, ding, yes! She's a writer. And she has/does all this cool stuff and she's not drowning in credit card debt, nor does she, you know, *shake it* on the side for extra cash. Although I bet Samantha would, if something happened to her PR agency. Miranda, too. My theory is she's dirtier than people think. A nice girl would never dye her hair that garish red. Although, really, their lives make me a little crazy. You'd think sometimes they'd just want to stay in and eat Raisinettes and watch old episodes of *Mystery Science Theater 3000* while tucked under a fluffy down comforter. All that grooming and trawling must get exhausting. Sometimes I want to yell at them, 'Hey! Stay home tonight for once! Balthazar will still be there tomorrow! Put a mask on, read something trashy in the tub, or, like, go take a pottery class. Slow down!' They're exhausted; no wonder they all look like they've served prison time on that show."

He nods and drawls, "I have no idea where you're going with this, but I'm certainly interested to find out."

"The point is Carrie Bradshaw set highly unrealistic expectations. I thought when I sold my book I'd have hundred-dollar bills hanging out of my pockets and it would be me commanding the best table at Balthy, sucking down their deep-cupped Goose Point Oysters, sipping Pol Roger Cuvée Sir Winston Churchill Brut '95. Or, if not rich, at least as cool as Carrie is so I'd make the kind of rich friends who'd have that kind of clout. Shoot, Mr. Big was probably always buying, you know? At the least, I figured I'd be able to live in the city without having to take mindlessly mortifying temp jobs before I get my advance check. But that's not reality."

"It's not?"

"Oh, *hel*— I mean, heck no. Don't get me wrong, I'm thrilled to have sold my book. But I still have to make some money so I can continue to live indoors until I get my first check."

"Have y'all been tempin' for a while? Aren't most assignments kinda like this one?"

"Yeah"—I laugh bitterly—"right."

"Are they so bad?" He makes "bad" into a multisyllable word—bay-ya-duh.

"Are you really interested or are you just humoring me because you think I'm unhinged and may go all Dick Cheney on you?"

He shakes his head. "Not sure yet. There's a possibility for this to go either way. Whyn't you tell me about some of them jobs and then I'll let y'all know?"

"Fair enough. Okay, so, after an entire year of working terrible and ridiculous temp jobs and putting together my book proposal, I'm ready for an enjoyable assignment. My recruiter tells me about this high-level, use-my-brain type of job at an architecture firm, and I'm like, 'Yes! Finally, a challenge!'"

"And was it?"

"If by 'challenge' you mean physically moving and sorting ninety filing cabinets full of musty, moldering, water-stained blueprints in the one part of the building without air conditioning, then yes. FYI? If you're looking for a manual laborer, the overweight, surly, ex–sorority girl wearing pearls may not be the best candidate."[7]

He chuckles and nods for me to continue.

"Anyway, when I wasn't busy hauling heavy, dirty things from Point A to Point B, my twenty-six-year-old, fresh-out-of-B-school boss enjoyed barking new and impossible tasks at me. Which was fun. Especially when I wasn't given tools to complete said tasks. For example, Little Miss MBA demanded I order more metal inserts for those fetid file drawers."

"That's not so awful, right?" he asks, leaning forward and resting his elbows on his sleek glass desk. He lowers his chin to his hands, still rapt with attention. His lips curve up and his smile makes his eyes all crinkly. I already adore this man—he's darling! Like I want to dress him in corduroy overalls and place him on a shelf in my bedroom.

"Correction—the custom-made file drawers. About which I had no manufacturing information. Or system upon which I could order them. Or official authorization to access said system if, in fact, one even existed. Or method to pay for the inserts, had I been able to track down the mystery drawers, gained access to said ordering system, and learned how to

---

[7] Seriously, I'm so lazy that many a time I've considered whizzing in our kitchen sink rather than climbing the stairs to our bathroom on the second floor.

operate it. My only resource was the girl? Who used to hold that job? And ended every sentence? In the middle of a phrase? With a question mark?"[8]

He covers his chin and mouth to suppress a grin.

"However, the beauty of being a temp is the ability to say with a straight face, 'Yes, I absolutely ordered them,' before dancing out of the building for the last time."[9]

"What'd y'all do before that?" They-ya-tuh.

"Prior to ordering imaginary items for architects, I had a short-term gig in the legal department of a company. This assignment wasn't so bad—a little collating, some filing, a bit of calendar management, and enough watercooler chat about last night's episode of *American Idol* to keep me if not happy, then at least relatively satisfied."

"That sounds kinda nice."

I agree. "Actually, it was, at least until the day the chief corporate counsel came back from his vacation. Prior to my arrival and his horrifically hairy-backed, Speedo-clad holiday in the south of France—by the way, I saw the photos and *I'm blind now*—"

Skip snorts a bit of coffee onto his French cuff. Without thinking, I grab a Starbucks napkin from his desk, dip it in my water glass, and hand it back to him.

"Start blotting. You don't want the stain to set. Anyway, the chief counsel had shipped four hundred thirty-page contracts to a client. Although he'd overnighted these docu-

[8] Do you care to guess? How helpful she was?
[9] Bonus superiority points awarded if you leave without stealing any office supplies.

ments, his client never received them. I suggested I call the client to confirm his correct address before reshipping them. However, he thought we—meaning me—would be better off simply faxing them on the office's miniature Playskool's My First Fax Machine. Now, let me see your cuff."

Skip holds out his wrist and the stain's noticeably smaller.

"See? Keep it up and it will be completely gone in a couple of minutes. Anyway, let's do the math, shall we? Four hundred contracts times thirty pages each on a piece of equipment practically covered in duckies and moo-cows.[10] As the attorney outlined the parameters of my assignment, I offered up a small prayer. *'Dear God, please allow me to walk the earth long enough to fax all twelve thousand frigging pages. Thank you. Amen.'* Unfortunately, the fax machine was not also blessed with such longevity and gave out around page 657. So, we went with my original plan, which was to ship the contracts."

Skip interjects, "It's all gone!" He turns his wrist over again and again, marveling at my mad stain-fighting skillz, yo. "But I'm sorry—you were sayin'?"

"While I prepared the mailing labels, I quickly assessed why the documents had never arrived. I popped into his office to explain the situation. *'Excuse me, sir?'* I asked, standing in his doorway. *'Um, I figured out why those documents you sent never arrived.'* Normally I'm not afraid of anyone, but there was something about this guy's steel gray eyes that really threw me. All flat and dead. Ick. Anyway, he was enraptured with his computer screen and he said, *'Uh-huh. And?'* *'Well,'* I

---

[10] The farmer says, "Be sure to use a cover sheet!"

told him, '*although I haven't been able to get the client on the phone to confirm this, I'm pretty sure you used the wrong address.*' '*Impossible,*' he replied with a gesture. I recall thinking, *Oh, hold the phone, did he just make* shoo-be-gone *motions at me?*

"I continued, '*But, sir, you sent them to the—*' He snapped, '*It's right. Ship it again.*' And yes, there was distinct shooing. Then he rolled his scary eyes and turned his back to me. '*But, this address was where the Wor—*' Before I could finish my statement, he rose and walked to the door. '*And that will be all, thank you,*' he said, shutting it in my face. So I dutifully completed the labels and sent the boxes off to Two WTC, NY, NY, which is better known as?" I ask.

Skip replies, "Ground Zero?"

I nod gravely. "The south tower."

"Wow. So, what'd you do then?" They-inn.

"Here's the thing—after 689 days of being unemployed (but who's counting?),[11] I totally appreciate the opportunity to work. But once in a while when I run into someone who's a bigger asshat than I could ever have been when I was a VP, I feel it's my duty to give them a gentle karmic reminder.

"On my last day with the legal department, I took it upon myself to do just that. I walked into his office and said, '*Excuse me, sir—hi, I'm Jen, you know, the temp who's been covering for Mary Ann? Anyway, I notice you shut your door a lot for privacy. And, I'm not really quite sure how to say this, but when you shut the door? It's not like a* magic *door or anything, so you don't actually become invisible when you close it. And you*

---

[11] Oh, yes. That's right. My mother was counting.

may not realize it, but anyone walking by can see in through your giant glass wall next to the closed door. And, the thing is, I was just thinking since you're chief counsel and all? It might be better if, um, the other employees didn't see you surfing teenaged-girl porn sites.'"

"No, y'all didn't!" He shrieks with laughter.

"Yes, I all did," I reply. While we giggle and wipe our eyes, the receptionist buzzes to inform Skip his next appointment has arrived and is waiting in the lobby.

"Well, Jen"—Jay-unn—"I think I got a purty good idea of what it would be like working together. Anything else I ought to know before y'all go?" Skip asks.

Minding my potentially dangerous buttons, I take a deep breath before delivering my final pitch. "Skip, I have to level with you. Working temp jobs is more than just a way to supplement my writing career and pay my cable bill. I mean, I used to be wealthy and obnoxious, spouting ridiculous sentiments like how I wouldn't ride the bus because 'the thing about mass transportation is it transports the masses.' But a while back I got a real wake-up call when my luxurious dot-com world came crashing down and I lost my executive position. However, as our financial situation improves, I sometimes forget those hard times. Given my propensity for raging narcissism, I occasionally need a coffee-carrying gig for reasons other than financial. Being someone's assistant, even temporarily, keeps me grounded. That's why I really want this job."

Skip tents his hands and hides most of his face behind it. "Jen, I've got to know one thang and it's important."

"What's that, sir, I mean, Skip?"

"If I look at teenaged-girl porn, are y'all gonna squeal on me?"

"Depends," I reply. "Are you planning on looking at any teenaged-girl porn?"

"I can't imagine I ever will." Wee-ill.

"Hmm, then I'd say we're good."

He extends his hand and reveals a huge smile. "All right, I guess I'll see y'all on Monday, maybe 'round nine a.m.?"

Wait, does that mean I got the job?

I got the job!

Knowing my suit can't possibly withstand a victory dance, instead I shake his proffered hand and reply, "I guess y'all wee-ill."

To: angie_at_home, carol_at_home, wendy_at_home, jen_at_work
From: jen@jenlancaster.com
Subject: *the shit list*

Haven't sent you one for a while, so please enjoy today's shit list:

My Tanning Salon—When your cheap door handle breaks and traps me inside the booth for ten fucking minutes, I expect you not to *laugh* at me when you're finally able to release me from my ultraviolet prison cell.

Coworkers at the Temp Job—Yes, I know you need an envelope and you're welcome to take as many as you want. But it might be nice if you *fucking said hello or something* before barging into my cube and riffling through all my drawers.

The Condo Association—We pay $2K/month to live here. Some of that money goes to condo assessments. This means someone is being paid to remove the one inch of solid ice on the sidewalk. Can you please make this happen before I break my fucking hip?

US Weekly's Cover Story—How can you be shocked Charlie Sheen and Denise Richards are getting divorced? It's *Charlie Fucking Sheen.* Your cover story *should* have read "Can You Believe It Lasted This Long?"

The Squirrel—You almost gave Fletch a fucking heart attack when you popped out of the garbage can and lunged at him à la *Christmas Vacation*. Excuse me, but he has *far* too much cholesterol in his arteries to sustain that kind of shock. (And I'm too young to be a widow.)

Also?

I don't appreciate laughing myself into a pant-wetting asthma attack upon witnessing my 6'2", 215-pound spouse screaming like a little girl while being chased across an icy parking lot by five pounds of furry rabid fury.

Off to go kick something,

Jen

P.S. Yes, I realize I dropped five f-bombs in this note. (Fuck you for counting.)

Church of the Magnificent Mile

A few years ago I used to take shopping so seriously it was less of a habit and more of a religion. Every chance I got, I'd steal away between appointments or at lunch in order to maintain my daily communicate status, worshipping at the Church of the Magnificent Mile. I'd make my way down Michigan Ave, stopping to pay my respects at the lesser deities: Sephora for their Fresh soy skin-care line and giant perfume selection,[1] the Body Shop for products with a conscience, Lord & Taylor for Jockey for Her underwear,[2] Marshall Field's for scarves and hair accessories, Pottery Barn for casual home décor except for glassware, which was Crate & Barrel's domain, Burberry if I felt like a little something plaid and pretty, and Les Vosges because carrying

---

[1] Yes, I only wore Dior J'adore. But I had to smell everything to make sure it was still my favorite.
[2] White and white only, thank you very much.

heavy shopping bags made me hungry for $30-a-pound chocolate-coated toffee. I'd tithe portions of my salary at each of these stores until I got to any one of the members of the Holy Trinity—Bloomingdale's, Nordstrom, Neiman Marcus—and the real purchasing commenced.

Bloomingdale's was my preferred spot for staples, such as fur-trimmed coats, bathing suits, and cashmere sweaters, while Nordstrom was the best place for multiple shoe purchases. (Really, those poor salespeople worked on commission—it would have been a sin to make them run into the back for only one pair!) Neiman Marcus was my absolute favorite place for ridiculous designer splurge items—jewelry, purses, and sunglasses. Plus Neiman's made it so damn difficult to buy anything—they wouldn't take Visa or MasterCard; basically they'd only accept cash, Krugerrand, and black diamond truffles—walking out of there with my shiny silver carrier bag always felt like a bit of a victory.

My shopping habit was so all-encompassing that I had to construct a list of rules so friends could better understand the process. But rather than sending them down on a couple of heavy tablets from Mount Sinai,[3] I simply e-mailed them.

The Jen Commandments of Shopping

Thou shall not buy on sale. Because sale? Is another word for shit not good enough to be purchased full price.

---

[3] Really, with the schlepping? Oy.

There's no such thing as too many twinsets. And you shall not rest until you have them in Every. Single. Color. (Except orange, because, you know, ick.)

Remember the three most important things when buying shoes: Italian, Italian, and Italian.

Life is too short to wear synthetic. Our Heavenly Father would not have placed all those goats in the hills of Kashmir[4] if He wanted you to put on something fashioned from a recycled Mountain Dew bottle.

Salespeople are there to carry the heavy stuff for you. So let them. See also: *Cold Beverages, Running to fetch*.

Coupons are for amateurs. What good is a $400 sweater if you can't tell people you paid $400 for it? See also: *Commandment, First*.

"Outlets" are for plugs and creative expression, not malls. Is style so trivial to you that you're willing to purchase your clothes at a store situated between the place where they sell the deformed Goldfish crackers and designer impostor perfumes? I think not.

Only shop in stores that have a philosophy. Hell, yes, you should pay 10 percent more for a store with a philosophy. (Even if that philosophy is, "Let's sucker our customers into paying 10 percent more.")

The harder to pay, the better it is. Self-explanatory. See also: *Marcus, Neiman*.

People who say "less is more" are simply jealous. More is *always* more. This is precisely the reason people go

---

[4] Do not give me the "Oh, but most cashmere comes from China now" argument. My point remains the same.

gaga over twins and litters of puppies and why a matched set of Kate Spade luggage is so much better than a single piece.

Even though I treasured almost every item sold in each of the Holy Trinity's bountiful departments, the merchandise wasn't the only draw. I loved the service and the personal attention. Nothing made me happier than when my girl Basha at Nordstrom's Dior counter called me to tell me about a new line of body shimmer. It made me feel like she had ESP; how did she know *that very morning* I'd looked at myself in the mirror and thought, *Yes, you glow, but are you luminous enough?*

No matter how chaotic Michigan Ave was, I knew I could enter the pricey enclaves of my favorite places and it would be calm, cool, and quiet. Clerks would speak in hushed tones—almost reverent—and would wrap my pair of capri pants and Lacoste shirt with the same care they would use to package Waterford crystal for shipping. There would be few other shoppers around, and we'd rarely interact because we were all too involved with our own expeditions.

My little boy-friend who worked the David Yurman counter would squeal whenever he saw me pass, sibilantly exclaiming, "Ooh! What are we treating oursssselvesss with today?" and before I could say, "Nothing, thanks," he'd be waving a black velvet-covered platter full of sssparkly thingsss at me. And it would have been rude not to try—and purchassse—at leassst one of them, right?

Obviously, I don't live my life like this anymore (a) because I can't, and (b) because I like to think I have some small capacity for "learning." I'll be honest—I still dig buying stuff, but that's mostly because at the nadir of our unemployment, purchasing anything other than dog food and toilet paper was a luxury. I still believe in the Holy Trinity, except now it's Target, Trader Joe's, and IKEA.

After selling off the bulk of our nice stuff while out of work, we began to replenish our household at Target when things turned around. I don't exactly know what happened to Target in the twenty years since I was a cashier there, but hot damn, have they changed! In 1985 I was mortified to get my off-to-college supplies at that stupid discount store. I remember grudgingly shoving a boring tan-and-brown comforter—the nicest-looking one they had—into my cart and then wanting to die a thousand deaths a week later when my adorable freshman roommate arrived with an equally adorable pastel tulip-sprigged Marimekko quilt.

There were no coordinated goods when I worked at Target and Cynthia Rowley for damn sure had nothing to do with my ugly-ass bedding. Yet now when I stroll Target's home department, there's nothing but gorgeous, high-quality, low-priced styles as far as the eye can see. What's your pleasure? The faded florals of shabby chic? Rich, shimmering jewel tones of the Far East? Nubby wools and flannels inspired by the North Woods? Any designer you'd prefer? Isaac Mizrahi? Michael Graves? Thomas O'Brien? Then step right up! Stripes? Plaids? Geometrics? Yeah, they've got it, and in every color, too. And don't forget the matching rugs and bathroom accessories, like toothbrush holders, shower curtains, and towels.

And can we please discuss their clothing? Twenty years

ago I'd have rather stayed in and studied than gone to a party in anything with a Target label. And yet recently when shopping for a new mop I passed by their women's section and saw a tan tapestry coat with a detachable fur collar. I tried the coat on and it fit as though I'd had it custom-made. As I had never seen outerwear this cute in my life, I forgot about the mop, threw the tapestry masterpiece in my basket, and made a mad dash for the checkout line, assuming the minute the rest of the female shoppers saw it, I'd have to fight them for it. None of the outerwear I bought at Bloomingdale's ever garnered the compliments I've gotten on my $60 Target coat.[5]

Recently my Target added a Starbucks *and* started selling wine, pretty much cementing it as my favorite store on the face of this earth, and if ever asked what the one thing is I'd take with me to a desert island, I'd say Target, of course.

That is, if I didn't have to take their current staff with me.

First, I have been a Target cashier, so I know that of which I speak. Although the merchandise has changed over the years, the basic exchange of goods for currency has not. Back when I worked there, we had no scanners. We had to key in every single bar code in order to check people out and we weren't supposed to look at the cash register when we did it.[6] If you bought it, we bagged it, and God help us if we put your cookies anywhere near your motor oil. The managers who stood at the end of the conveyor helped us speed things along

---

[5] Ever seen Carrie Bradshaw in a Target coat? No? I didn't think so.
[6] Uphill! In the winter! With no shoes on! For five miles! With hungry dogs chasing us!

not by bagging but by loudly providing constructive criticism about every single one of our stupid mistakes.

The managers in my store were particularly sadistic and would run time and motion studies on each of us cashiers, making wagers on who could process the most customers per hour. Then they'd place our scores up on the break room wall with our names on them and helpful motivational phrases, like "Ring faster, you loser!" Also, we had to dress professionally under our smocks with earrings no larger than a dime, clear nail polish, no facial hair,[7] and panty hose, managers reserving the right to yell at us like drill sergeants were we to be remiss in any of the above areas. One day I forgot to put on knee-highs and flashed an inch of bare ankle; from the reprimanding I received, you'd have thought I'd kicked each and every customer in the big box.

Let me just say this—my old managers do not work at the Target where I shop. There's one kid there who sits on a stool to ring people up, and he wears a towel around his neck to mop up where he sweats from all the not-standing. He won't even lift your purchases, making you scoot them across the scanner yourself. Yet I've seen him literally run out the door to smoke, and am pretty sure I once saw him hoist a case of beer onto his shoulder at my grocery store, so I don't know why he merits a stool. And does he bring his own towel? Or just rotate the sweaty one back into stock? I kind of don't want to think about it.

As for the rest of the staff, they don't quite adhere to the

---

[7] Really not a problem for me. At least until I hit my thirties. Ha! Kidding! (Or am I?)

rules of yore, either. Neck tattoos? Check. Hickeys *and* neck tattoos? Check. Giant gold nameplate necklaces that spell out M-u-t-h-a-f-u-c-k-a? Muthafuckin' check! I imagine if these cashiers manage to show up wearing pants not tenuously clinging to their kneecaps, their bosses are probably happy.

In my day,[8] we got in big trouble if we didn't say, "Welcome and thank you for shopping at Target," to every customer as they approached our lane. Apparently these rules no longer apply, as usually my cashier will look at me with dead shark eyes, ring up my wonderful new items without a word, and then stare at me once the total appears on the register while the bagger carefully mixes my bleach, ammonia, and Pringles in the same bag. I'm at the point where I now say, "Hi, thanks for ringing me up here at Target. How much is my total?"

In all fairness, I've read mine is the busiest Target in the world per square foot, so maybe everyone is just really jaded and tired of the crowds? Plus, I've heard their cashiers speaking ten different languages, so I, Miss Whitey McXenophobe, should perhaps cut them some terry-cloth-covered, stool-seated slack.

The downside of the Target experience, at least at the urban Targets, is that something ridiculous happens every time we visit. Sometimes we get to see shoplifters get busted; occasionally it's a bit of domestic violence with a dash of stock-boy bitch-slapping when a rain check is offered in lieu of the sold-out sale Pampers. (Fortunately, there's never less than

---

[8] Yes, I know exactly how old that makes me sound.

one of Chicago's Finest shopping there, squad car perched right on the curb, so it's totally safe.)

Not long ago, I'm on my daily pilgrimage to Target and have just finished paying for an *Us Weekly* and some mini Hershey's bars when I see another customer's child do something troubling. "Excuse me, ma'am?" I say to the woman behind me. "Your son just ate a piece of gum stuck to the construction barrier in front of the new Starbucks."

With zero clue as to what I've said, she asks, "*¿Qué?*"

"I said your child is chewing someone else's gum. He picked it off the wall and put it in his mouth. I thought you might want to know."

She frowns at me. "*¿Qué?*"

Damn it, how do I make her understand? "The baby?" I point at the little boy in the shirt with the rooster on it. "Over there? He's yours, right? He's chewing old gum and—ugh—right now, look, he's peeling more off the wall and stuffing it in his mouth."

"*¿Qué?*"

I raise my voice. Fletch says everyone understands English if you speak loudly enough. Or maybe he says everyone speaks English at gunpoint? I forget. "Your boy. Your, um, damn it, what's the word? I know how to say it in Italian. Um, niño? Bambino?" I point at Little Rooster Boy. "Ate gum." I point at the wall and the Wrigley display behind us. "That had been in someone else's mouth." I point at my own mouth and Fletch's, making chewing motions. "He's going to get worms!" I hold my hands up to my face and make little squiggly motions with my fingers.

"*¿Qué?*" She turns to the cashier and asks, "*¿Qué dijo la* *ramera loca?*" and the cashier then rattles something back at her in rapid-fire Spanish and they both shrug. The woman yells some gibberish to the Little Rooster Boy, who toddles back over to be picked up and placed in the front of her cart.

Aha! Now we're getting somewhere! "Yes, yes, exactly! No more stinky danger gum! You're welcome!" We walk out of the store and I'm delighted to have been a Good Samaritan. "See, Fletch? You always tell me not to get involved, but I did and it paid off. They were glad that I stepped in. People really appreciate it when you try to help."

"Um, Jen? I'm pretty sure she just called you a crazy bitch," he tells me.

"Oh." I *really* need to learn Spanish.

But no matter what language you say it in, Target is a little slice of heaven.

The second prong in my revised Trinity is IKEA, the Swedish home store monolith. If you're unfamiliar, they carry every single thing you could possibly ever need to fill your home and garden at low, low prices, but in obscure Swedish sizes so those items won't coordinate with anything else you own, like, say, if you want to put a regular Target lamp shade on your IKEA lamp. Fletch thinks it's Sweden's master plan to make Americans so busy trying to construct furniture with Allen wrenches that we don't notice they've invaded us. (Personally, I think it's payback; the Swedes are pissed that we aren't buying ABBA albums anymore.)

The IKEA I frequent is in the suburbs and is so big you can actually see it from space.[9] Seriously, it's three stories tall and has special escalators for your cart to ride down next to you. There are also giant multilanguage signs in front of it saying:

DO NOT PUT YOUR BABY STROLLER ON HERE YOU DUMBASS BECAUSE IT'S A CONVEYOR BELT AND YOU DON'T PUT YOUR BABY ON A CONVEYOR AND EXACTLY HOW STUPID ARE YOU THAT WE HAVE TO REPEAT THIS TEN TIMES AND WITH A PICTURE OF A BABY STROLLER WITH A SLASH THROUGH IT AND HOW DID YOU NOT NOTICE THIS SAME SIGN POINTING TO THE NICE SAFE ELEVATOR TEN FEET AWAY?

Which would lead you to believe we wouldn't see people trying to put their strollers on it every time we visit. (And you wouldn't think Fletch and I laugh ourselves stupid every time we see this happen either, yet here we are.)

Except possibly Las Vegas, there's no better place to people-watch than our IKEA. Were the FBI to pay attention to my helpful suggestions (or return my calls), they'd know to set up a camera at the front door, because at some point every single person on the face of the earth eventually passes

---

[9] Probably not true, although technically not confirmed one way or the other. But wander around the joint for four or five hours and it will certainly feel true.

through it. I don't care how rich or poor you are, the draw of purchasing twelve hundred tea lights for thirty-seven cents is too great for anyone to resist.

Fletch and I are fortifying ourselves with big plates full of delicious Swedish meatballs and lingonberry sauce with lingonberry soda and lingonberry tarts for dessert[10] at a table overlooking the scratch-and-dent section two floors below us before we commit commerce.

Fletch chews a meatball thoughtfully and then says, "You know, coming to IKEA is a lot like doing tequila shots."

"Why's that?" I ask.

"Because when someone suggests it, it seems like a fantastic idea—big fun and all—but in the morning you wake up nauseous in the middle of a pile of table legs, with no idea how you got there, and swearing to never do it again."

I agree. "And then once your hangover's gone, you forget all about it, so the next time someone says, 'Hey, let's do shots!' you're like, 'Capital idea!' and the cycle continues."

"But not us. Because today we're just going to look at that one lamp shade and a nightstand and we're out of here. We're not going to spend four hundred dollars and we aren't going to be here for three hours. Agreed?"

"Agreed." As we eat I notice a pattern occurring in the scratch-and-dent section. "Fletch, check out that dresser down there."

"Which one? The maple laminate one like we have in our bedroom?"

"Yes. Watch—every single person who goes by it is going

---

[10] You know what we need more of in this country? Lingonberry products.

to open the drawers, even though I bet they have no plans to buy it." We keep an eye on the piece for the next five minutes, and sure enough every single passerby opens a drawer.

"Whoa, Fletch, watch that lady—she's opened the drawer at least forty times. Drawer open, drawer close. Drawer open, drawer close. What is she checking for? 'Perhaps if I open the drawer this time, it will be full of kittens? Nope. Better close it and try again.'" We continue to observe and giggle. "Ha! Her daughter joined her and now *she's* opening and closing the drawers. Drawer open, drawer close. Drawer open, drawer close. Once you establish that each of the five drawers is properly on the track, why would you open and close them eight thousand more times?"

A gentleman joins the mother and daughter and Fletch says, "I don't know, but we'd better let Dad give it a whirl!" We laugh until we choke as the man begins to work the drawers again and again.

"Fletch, suddenly I feel like the smartest person in this store."

"No kidding. Okay, let's bus our trays and get busy. Fifty bucks and fifteen minutes—we can do it." To confirm, we bump our fists together in Wondertwin solidarity.

Three hours and $400 later, we're a whole lot less smug.

Trader Joe's is the third prong in our shopping Trinity and definitely rivals Target for my affection. Such is my crush on Trader Joe's, it's all I can do to not ride by it/him ten times a day on my bike. I want to pass Trader Joe's little origami notes in study hall asking, "Do U Like Me? Circle Y or N." They have hundreds of house-branded groceries so they're not only inexpensive but also really good. Plus a lot of their merchandise is organic so I actually feel like I'm doing something healthy for myself when wolfing down an entire box of their private-label imitation Oreos.

Even though Trader Joe's draws from the same employment pool as the Target tattooed troglodytes, they must do some sort of special training because their staffers are chatty and enthusiastic. Like if you buy dog food, they start a conversation about what kind of pup you might own and are *so damn happy* to know yours are from a shelter. Or if you get a bunch of steaks, they inquire about your possible barbecue and *how much fun you'll have and isn't the weather just great for it?* What's nice is when you buy a cart full of their fine, fine Charles Shaw wine,[11] they're also kind enough to not mention *your raging alcoholism*. They just smile and pretend they don't notice your gin blossoms.

I love every Trader Joe's I've visited, but my particular Trader Joe's is special—I go to the one in Lincoln Park and it's on the second floor of the shopping center. To get in, you have to drive up a ramp and then park inside. As a very, very lazy person this is extraordinarily appealing to me, as it's but a step away from actually getting to drive down the aisles.

Alas, my Trader Joe's is a harsh mistress[12] because there's something about him that brings the cell-phone users out in droves. *Droves*, I tell you! Most of the time Fletch and I are

---

[11] A.k.a. Two Buck Chuck.
[12] Master?

the only ones in there not on the phone; not surprising, because we only call each other.

I'm in the middle of a very important decision—Trader Joe's delicious capellini or farfalle—when some stupid girl cuts in front of me and begins to rant about her problems with her sister on her Sidekick. No matter which way I try to maneuver around her, her blathering gets in my way. You know what? I don't care if your sister hates the yellow bridesmaid dress and it's throwing your big day into chaos. All I care about is getting some damn pasta. But it's impossible because you are in my way and I can't get around you and your fucking fantasy wedding.

Remember when the only people who had cell phones were doctors and Wall Street types? If they were in public and on their mobile, they were either saving lives or brokering the merger between Salomon and Smith Barney—serious stuff, right? Yet now I can't get my shopping done because some woman I will never meet prefers buttercream-colored satin to lemon and is making her sister apoplectic.

When did the cell phone become a license to be rude? And why must I be subjected to your personal conversations?[13] Five years ago, while at Cucina Bella on Diversey, a dot-com wunderkind was seated at the table next to me. During the course of our dinners, his phone rang twenty-three times. No shit, twenty-three times; I know this because I counted. And it was a loud ring, not just a beep. Better, he actually answered the phone and had conversations with every caller while still seated at his table. I knew that this kid ran a

---

[13] Believe me, if I wanted to eavesdrop, I would.

successful Web site, so I initially let it slide, thinking he might have been doing business. But as his conversations were peppered with the words "dude," "bong hits," and "Jaeger shots," I realized he was simply yammering with his buddies and I wanted to dice him, deep-fry him, and serve him with a ramekin of cocktail sauce. (Instead, I cornered his date in the ladies' room and convinced her to dump his inattentive ass.)

I know I'm fighting a losing battle to stop people from talking on their phones in public. For some reason, most people need that constant stimulation. God forbid anyone be quiet for a minute, because that's when they begin to hear the voices in their heads. You know, those little voices that make them question their views on society, ethics, organized religion, etc.? And we can't allow *those* thoughts, now can we?

My rule of thumb is this: if you're going to be boorish and subject me to your cell-phone conversation while we are sharing a public space, it had at least better be out of the ordinary. Hearing you prattle on about your lousy boyfriend? Not remarkable. Listening to your discourse on your lousy boyfriend, Che Guevara, who had you running arms through Colombia? Start talking.

But until then, remember, you're in *my* house of worship.

So kindly shut the fuck up.

To: angie_at_home, carol_at_home, wendy_at_home, jen_at_work
From: jen@jenlancaster.com
Subject: *casa chaos*

Hey, girls,

Alternate e-mail title—why Fletch hates working from home.

Setting: Our living room, 7:58 a.m.

>   **Fletch:** Jen, I'm about to be on back-to-back conference calls. Can you please keep everyone quiet?

>   **Me:** Of course.

>   **8:05 a.m.**—*I accidentally set off the security alarm when I open the front door.*

>   **8:18 a.m.**—*Cat knocks his feeding tower off the top of the refrigerator, showering the entire kitchen with cat food pellets.*

>   **8:29 a.m.**—*Dogs go monkey-shit crazy with barking when a leaf blows across the patio.*

>   **8:32 a.m.**—*Dogs go monkey-shit crazy when they see a bird on the patio.*

>   **8:39 a.m.**—*Dogs go monkey-shit crazy for no good reason.*

8:47 a.m.—*A different cat projectile vomits on the counter.*

8:48 a.m.—*Same cat takes out her anger about throwing up by attacking Maisy. Much howling and hissing ensue.*

8:50 a.m.—*Maisy is so upset she poops on the stairs and then hides in the corner, shaking.*

8:51 a.m.—*Feeling sympathy for Maisy, Loki begins to heave while I scream, "Not on the rug! Not on the rug!"*

8:52 a.m.—*Fletch hangs up the phone and bangs his head against the counter.*

I told him the day he goes out for cigarettes and never comes back? No one will blame him.

Later,

Jen

The Butt-erfly Effect

id you know *The Butterfly Effect* is more than a lousy Ashton Kutcher movie?[1]

As a principle of chaos theory, the butterfly effect can be demonstrated by how the change in air currents generated by a single butterfly flapping its wings in an Amazonian rain forest[2] can create an Indonesian tsunami, the likes of which will leave world-renown supermodels clinging to palm trees.

My own butterfly effect occurs when one small idea inspires one minuscule decision, which ultimately throws my whole world off its axis.

The thought? *Saving a couple of dollars.*

The idea? *Getting a library card so I could borrow books instead of buying them.*

---

[1] In fairness, I haven't seen *The Butterfly Effect*. Maybe it's *not* a lousy movie. But based on his performance in *Dude, Where's My Car?*, my expectations aren't terribly high.

[2] Through the magic of science, humidity, and possibly Steven Spielberg.

The decision? *Putting a utility in my name so that I could prove Chicago residency in order to get said card.*

The result? *Getting an up-close-and-personal look at a stranger's bunghole.*

But instead of a butterfly, I blame Fletch for what happens next.

Anyone who's ever been assigned an essay for class will tell you the best thing about writing is *not* writing. I've found when I'm on a deadline, the temptation is there to do anything but put down words. Personally, my favorite "avoid writing" activity is redecorating, because a blank page doesn't look nearly so bad when you've filled a whole wall with rose-colored paint! Plus, I have it on good authority[3] that electricity was discovered, television was invented, and the theory of relativity proved simply because those guys didn't want to face their English 101 term papers. (Ditto on the PlayStation and the knit beer can cap.)

I'm trying my hardest to treat writing like it's a job. So, to combat my creative avoidance I force myself to sit in front of the monitor—much like my early professional days of doing data entry—until I run out the clock. My discipline about sitting down at the computer is admirable, but that still doesn't mean I'm always productive once I get there. Again much like my data-entry job, except now I get to work in cutoff sweatpants and an old Lacoste shirt that may or may not be covered in barbecue stains.[4]

---

[3] Meaning I made it up in my own head.

[4] Eating "a mess of ribs" is also an excellent way to procrastinate.

Today's been a bad day in terms of creativity, as I've holed up in my two-tone pink[5] plaid office for hours, trying unsuccessfully to coax words onto a blank screen. I feel a frisson of failure as the cursor blinks at me and I finally give up and play a few rounds of FreeCell before IM-ing all my little online buddies. I glance at the clock and see I have hours yet to kill, so I Google-stalk old coworkers, catch up on conservative news at DrudgeReport.com, and reread the entire GoFug Yourself.com archives, hoping to draw inspiration from Heather and Jessica's biting wit . . . with no luck. At four o'clock—my prescribed stopping time—I finally stroll down the stairs to bother Fletch. If *I'm* not getting any work done, then no one else in this house should be allowed to, either.

Fletch is working at our breakfast bar, leaning over his laptop in deep concentration, his BlackBerry and cell phone stacked neatly on top of a bunch of folders.[6]

"Whatcha doin'?" I ask, drawing out the words while riffling through his paperwork.

"The usual."

"Like what?" I begin to flip open his folders and accidentally spill the contents of one on the floor. I quickly scoop them up and attempt to reassemble them.

"Regular work stuff.[7] Pretty much what I do every day."

"I know that. Like, *specifically* what are you doing?"

He glances up from his computer with an exasperated expression. He grabs the papers I've haphazardly shoved in the

---

[5] Colors chosen during a heroic bout of creative avoidance.

[6] Fletch works down here instead of in our office on the second floor. Something about the pink walls making him feel all stabby?

[7] Network design, FYI.

folders, reorganizing and restacking everything I just pawed. "*Specifically* I'm trying to earn a merit badge by helping an old lady across the street. One more and I'll get to lead the campfire sing-along at the jamboree."

"Is being a smarty-pants really necessary? I asked a legitimate question."

"Well, sorry, but I'm trying to concentrate and you're making it hard by talking and moving my things out of order."

"Oh. Sorry." I sit down next to him, place my chin in my hands, and sigh deeply.

No response.

I sigh deeply again.

Nada.

I sigh deeply a third time and add a little moan at the end.

He presses his lips together and asks in a distinctly patronizing manner, "Jen, can I help you with something?"

"Yes, now that you've asked. I'm bored. Stop working and talk to me." Seriously, writing is a lonely enterprise. Often I have words to keep me company, but an unproductive day highlights just how isolating this profession can be.

"For my job, working from home actually entails 'working.'" He makes air quotes at me when he says this. "I've got to get this RFP out today and I'm sorry, but I don't have time right now. I'll give you my undivided attention over dinner, okay?"

"But I need some interaction *now*. I couldn't write anything good and I'm so bored I might die," I reply.

"Then I'll miss you when you're gone. Fortunately, my productivity may improve." He toggles back and forth between making notes on graph paper with a sleek silver ball-point and inserting objects onto a Visio diagram.

"Hey, neat pen. Can I see it?"

"Okay, right now? You're Homer Simpson and I'm Frank Grimes.[8] I expect you to show me your mansion and your lobsters before you try to drink a beaker of sulfuric acid. Except unlike Grimey, I wouldn't stop you."

Well, *that* was uncalled for. "You—you're a mean, mean meanie and I hope staring at your laptop gives you eye cancer." I grab a pillow from the love seat and throw it at him to punctuate my sentiment.

"I see all that time with the thesaurus has really paid off." Oh! Straight to the heart! He sees I look stricken and his voice softens. "Listen, I'll make you a deal—I've got to get this crucial part done. But I'll talk to you when I finish, okay?"

"I guess so."

"See you in a while."

I continue to hover next to him. He scoots down one barstool to get away from me. "For now, you have to find something else to do. Maybe talk to your imaginary online friends."

I cross the room to lie upside down on the couch and begin to kick my feet against the wall. It is Time to Whine. "They aren't make-belieeeeeve. Besides, I already did that. Now I'm booored. If you won't talk to me—which I'm pretty sure is a violation of those marriage vows that guy in the casino made us repeat—then help me find stuff to doooo."

....

[8] "Homer's Enemy," episode number 176 of *The Simpsons*—Best. Episode. Ever.

Because we're on a budget, I haven't really left the house for a while. And since I've not been out in the world having new experiences, I've got almost nothing to say. I'm bored and uninspired. I feel like I did in grade school during our vocabulary tests when I forgot a definition—I could write the equivalent of *"The girl could not think of a way to use 'acrimonious' in a sentence,"* but I imagine that would please my editor as much as it did my fourth-grade teacher. Which is not at all.

"Watch some TV."

"There's nothing on but sports and soap operas. Blah."

He throws his hands up and gestures at me in disgust. "You realize this" —he taps the counter with his pointer finger—"this *right here* is why we aren't having children." We plan to remain child-free not because we hate them but because we fear what our combined genetics may create. We think our kid would be some sort of supervillain, or at the very least have the kind of sarcastic mouth that would ensure he or she would never date and would thus live with us forever. (However, we reserve the right to adopt a kid from a foreign country if we ever have a big yard and no riding mower.)

I throw another pillow at him.

"Okay, okay, you obviously aren't going to get out of my hair until you find something to do. Why don't you go to the gym?"

I sit up straight. "I'll never be *that* bored."

"I don't know then, um, how about . . . make dinner?"

"We don't have any food."

Fletch rests his face in his hands. "I don't know, maybe read a book?"

"I read them all." The problem is I go through books like tissues. I pretty much inhale them in one or two sittings because I read so fast. Generally this is good, except occasionally I end up missing important details, and thus, the entire point. For example, in *The Sun Also Rises* by Ernest Hemingway, I glossed over the bit on the first page where it mentions Jake Barnes has a weird war injury and has been rendered impotent. So, instead of spending my time with the book marveling at everything that makes Hemingway an American treasure—the majesty of his phrasing, his ability to paint a complex picture with an economy of words, the way every tale turns both epic and tragic, yet ultimately uplifting—I interpreted his story as though it were a pink-jacketed, shoe-covered bit of chick lit. I scratched my head over why Jake and that Brett girl from the cool crowd didn't just *do it* already and cheered him on from the sidelines with my helpful suggestions, like "Dude! She totally likes you!" and "You're way funny and cute—you should *so* go for it."

(As soon as you're done calling me a philistine, I'll continue.)

Anyway, now that I think about it, reading sounds like kind of a good idea. I mean, maybe the new Sedaris will inspire me? "Okay, yeah," I tell Fletch, "yeah, I'll do that. Thanks for the suggestion! But I'll need to get some new books. Can I have two hundred dollars? I want to restock my bookshelves."

"Sure. Of course, if I give you two hundred dollars, we can't buy groceries. But going hungry would almost be worth it to get you out of the house."

"Then how am I supposed to get something to read?"

"You can either spend less than two hundred dollars or go to the library."

"Those bastards at the Palatine Public Library confiscated my card after they found out I'd moved out of town almost a decade ago. Sucks, too, because it was a really good library. Didja ever see their mystery section? Stacks and stacks of books, far as the eye can see."

He closes his laptop and begins to gather his folders. "And . . . this is why I drink. Do me a favor and go to one of the Chicago Public Libraries. Not only are there branches in every neighborhood, but the one downtown takes up two city blocks and is nine stories tall. Surely they will have something you like. And now if you'll excuse me, I have to finish this proposal so I, you know, don't get fired."

"Hmm, the Chicago library, you say? This intrigues me. But I don't have a library card. What do I— hey, hey, *hey!* Where are you going?"

As I watch Fletch climb the stairs, I make a decision.

The library it is.

As soon as I figure out how to get a card.

Here's an interesting lesson—when you call the library with an important question, talk to the librarian, not one of the little thugs who's there doing community service.

Why?

Because the librarian will give you *accurate* information about obtaining a library card, and won't just blithely agree when you ask if it's necessary to bring in a utility bill with your name on it in order to prove residency.

And thus, you won't make the mistake of canceling your husband's natural gas account and opening a new one in your name in order to do so.

And this won't give the local gas monopoly the option to claim they have no idea about swapping out an established account for a new one, and so they simply disconnect your husband's service, per his[9] request.

And then you won't have to go fourteen days without natural gas until the whole mess gets sorted out because their technicians are *busy* and if you're the kind of dumbass who accidentally cancels service based solely on the advice of a juvenile delinquent, then it's not really an emergency on *their* part.

The nice thing is, if you have to lose a utility, gas is the best.[10] Having no electric service is pretty traumatic, especially if you've just stocked the freezer with a Costco porkchop run. And not only can't you operate the AC or keep your wine chilled, you can't watch TV or vacuum . . . unless you figure out how to burrow under your deck and over the fence with an extension cord and tap into your neighbor's power supply. Which I do not recommend, unless the circumstances are dire.[11]

Losing phone service is no big deal because I couldn't care less if I never called anyone again. I'm generally loath to chat on the phone, and rarely answer it when it rings. I figure

---

[9] Meaning *your*.

[10] In my expert opinion, formed from losing every utility during my extended unemployment.

[11] Yes, watching the *American Idol* finale is totally considered dire. Come on, Justin versus Kelly? It was history in the making!

if I need to talk to someone, then I'll simply e-mail to arrange a lunch. However, our DSL runs through the phone line and I need Internet access like I need a heartbeat. Ditto on satellite, because, really, why would Jack Bauer bother to save the world if I'm not watching?

Gas provides our heat, but we barely need it because this place is a three-story brick sweatbox. Until the thermometer dipped below forty degrees outside, we had to run the air conditioner. It's in the high thirties outside right now, yet it's a balmy seventy-two degrees in my office.

The bonus to our not having gas is I'm no longer forced to yell at Fletch for cranking up the thermostat when he thinks I'm not looking. Good God, you'd think the man was a reptile or something—he won't be happy 'til he has a steaming hot rock to lie on in the baking desert sun.

I wonder, though, if I'm simply insensitive to the cold? After Fletch moved in with me in college, he kept complaining about how the apartment was freezing. Except for the ice on the wall of the shower, I didn't see a problem, even after living there two and a half years. One day he couldn't take the cold or my stubborn streak anymore and he brought home a thermometer. We found the temperature was a consistent forty-five degrees. *I* suggested he borrow my L.L.Bean Norwegian sweater (cozy!) and *he* suggested we get it fixed. But once I thought about it, I became angry on principle at the apartment being cold, considering I paid for heat as part of my rent. A couple of quick calls—first to my landlord, and then to Action News—and the situation was resolved.[12]

---

[12] Lafayette, Indiana—home of the slow news day. (We were the top story!)

Anyway, our stove is gas, and without the benefit of burners I can't cook those elaborate pork-chop dinners that have definitely become my least favorite part of the *Fletch Works a Real Job While I Stay Home and Attempt to Write* deal. However, I'm still in charge of meals, so I have to get creative after Fletch complains about all the microwave soup and hot dogs I try to force on him. The subsequent *All McDonald's, All the Time* episode does not go well either, regardless of how it may have worked out for Morgan Spurlock. So I buy six kinds of freshly sliced meat and three interesting cheeses from the deli and get in touch with my Inner Sandwich. I also give the George Foreman grill a whirl, with mixed results.[13] However, this week I've discovered the easiest-to-prepare, most satisfying meal yet. You may now address me as *Jen, Queen of the Crock Pot!* I throw meat, vegetables, and some dry soup mix in the crock around nine a.m., stir a couple of times throughout the day, and by six p.m., voilà! Dinner is served. Fletch picked out the recipes, so he's happy, too.

I'd almost be tempted to not get the gas turned back on, especially because I'm so terrified of explosions. Seriously, it seems like every week you see some idiot standing outside next to a gaping hole that used to be his bungalow, saying, "Yeah, I kinda smelled gas, but I didn't think nothin' of it." Granted, I have *a lot* of irrational fears, such as opening the toilet lid and finding a severed head, drinking a can of soda and swallowing the fingertip or hypodermic needle floating inside, and being killed by a gigantic falling icicle. But this last one actually happens every year! I used to save the newspaper

---

[13] Meaning I burned my hand on it, damn it.

clippings about the incidents until Fletch found them and laughed at me.

The only problem is no gas equals no hot water and our tap water is cold. Like fresh from a mountain stream in a beer commercial cold. Like, "Hello, hypothermia, nice to meet you!" cold. While we wait for the gas servicemen to get around to us, Fletch has been showering at his gym. He told me I could get a temporary membership, but I'm not sure I want to run on a treadmill solely to make it look like I'm not there just to use their shower. Until I take that plunge,[14] I've come up with an in-house ablution solution.

I fill the tub halfway with freezing tap water and I let it come up to room temperature. Then I dump in pots of boiling water I've heated in the microwave and the electric kettle. The upside is all the heating and pouring makes me feel like Laura Ingalls Wilder in her Little Condo on the Prairie, but the downside is it takes a good two hours of pouring and dumping and I can only get tiny snatches of writing done between boil cycles.

But so far, it's still better than going to the gym.

The gas man cometh tomorrow, which is good because if I have to fill that goddamned tub one more time, something very bad is going to happen, like me going to a cardio funk class. I haven't felt fully clean in almost two weeks. Yes, I normally love baths and I take them all the time, but for reasons

---

[14] Rim shot!

more literary than hygienic.[15] I will actually shower after sitting in the tub because I hate the idea of rinsing in dirty water. At present, I feel all filmy and oily and I'd be willing to commit a felony for five minutes of hot running water.

I'm almost ready to brave step aerobics when I remember a place on Belmont Ave. Back when I consumed spa services like coffee and Prada bags, I had a bead on every good facility in the city. I'd heard tons of enthusiastic praise about Thousand Waves Spa for Women on Belmont, although I'd never gone. Their specialties were herbal wraps and massages, whereas I was more of a facial and pedicure kind of girl. I never got comfortable with the idea of people touching me and not accomplishing anything (for example, sloughing off excess skin), and now the idea of a massage makes me a bit squeamish. (It goes without saying whatever service I purchased entailed wearing a full set of underwear.)

However, I also remembered this place sold spa passes, and for $20 you got to indulge in their Jacuzzi, redwood sauna, eucalyptus steam room, lockers, beauty products, new age tea, and shower facilities, exactly what I need today. With a quick phone call I verify this information. Confirmed, I shove my swimsuit in a bag, and off I go.

I'm greeted at the door of this Japanese-style spa and leave my shoes next to all the others lined up against the wall. The receptionist talks about how this place is a calm oasis and their goal is to help me relax and find balance. They ask that I respect the other patrons by refraining from cell-phone use and

---

[15] I do 50 percent of all my reading in the tub.

keeping my voice down. "No problem!" I heartily agree before clamping my hand over my too-loud mouth. "Sorry!" I whisper.

I make my way down the long hall and am greeted by the most wonderful fragrances—fruity floral body wash, clean linen-scented candles, tangy, sinus-opening eucalyptus, smoky wood warmed by the sauna, and the chemical bite of the hot tub's chlorine. To most people, chlorine's kind of a repulsive smell, but for those of us who spent their summers submerged, it's as pleasant as a sunny day when your only chore is to lie on a raft until you feel like riding your bike to the pro shop to buy a new Izod.[16]

After an extra-soapy preliminary shower, I ease myself into the hundred-and-twenty-degree Jacuzzi, wallowing up to my ears. I bring the book *Wicked* with me as it's already misshapen from too many spills into the bath. The Jacuzzi is huge and I'm able to float in the very center, spreading my arms wide, without touching any of the sides. I look like the Vitruvian Man—if he were wearing a pink-and-black Miraclesuit, that is. As the bubbles begin to buffer me against the sides, I feel clean down to my very soul.

Since I'm here, I may as well give my pores a treat, so I leave the tub and enter the sauna. I grab a cold drink and lay down my towel before ladling water over the hot rocks. The stones hiss and pop and the room practically reverberates with heat. I take a washcloth filled with icy water and wipe all the toxins off my face. I squeeze it over my shoulders and the water evaporates before it even hits the wooden bench.

---

[16] When Lacoste split with Izod? Most. Tragic. Divorce. Ever.

The great irony here is I hit the cold-water-plunge shower between services, and it's the exact same temperature as the water I'm paying $20 to avoid at home.

The heavily scented steam room is a soppy slice of paradise. I breathe in as deeply as I can, and I can practically feel the little bitty alveoli widening. When I was in sixth grade I had to be hospitalized for a severe case of pneumonia—ever since then, my lungs have felt tight. But today after spending so much time in the steam room, air trapped since the Carter administration comes out when I exhale.

Even the plain old shower is plain old terrific with all the water pressure and fine assortment of scented body products. And yet the experience is just shy of ecstasy.

Why?

Too much naked!

Everywhere I look there's, gah!—more exposed flesh. And I am just not a naked person. I'll happily wear a bathing suit on the world's most crowded beach and feel okay about myself, so it's not so much a body image thing. Pretty much it's an uncomfortable-with-naked thing. Also, I'd prefer to avoid *your* cooties,[17] and the best way to do that is to keep as many layers of spandex between us as possible. Point? If I glance up from my book and notice your Brazilian wax headed toward me, don't be surprised when I fucking *fly* out of the hot tub. Because, really? I can live a long, happy life without ever knowing you've shaved your pubic hair into a clever shape. And your **shudder** piercings? Well, those should be between you, your physician, and the guy who works the

---

[17] No offense.

metal detector at the airport. (I've adopted a strict Don't Ask, Don't Tell, and For God's Sake, Don't Show policy.)

I can't help it—I'm extremely modest. When I was a kid, I'd put on a bathing suit to play with Barbies in the tub. As an adult, nary a single Vegas hotel Jacuzzi has seen my pasty white rear end, even when I'm staying alone. (Yes, room service thinks it's hilarious when I tell them "Come in" and I'm floating in the giant tub wearing a one-piece. But I don't want to drip on the floor or slip on the marble and that wine's not going to serve itself.) (Shut up. I tip well.) Even during my most trash-can-punch-soaked sorority days, I never crowded in an open fraternity bathroom and peed in tandem with all my sisters.

I think spas are supposed to have a bit of an "Amazons at Paradise Island" vibe to them and that's all right, I guess.[18] And I totally see how someone would prefer not to sweat all over her $125 Miraclesuit while sitting in the steam room—considering all the struts and trusses they contain, they'd probably rust. I even get that there's something incredibly liberating and primordial about floating nude in the hot tub, yet there's still no way I'm going to do it, so please don't give me the "it's perfectly natural" speech. Bowel movements are also perfectly natural, but you'll forgive me if I don't want to take one in the center of Nordstrom's shoe department.

But these women who are walking from one service to the next without benefit of a towel? Un!Comfortable! I grudg-

---

[18] Having just Googled "island where Wonder Woman is from," I ran across a bunch of photos of Lynda Carter from the series in the seventies. No wonder my dad always watched the show with me.

ingly understand if you want to scoot from the hot tub to the sauna without dampening your robe. Personally, I wouldn't do it; however, this is totally appropriate behavior. You know, naked now, nice warm, dry robe later. So I would probably get in trouble for violating everyone's calm if I were to yell, "Cover your shame, damn it!" And yet the temptation is large.

I feel about as clean as I can get without actually shucking off a layer of epidermis, so I decide to spend my last half hour in the Quiet Room. Yeah, I'd like to remain in the Jacuzzi, but I just can't take any more naked because, really, how do you *not* look? As competitive as I am, I've been comparing myself to everyone else here and so far I am not happy with the results. I do have a better figure than that one chick, but it's only because she's at least seventy and had a mastectomy. *Yep, you may have beat cancer, but I beat you!*[19]

I towel off and put on my underwear before wrapping my robe tightly around me. I walk down the stairs to the dim, serene Quiet Room, where everyone is delightfully covered in layers of white terry cloth. Wicker chairs with big squashy cushions are scattered throughout the large room, with lots of space between them in order to foster peace and serenity. I grab an *Us Weekly* from the magazine rack and a cup of organic green tea, swirling in lots of honey. Save for a faint bit of whale music, the room is so still I can practically hear my heartbeat.

Magazine unopened, I sit and sip the scalding tea. As I silently reflect on the day, I have to laugh at myself. God, how did I ever get so uptight? I mean, I really need to (a) relax,

---

[19] Do you think the Devil will get a kick out of me and perhaps allow me a small fan in Hell?

and, barring that, at least (b) learn to mind my own business. What right do I have to be uncomfortable if someone decides to shed her clothing before getting in a well-chlorinated, single-sex hot tub? This place isn't exactly a set for *Girls Gone Wild*, so it's not like anything untoward is going to happen once people have derobed. Grandma is not about to shake her remaining breast at the camera. And who died and made me the Clothing-Always Police? No one here's done a thing wrong, yet I have the nerve to sit in judgment based on my own ridiculous prejudices. It's not fair and it's not right and I recognize that. And I'm more than a little ashamed of myself.

Resolved: Naked is a natural state and totally appropriate in a spa setting.

And I am fine with that.

For *you.*

I sit back and enjoy my tea, pleased at the idea of possibly being a better person.

However, when some random girl, naked as a jaybird, strolls into the Quiet Room of the Thousand Waves Spa and spends ten minutes bent over *right in front of me* with her little brown starfish waving hello to God and everyone while she paws through the magazine rack in search of the most current issue of the *New Yorker*, please know the line between "appropriate spa behavior" and "graphic peep show" has been crossed.

And if the air disturbed by my resulting scream causes yet another Indonesian tidal wave, well . . . I'm sorry.

But it's totally Fletch's fault.

To: angie_at_home, carol_at_home, wendy_at_home, jen_at_work
From: jen@jenlancaster.com
Subject: *more tales from a terrible wife*

Setting: Skybox at Wrigley Field, last Saturday afternoon.

Fletch: Our wives are going to die when they find out who we met.

Jeff: They'll go apeshit. My wife watches every week.

Fletch: Jen watches a lot, too.

Jeff: You know what we should do? Let's not tell them—we'll wait until they see the pictures.

Fletch: Good idea. I'm sure Jen's reaction will be priceless.

Fast-forward to today at the Costco photo booth, 4:30 p.m.

Me: These pictures are very nice, sweetie.

Fletch: *(picking one out of the stack)* And what do you think of this one?

Me: Your shirt is cute.

Fletch: *(trying to suppress a smile)* Uh-huh? And?

Me: And what?

Fletch: Anything else you want to say?

Me: Your hair looks nice.

Fletch: And?

Me: Um, you aren't quite as bloated as those photos from the Bears game where it looks like you swallowed a whole keg?

Fletch: And??

Me: *(glancing at the photo again)* Who's the little guy? Is he one of your clients, too?

Fletch: Does he look familiar?

Me: Kind of. Wait, is that . . . is that . . . Ferris? My old boss from when I worked at that bar in college?

Fletch: No. Look and think. You *know* him.

Me: Errr . . . one of your account managers? Although it seems like if he were entertaining clients, he should have dressed a bit more professionally.

Fletch: *(exasperated)* No, it's James Denton.

(silence)

Fletch: From *Desperate Housewives?*

(silence)

Fletch: Which I know you watch because you *make me watch it with you?*

(silence)

Fletch: *The plumber??*

Me: Oh, okay. I didn't recognize him without Teri Hatcher attached to his face. Yeah, I see it now.

Fletch: That's it? That's all you have to say?

Me: I guess I didn't realize he was scrawny. No wonder those housewives are so desperate.

All Quiet on the Westerville Front

Someone has broken into my house!

And, aahhh!! They are naked!

But . . . I've been here in the kitchen this whole time. Wouldn't I have heard someone breaking in through the glass door fifteen feet directly in front of me? Or maybe have seen them through the open blinds?

And wouldn't the dogs be barking instead of snoring away on the couch?

And if someone were going to home invade me, why naked? That's dumb simply because it would be so easy to identify them to the police afterward. "Can you tell me what he was wearing, ma'am?" the officer would ask. "Yes—a guilty smile and a pair of tube socks," I'd reply. Besides, it's forty-eight degrees outside and raining sideways. It's curl-up-by-the-fire-with-cocoa weather, not run-around-naked-and-steal-my-stuff weather. Plus, with no pants, there are no pockets, so where would the intruder put my cash and jewelry?

Still, I'd better grab that big-ass machete Fletch bought when he went to Thailand so I can stab the intruder. Yes, sir, I shall stab them good because I am half Sicilian and stabbing is my birthright.

Oh, wait . . .

That's not a naked person. That's my tan tapestry jacket hanging on the coatrack.

And I almost stabbed it. Heh. Wow.

Fletch should never leave me alone again.

Fletch left today for an indeterminate amount of time. He works for a telecommunications company and their hourly employees are going on strike, so managers like him have to do union members' jobs during contract negotiations. He could be gone anywhere from a day to a month, depending on which side is willing to make more concessions. Contract negotiations broke down over benefits; the union has balked because the new contract would give them a $5 pharmacy copay instead of paying nothing. Interesting, because management employees pay $30 per prescription, and that's only after meeting a $2,100 deductible. But at this point, I'm thrilled to have any medical coverage so I can't complain. I take comfort in knowing the *next* time I almost bite my finger off eating French fries, I can have someone other than the kid who works the drive-thru look at it.

Although I'll miss Fletch while he's away, that's not really the issue. We'll talk and e-mail whenever he has a free minute. I remember the great conversations we used to have on the phone when he'd graduated and I hadn't yet joined him in Chicago; we connected on a whole different level.

The problem is I really should not be left to my own devices for any period of time. Fletch is the stabilizing force that keeps me "adorably eccentric," instead of "that fucking weirdo with dirty hair who talks to her dogs while gardening in pajamas." I don't know what happened to me—I was fine living alone in college.[1] But there's something about an urban environment that brings out the propensity for insanity in all of us. Every week you hear about some bat-shit-crazy old lady who's found harboring thirty pit bulls in her tiny apartment. The newscasts always start: *In downtown Baltimore today* or *"Police raided a squalid Detroit home,"* because it seems like this kind of stuff never happens out in the country. Or maybe it's just if you live on a forty-acre farm, your neighbors would be fine if you kept your goat indoors. *Smoke up! Enjoy! Be careful he doesn't eat your pillows!* But in a creaky old three-flat with a shared stairwell? Not so much.

I need Fletch around to remind me it's not appropriate to eat Lucky Charms three times a day simply because I despise cooking. He's the one who gently leads me away from the phone after a night of drinking.[2] And without him to tell me no, I'm sure *I'd* be the bat-shit-crazy old lady with thirty pit bulls. Basically, Fletch keeps me off the evening news.

It's already well past dinnertime and the only thing I've had to eat today is a couple of slices of Buffalo chicken pizza served with a side of mayo.[3] I don't know what to make that

---

[1] For the most part.

[2] I had a bit of a beer-induced 1-800-PSYCHIC FRIEND addiction before we met. I've yet to have another $300 phone bill since we've been together.

[3] All the bleu cheese dressing was gone, so I thought the mayo would be an adequate substitution. It wasn't.

doesn't involve the stove or a box of cereal, so I'm sitting here hungry.[4] I wish I could remember what I used to do before Fletch came into my life and decided we'd have pork chops.

I lived alone for three years before him—surely I must have eaten, if only because I don't remember Sally Struthers or a TV crew filming my dirty, fly-ridden face and distended belly. I know I didn't cook back then because I had a gas stove and it terrified me. My parents had an electric range so my only experience with a gas stove prior to moving in was the fifty-year-old one at my Noni's[5] house. Long story short, I was in the kitchen when in our youthful attempt to bake a cake, it blew my cousin Stephanie's eyebrows off and she had to run upstairs, shove the dog out of the way, and stick her flaming head in the toilet.[6] And I've worked too long to attain the perfect eyebrow arch, so I disconnected the gas and used my college oven to store my shoes.

And yes, I know I live in the middle of a city and there are hundreds of places ready, willing, and able to deliver a global variety of meals, but without Fletch here to confer with on what sounds good, I'm mired in pizza-and-mayonnaise fiascos. Maybe I'll call him to see what I should do.

I pick up the phone and dial. Damn. Voice mail. I guess I'll try his e-mail.

---

[4] And kind of stupid, if I'm being perfectly honest.

[5] Speaking of crazy old ladies . . .

[6] You know what didn't help? Me trailing along behind her singsonging, "Yooooou're in trooooooouble!"

To: jen_at_home
From: fletch_at_work
Subject: *Reporting from the Front Lines of History, Day One*

It dawned on me that I might be witnessing firsthand a significant event, the eternal struggle between the Proletariat and Bourgeoisie. The exploitation of The Worker by The Man, the death of The American Dream done in by corporate greed and ruthless management. And given such a rare glimpse into actual politics and economics in action, I feel I have a duty to document it and shall be keeping a journal of my time here. Just as I have a sworn duty to provide the good people of Westerville, OH, with a reliable telecommunications infrastructure.

I'm signing off now so I can begin the diary. Before I do, I'll remind you that you worked in a restaurant when you lived alone. You ate there every day and that's why you didn't starve. I was kidding when I offered to leave you the number to Adult Protective Services. Now I'm not so sure.

To: jen_at_home
From: fletch_at_work
Subject: *RE: RE: Reporting from the Front Lines of History, Day One*

Okay, Jen, jelly beans are not an acceptable dinner. I can't believe I just had to write that sentence. And, no, the Garbage Fairy is not "on strike," too. I'm sorry to hear that in less than twenty-four hours the trash is stacked to the ceiling by the front door, but did it ever occur to you that maybe I do more around the house than that for which I get credit? I get the feeling you're a can of shaving cream shy of running around slapping yourself in the face à la Macaulay Culkin.

To: jen_at_home
From: fletch_at_work
Subject: *Day Two*

We had two picketers today at 6:00 a.m., parked in lawn chairs on the sidewalk. Reports from the early shift are that more arrived later in the morning, bringing with them a small tent and barbecue grill. They were gone when I arrived at 6:30, but who could blame them after a day of scarfing down weenies?

Oh, and yes, to answer your question, 9:30 a.m. is far too early for a margarita.

To: jen_at_home
From: fletch_at_work
Subject: *RE: RE: Day Two*

No, I was unaware we had twenty-eight pillows in our house. They aren't something I would ever think to count.

And no, I'm sorry to disappoint, but I don't think our e-mails to each other are just like the ones Elizabeth Barrett and Robert Browning used to send, for a variety of reasons, the first being he never worked for the phone company and to my knowledge, she never got her fist stuck in a peanut butter jar.

To: jen_at_home
From: fletch_at_work
Subject: *Day Three*

The picketers are back. Today they brought lawn chairs and a picnic blanket. I believe protesters should walk, or at least stand. But I'm a traditionalist. Who would take the "Million Man Picnic" seriously? Anyone, that is, besides the Kingsford Charcoal Company?

Also, you'll take the pink polish off the dogs' toenails if you ever want me to walk them again.

To: jen_at_home
From: fletch_at_work
Subject: *RE: RE: Day Three*

Remember what I told you about moderation? Blacking out after drinking a whole pot of coffee today is entirely preventable.

Perhaps next time you'll choose to go to the store to buy more half-and-half, rather than cutting your coffee with whipped cream.

To: jen_at_home
From: fletch_at_work
Subject: *Day Four*

Did you know Westerville is in a dry county? In fact, it was the home of the Anti-Saloon League from 1893 to 1933. Please note for future reference: we are *never* moving to Westerville.

See you tomorrow night—and for the record, yes, I *will* be aggravated if you don't disassemble your couch-cushion fort before I get there.

Fletch returns home today to an orderly, non-couch-cushion-forted home and we celebrate with a lovely pork-chop-and-green-bean dinner, followed by a pie à la mode chaser. I'm so glad he's back because that means everything can return to normal.[7]

After an uneventful evening of dog-walking and reality TV, I'm preparing for bed by brushing my teeth when I hear something that sounds like *"Yeaarrggghhhh!"*

"You say something, sweetie?" I spit, rinse, and return my

---

[7] And thank God, because I can't take any more Lucky Charms.

toothbrush to its holder before entering the bedroom to find the source of all the yelling.

Fletch, holding his pillow in one hand, points at the bed and shouts, "What is *that*?"

I look. "Oh. That's a machete. It's yours. Don't you remember buying it? Did Westerville make you all forget-y?" I ask. I guess now would be an excellent time to mention the paranoia I developed when I used to live alone.

To backtrack, like any other kid, I used to keep my hands and feet far away from the monsters who lived under my bed. One night I felt a bit daring and let my hand dangle over the side. Instead of nothing, I actually touched *another hand*! I didn't realize my brother had come into my room (I had a window unit and it was a hot night) and climbed into the twin bed right next to mine. He sprawled in such a way that his hand hung off the side of his bed, and that's what I felt when I reached out. I screamed bloody murder, causing my brother to wake up and bolt out of bed, thus knocking over the box fan, which then led my parents to believe one of us had fallen out a window. And then my dad yelled at me, which was kind of unfair. Like *I* was responsible for the monster?

Fast-forward to the house I lived in before I met Fletch—it was at least a hundred years old and had not been well maintained. Plus, it was directly between the bars and all the fraternity houses on Littleton Street.[8] So, drunken fraternity guys were always wandering by and messing with the place, as drunken fraternity guys were wont to do. The West Lafayette

----

[8] Yeah, like I didn't plan *that* intentionally. Like a spider and her web, I was.

Police got a bit tired of me having them on speed-dial, so I decided I'd take matters into my own hands. To make another long story short, I've slept with a weapon close by for years.

But at some point, I probably should have related this explanation to Fletch. It's just that when we first started dating, I wanted him to believe I was normal, so it never came up.[9]

"I know what it is, *thank you*." He holds up the knife and turns it over in his hands. The handle is wrapped in green cord Fletch calls *Hundred Mile an Hour Tape*. (I've never asked for an explanation because if Fletch starts in on his army stories, I'll pretty much end up stabbing myself in the ear.) The blade is over a foot long and almost four inches across at its widest point, and it tapers down to a deadly little point. It's possibly the scariest thing I've ever seen and is *so* much cooler than the variety of steak knives I used to sleep with in college. "My question is, why is it *under my pillow?*"

"I kept it there for protection while you were gone."

"So if someone broke in, you were going to *stab* them?"

"Uh-huh. Or cut something off. Guess it would depend on what was more expedient. Ooh, also, I sat in the front window every night and sharpened it, just in case any bad guys were casing the joint. Be careful when you pick it up—it's quite sharp now." I begin to arrange the pillows on my side of the bed into a proper sleeping nest. I like the flat acrylic-filled one as a bottom layer, then I have my feather pillow from childhood stacked on top of it at an angle. I also snuggle with a big body pillow that I call President George Squashington,

---

[9] He didn't find out otherwise until it was far too late.

but it's not on the bed. I cross the room to retrieve it. "Honey, did you forget? You moved President Squashington! I need him so I can sleep."

"Sorry, didn't recognize him without his powdered wig. But back to what we were saying—you've been sleeping with this mammoth knife because you're concerned about your safety."

"Deeply." I fluff the president and place him perpendicular to the others.

"Despite the fact we live behind two security gates?"

"Uh-huh."

"And have an alarm system."

"Yep."

"And 165 pounds of shepherd and pit bull."

"Duh. Who's going to protect the dogs? Me and my knife, that's who."

Suddenly Fletch looks very tired. "Tell me, how do you counter the fact our area has one of the lowest crime rates in the city?"

I toss a cat off the bed so I can shake out my quilt. "Well, it's not as low as I'd like. You realize I go to the Chicago Sex Offender database all the time and look up the local addresses, don't you? There are eight registered child molesters in our police beat! Eight! That's eight too many." I walk over to my dresser, open a drawer, and pull out a laminated folder. "Would you like to see their dossiers?"

"You *did not* print out their information."

"Of course I did! I'm constantly vigilant, and since I wasn't busy cooking, I needed a project while you were gone." I hand him my stack of mug shots. "I figure if these guys are prowling around—and have suddenly lost their taste for children—I need to know. Besides, if I didn't print them out, I'd have to look up their addresses whenever I take the dogs around to pee on their lawns."

Fletch shakes his head and opens his mouth but no words come out.

"What? The dogs have to relieve themselves somewhere, right? Plus, I like the whole retribution aspect of it—*no green lawn for you, you pervert!* Kind of like a Scarlet Letter, only in dead grass. I swear, Loki seems to whiz battery acid. Anyway, I've decided it's my civic duty to keep an eye on their homes to make sure I never see a Big Wheel parked in their yard. I'm telling you, if you're not constantly vigilant, you aren't safe."[10]

He hands the papers back to me and I file them away in my underwear drawer. "If safety is such a concern, tell me again why we can't have a shotgun."

"Pfft. A home invader would assume you'd have a gun, but a machete? That's completely out of left field. Really, that's some *Monty Python, Nobody Expects the Spanish Inquisition* shit. Plus, if you hack off a bad guy's hand, his days of B and E are over. Stabbing is nice because it allows for deep hurting *and* an object lesson." I return to the bathroom, swish tooth-whitening mouthwash around, and then rinse again before we both get into bed. "Shooting just doesn't afford the same nuance."

Fletch finishes fluffing his solitary pillow. "Sometimes I

---

[10] See? I am all about the locked door, unlike one Miss Carrie Bradshaw, who'd sit in her apartment with her window wide open. So either Giuliani really did turn New York into Disneyland or something wasn't realistic.

forget you're half Sicilian. Too bad you weren't in Westerville. It would have been hard for the strikers to walk the picket line with broken ankles."

I kiss him good night and settle into my side of the bed. "Mm-hmm. We're a stabby, vengeful people. No bedbugs and such, Fletch."

We're silent for a few minutes and I'm just about asleep when Fletch shakes me. "Hey, Jen?"

"What is it, sweetie?"

"I'm never leaving you alone again."

I hide my smile in the pillow. "Good."

Dear Google Management,

I love your services and access them so often that I've come to use terms like "Googleicious" and "Googleholic" to describe said affection. That being said, we have a problem.

The dilemma is that old-school, semi-repressed grandfather types like my dad have also discovered the utility of your service. Now, the search engine is just dandy when older gentlemen need to find pastel plaid golf pants, local Lincoln-Mercury dealerships, and discount plane tickets to Florida.

However, a crisis occurs when they employ amorphous search criteria. For example, when my father decided to do some reading on Stephen Hawking's theories of the nature of space and time, he Googled a variation of the term "black holes" and ended up on an entirely different type of Web site.

I could hear his shrieks one state away.

To compound this quandary, this retired executive class spent a professional lifetime with the aid of a competent secretary. Thus, they never developed an eye for the small details—that's what "their girl" was for—because they were so busy running the world. Point is, if my dad's right-hand Barbara had been around to assist him, he would have never accidentally clicked through to join the Log Cabin Republicans while looking for information on building a rough-hewn timber home.

I beg you to please add an "Old Businessman" parameter to your search engine. These fellows, although tigers in their prime, have been weakened by a lifetime of unfiltered cigarettes, double Manhattans, triple cheeseburgers, and quadruple bypasses. Their cardiovascular systems simply cannot handle the sustained and perpetual shock that can result from a bad Google.

Please fix.

Best,

Jen Lancaster

P.S. My friend had a similar issue when searching for a Catholic school uniform for her daughter. A "Soccer Mom" button may also be in order.

To: angie_at_home, carol_at_home, wendy_at_home, jen_at_work
From: jen@jenlancaster.com
Subject: *the king's on his throne (and all's wrong with the world)*

Ladies,

The dream is over.

Our lives will never be the same.

I blame the dog.

You guys know in the ten years we've been together Fletch and I have purposefully kept a bit of mystery in our relationship by attending to personal bathroom business behind closed doors. And much as I love him and desire to be privy to his innermost workings, I'd happily live the rest of my life unsure if he's a back-to-front or front-to-back kind of guy or employs the one- or two-hand technique. (Carol, stop calling me "repressed." Think about it—Elvis never felt the same about Priscilla after seeing little Lisa Marie born. Laugh at me all you want, but this is a boundary I won't willingly cross.)

Anyway, I was sitting on the bed folding laundry, watching *Fox News* while Fletch used the mug off the master bedroom. Maisy, having found herself alone for thirteen seconds and deeming this wholly unacceptable, charged up the stairs with such veloc-ity that she couldn't stop herself when she reached the summit, thus exploding open the bathroom door located eight feet away, like a small, corn-chip-scented cannonball.

And there he was, Fletcher in all his mystical glory, pants around his ankles, *Star* magazine in his hands, reading an article on Nick and Jessica while nature and all the fiber in our diets took its course. Our eyes locked with the kind of paralyzed horror one thief might have when bumping into another thief, finding themselves in the awkward, unfortunate position of having broken into the same home at the same time.

I was the first to react by shrieking and pulling the covers over my head while Maisy bounced back and forth between the bathroom and the bed, delighted to have united us all in the experience.

When the screaming on both parts finally subsided, I stumbled across the room, eyes clamped shut, and gently closed the door.

We shall never speak of this again, he and I. Yet the image will be burned into my retinas for eternity.

Hold me.

Jen

P.S. Am not a drama queen. *Am traumatized.*

Tuesday Afternoon Drinking Club

*I*n my former, auspicious career I addressed crowds of thousands without breaking a sweat. I negotiated with dour, gray-suited hospital administrators so hostile they'd drag me into the desert and leave me for dead given the opportunity, yet I stood my ground in demanding they accept my company's contract, "Or else." And I've guided corporate executives through the most dire of crises with a smile on my face the entire time. So you'd think chatting with a kindly medical professional in the privacy of her office wouldn't be but a blip on my radar.

And that would be true.

If I were wearing pants.

Today I've got an appointment with the girlie doctor and I'm nothing less than terrified. I've put off my annual well-woman exam for four years because I'm so cowardly about this sort of thing, no doubt stemming from my Quaker-like sense of modesty. Sure, it's all well and good to litter my conversations with every variety of f-bomb,[1] but when it comes to showing my unmentionables to a complete stranger? Regardless of her impeccable medical education, extensive experience, and board certification? I think not.

However, I'm really trying to act more like an adult lately,[2] so I force myself to make the appointment. Of course, I have to down a whole bottle[3] of wine to do so. And then I cancel it three times before Fletch, disgusted by my lack of courage, threatens to (a) drag me to the appointment on a leash like we have to when we take Loki to the vet to have his nails clipped, and (b) check me into the Betty Ford Center if I don't stop inhaling boxed wine every time I look at the phone.

I *have* to honor the appointment this time and the only way that's going to happen is if there's an elaborate system of treats and rewards in place. I decide my beforehand treat will be a trip to the bookstore, so I ask Fletch to drop me off at the Michigan Ave Borders an hour before my appointment.

We've just gotten in the car when I start to hyperventilate.

"Funny, but Loki doesn't start to panic until after we've exited our parking lot," Fletch observes. "You need to breathe in a paper bag or something?"

"No." Gasp. Gasp. Gasp. "I'll (gasp) be (gasp) fine," I reply.

"I don't understand your anxiety. Are they going to cut you at all?"

---

[1] "Fucktard" being my all-time favorite.

[2] Other attempts include paying bills instead of stuffing them in a cabinet and fewer Pepperidge Farm–based dinners.

[3] Read box.

"Oh, sweet Jesus, no!" I shriek.

"Then they're just going to look at stuff?"

Gasp. "Right."

"Alone, in an exam room—just you and the doctor, and no one else, right?" We cross the bridge over the north branch of the river at Division and begin to drive past the projects.

"Yes." Gasp.

He glances at the boarded-up buildings with their broken windows and concertina wire and poses a question. "Okay, which would you rather—to be dropped off in the middle of Cabrini Green at midnight with a handful of cash or to see your gynecologist for a routine visit?"

I don't even have to consider the choice. "The Green. Definitely the Green."

He turns to face me. "You're kidding."

"No, really—maybe Florida and J.J. still live there? And Thelma and Ralph, too. But not James. Poor James. He was killed in a car accident before the family could move to Mississippi for his excellent new job. And that? Was not dy-no-mite."[4]

"I wouldn't know. My racist parents refused to let me watch *Good Times*. However, they *were* able to decipher fantasy from reality, which is more than I can say for you right now."

I begin to hyperventilate again as we turn down Michigan

---

[4] You know who never referenced her childhood influences? That's right. Miss Carrie I-Have-No-Past Bradshaw. I also don't remember her ever freaking out over a routine well-woman exam, so I'm calling this one a draw.

Ave and idle in front of Borders. "Okay, you're here," Fletch says. "Good luck today."

"Do—do—you have any last-minute advice for me?" I stammer.

He looks thoughtful for a moment. "Yes. Yes, I do."

"Well?"

"You should try to be less of a pansy. See you later!"

I escape into the safe confines of the bookstore, secure in the knowledge no one there is going to make me pull down my pants. I linger over the new releases and peruse the sale table. I go upstairs to the café and eschew coffee in favor of herbal tea, figuring the caffeine would make me even jumpier. Beverage in hand, I cruise the self-help section but don't see any titles that might make me "less of a pansy."

I buy a few new reads before heading down the street. I trudge past many happy places—Cartier, Coach, Tiffany, and, of course, Garrett's Popcorn, but window-shopping fails to make me smile because I feel like Dead Man Walking.

I pray to get hit by a bus as I turn down St. Clair Street, figuring the doctor could check out my girl parts while I was under sedation to fix my broken leg, but no such luck. I arrive at the office not only intact but early, damn it. As I climb the wide marble steps to the front door, I'm overwhelmed by the desire to run. However, my inner adult forces me to press on and take the elevator to the eighth floor, likely because my inner adult fears running slightly more than pants-dropping.

With a quavering voice, I check in at reception. The office is gorgeous—clean, sleek furniture, lush plants, and an unobstructed view of Lake Michigan through enormous picture windows. The skies are steely gray and it's windy today so the lake is choppy with whitecaps and is kicking up six-foot waves. Water crashes and foams over the concrete barriers protecting Lake Shore Drive, launching huge plumes of icy spray all over the abandoned running path. If I didn't know I was in Illinois, I'd swear I was looking at the Atlantic Ocean. This magnificent body of water is precisely one of the reasons I choose to live here. Were I not about to show a stranger my yahoo, I'd be enthralled by the vista[5] and likely to break into a chorus of "The Wreck of the *Edmund Fitzgerald*," but today it barely registers.

The receptionist gives me the insurance form clipboard and a pen sporting an Ortho-Novum logo. I feel like I'm going to throw up and my hands are shaking so badly I can barely scrawl my name on the paperwork. I'm about to toss the clipboard, dash out the door, and catch the first steamer to Venezuela when some girl comes in with a "problem." I can't hear everything but I do catch the bit where she tells the receptionist, "I don't know what it is, but I want it gone immediately." I snicker so loudly the entire desk staff shoots me murderous looks, but I don't care. Laughing at someone else's misfortune makes me momentarily forget my fright and I remain in my seat, keeping a healthy distance between myself and Miss Scratchy McUnderpants. (Because, really? What's funnier than venereal disease?)

I'm barely on the second page of the new Janet Evanovich when my name is called, so I gather up my sack of books and head down the Hallway of Doom. The nurse is wearing

---

[5] I once took a lousy job in the Chicago Board of Options Exchange building because of a similar view.

Dansko professional clogs and my loafer heels are rubber, so the only noise I hear as I'm walking down the hall is that of my own pounding pulse.

The walls leading to the exam room are covered with beastly graphic charts of internal workings. Squeamish as I am, the idea of all those pipes and tubes and fluids makes me weak in the knees. I prefer to think of myself as having a thick peanut-butter center. Or possibly creamy caramel.

Once I get to my room, the first thing I have to do is step on the scale. "Well," I tell the nurse, "you certainly know how to add insult to injury in this joint." And it's no surprise when she points out I've gained fifty pounds since my last visit. "Really," I exclaim, "is that why I can no longer get my old pants past my knees? Goodness, I'd simply assumed I'd had twenty-seven separate dry-cleaning incidents!"

Note to self for future reference: *Tubby girls with smart mouths will be given paper robes, not cloth, by nurses who lack senses of humor.*

Nurse Ratched advises me to strip completely, and as I undress I wonder if "completely" includes my socks. Erring on the side of caution, I toss them aside first, pleased with having the foresight to have given myself a fresh pedicure. Earlier this morning, I also brushed my teeth a second time and flossed. Fletch noted my excellent dental hygiene and asked, "Is that the end they're going to examine?"

With much trepidation, I take off my sweater and bra and begin to struggle into the miniature paper gown. Because of my rampant modesty, I'm trying in vain to keep everything covered. While I wrestle with the tiny plastic belt-tie, I *burst* out of the left side of the robe, thus exposing my long, flat, completely non-gravity-resistant breast to the wall of *Your Cervix and You* brochures.[6] *Gah!*

So, I do what any good little prude would do in this situation . . . I grab a stapler from the doctor's desk and attempt to put the side back together in a panicked frenzy. While I twist around to work on fixing the left shoulder, I *burst* out of the right side of the robe.

I begin to get very angry at the exploding clothing. Exactly when did I turn into the Jen-credible Hulk?

In my haste to cover my naked parts, I then staple the right side of the robe all crooked. I glance at myself in the mirror and see that what I'm wearing no longer resembles anything like a robe. Jagged bits of paper are sticking up everywhere, with random clumps of staples littering the sides and shoulders. I look like a mental patient who escaped to a paper factory and crafted a paper suit before attempting to create a paper getaway car to drive to paper Mexico. All I'm missing is a touch of (paper) crazy about the eyes.

After inspecting my handiwork, I inadvertently bend over laughing, thus causing the one untorn part of the robe to *explode*. And in trying to fix it, I accidentally staple the back of the robe to my khakis. I'm hunkered over in my paper straitjacket, struggling to remove staples from my pants, when my gynecologist enters.

The doctor then excuses herself while she tries to stop crying.

Fortunately, when she returns she's carrying a cloth gown,

---

[6] Coming soon to a theater near you!

which I manage to put on upside down and backward. However, she's got access to all the forbidden zones, so we leave it as is. She apologizes for giggling and says this sort of thing happens all the time. Yeah. Of course it does. Ten bucks says six months from now an entire table of conference-going, Chardonnay-swilling, lobster-tail-eating OB/GYNs will be laughing at me when she recounts this scene.

To the good doctor's credit, she senses how scared I am, although perhaps my inability to clothe myself tipped her off. Or possibly me shrieking, "I am fucking terrified!"

Which is why I'm not surprised her first question is, "Do you use recreational drugs?"

I think for a moment before replying, "I don't know. Do you consider NyQuil recreational?"

"I guess that would depend on the frequency," she replies.

"Maybe every couple of months?"

"I'd say that's okay. Any other drug usage? Marijuana? Ecstasy? Cocaine?"

"Ha!" I reply. "Look at my butt; is this the ass of a coke fiend? I think not. However, sometimes when I'm tense, I have an OTC sleeping pill and follow it with a champagne chaser. Actually, it's my signature drink and I call the combination 'The Judy Garland.'"

After the doctor explains why she can't just "remove the whole shootin' match so I don't ever have to suffer through this again," she puts on her rubber gloves, at which point I may or may not pass out.

When I snap to, I inform her, "My middle name is Ann, my favorite movie is *Pulp Fiction*, and I have a naughty pit bull named Maisy. Seems like if you're going to poke around *down there*, you should know a bit more about me."

She nods thoughtfully and tells me, "My middle name is Elizabeth and I like *Law and Order* reruns. I backpacked in Europe after I finished undergrad and I adore Indian food. Now can you please uncross your legs so I can get a look?"

The whole exam takes less than five minutes and . . . yes, I realize I probably overreacted. No matter how unpleasant the circumstance, if I can hold my breath for the duration, it can't be *so* bad. After I dress,[7] the doctor reenters the exam room and wants to discuss breast health. The only thing slightly less mortifying than *being* naked with a stranger is *talking* about it.

Stab me in the eye with a fucking fork, why don't you?

Anyway, the doctor tries to give me a little kit that includes a journal to document my monthly cancer-screening self-exam.

A *journal*?

What the hell am I going to record in a *boob journal*?

> *January 1*—*Got to second base with myself. Heh.*
> *February 1*—*Got to second base with myself. Heh.*
> *March 4*—*Forgot about the screening and only re-membered four days later when I almost slammed my boob in the car door. Got to second base with my-self. Heh.*

Sorry, but I do not possess the kind of maturity required to write about me ol' knockers on a regular basis. I politely refuse the

---

[7] I've lost a sock in the process—WTF?

offer, claiming I couldn't see me using it, what with all the gig-gling. Although I have to wait for the pap results to come back from the lab, everything else looks fine and I'm free to go, *thank God*.

Pants securely on, bags packed, and sock-free, I leave the scary, scary office with a spring in my step and a bit of a speculum-induced waddle. I did it! It's over! I congratulate myself for being brave, so very brave,[8] and decide it is treat time. *Woo-hoo!* But what to get? When I was a kid, my mom would take me to Dairy Queen after a particularly traumatic allergist appointment, but (a) she's 150 miles away, and (b) it's fourteen degrees today. So a Peanut Buster Parfait is probably out.

I practically dance the ten blocks from my doctor's office to One Magnificent Mile and spend the whole time vacillating between the idea of high tea or a cocktail. Sure, orange pekoe and finger sandwiches in the vast parlor at the Drake Hotel sounds lovely, but that's really more of a shared experience. Also, my hands are still trembling and I'm not sure I could keep my tea in its bone china cup. Instead, I choose the warm embrace of my old friend alcohol.

I head to the gorgeously appointed mahogany-and-leather bar at the Four Seasons on Delaware and I survey the array of squashy couches and brocaded chairs. Oh, how I love the Four Seasons! We used to come here all the time during the dot-com era, but now that we're barely middle class we save it for very special occasions.

---

[8] Yes, yay, me! I was able to do something once in ten years that every other woman in America does on a routine basis without blinking an eye.

I've always adored the service here; I guess I appreciate any place that lets me make an ass out of myself without raising an eyebrow. One time a group of us came here after some drinky-drinky event downtown. Right as we were about to pour ourselves into a cab, I spotted a gigantic laminated "George Bush Is Hitler" poster and I thought, "Oh, *hell* no." Sure, I get why people don't like him and I'm fine with that. I understand those who protest his decisions and can totally see why folks might think he's a dummy. However, I cannot agree with comparing him to the fiend who almost single-handedly exterminated an entire race of people. So I tore the poster off the telephone pole and was barely able to wedge it in the taxi with us.

Anyway, we spilled out of the cab and washed onto the sidewalk at the Four Seasons. Valets helped us up and out, gingerly handling my mammoth placard. "Here you are, miss," they said without batting an eye. They acted as though drunken girls carried giant posters of a swastika-covered president into their facility ten times a day. We paraded past all the staff—doormen, bellhops, concierges, etc., each of them smiling graciously, while I struggled behind my colossal sandwich board. We sloshed into the bar and the maître d' met us at the door to show us to our seats.

And this bit? Right here? Is why the Four Seasons rocks.

With nary a smirk, he asked, "Might I check that item for you, miss?"

To which I replied, "Ssshhank you, but I shhhannn't be requiring your sssshhhhervichhes," before hooting and snorting at my own savoir faire. And then Fletch, our friends, an unfortunately mustachioed photo of the commander in chief, and I spent the rest of the evening sitting on barstools swilling $14 cocktails.[9]

As I settle into a plush couch in the corner next to a porcelain reading lamp, a waiter approaches with a dish of mixed nuts and wasabi peas. "Miss, what might I be gettin' you?" he asks in a melodious Irish accent.

"Hmm," I say. "I'm not sure. I've had a *really* stressful day. Doctor. Girl parts. Total nightmare. But I don't want to talk about it. So, what can you suggest that might be hot, sweet, and full of liquor? And I don't mean Tara Reid!"

With a heroic amount of patience, he waits until I finish chortling myself stupid to detail the finer points of the winter drinks menu. We settle on a cider-and-whiskey beverage, which I belt down in about thirteen seconds. After the first cocktail, I begin to pace myself, spacing out my drinks with sips of water from my crystal goblet and nibbles from the gratis nut tray. (Whatever profit margin the Four Seasons may have realized from the overpriced ciders is neatly eclipsed by my cashew consumption.)

Since I spend all my money on fancy drinks, I have to take public transportation home. Mumbling to myself about girl parts and shuffling, I make my way down to the Chicago Avenue stop. The bus and I arrive at the same time (how did that happen?), and wafting whiskey fumes, I manage to stagger over discarded newspapers and empty Starbucks cups to the back of the vehicle.

---

[9] Two things to note for future reference—sashimi is a *terrible* drunk food, and if you have to throw up in a public place, there's no finer washroom than the one at the Four Seasons.

And you know what's nice?

Today I finally smell like everyone else on the midday bus. Hooray for Tuesday Afternoon Drinking Club!

Y

Before leaving the Four Seasons, I apparently call Fletch at work and leave the following message: *"Hi, iissch me! My girly partschss are fiiiine and I'm drinking whooshkey! Bring home many beers."* Smirking, Fletch informs me he and his work pals had a delightful time passing the phone around and laughing at my expense.

Yes, *har-de-har-har*, fat boy. Laugh it up.

I hope you enjoy doing your own laundry when I check myself into the Betty Ford Center.

from the desk of Miss Jennifer A. Lancaster

Dear *Fox News* Channel,

I love you and would watch you 24/7 if I didn't have to sleep,
shower, and cook pork chops. And you're aware that every TV
in my house defaults to your station. And that I leave them on
all day so that when I walk from room to room, I never miss a
second. My home is like a sports bar—only with conservative
news.

Here's the thing—when you *burst* into an interview with your giant, multi-exclamation-pointed FOX ALERT banner, you cause
my heart to seize up in the process. So if you're going to do this, I
expect to hear *real and accurate* breaking news. I just wasted an
entire beautiful Saturday indoors waiting for information on the
evacuation of LAX because you convinced me that we were under
siege by terrorists.

Oh, Fox, Fox, Fox . . . a sparking flashlight is not an
explosion.

A stupid teenager running the wrong way up an escalator is not a
terrorist.

For future reference, please keep in mind that discretion is the
better part of valor. And that I am on the wrong side of my
thirties with high cholesterol. My small, clogged, black heart

can only take so many FOX ALERTS, so let's make 'em count, okay?

Your biggest fan,

Jen Lancaster

P.S. Please give Sean Hannity a raise.

Dear America,

Okay, what the hell is going on here?

Is there a bizarre weather front passing through, thus making you completely and utterly goofy?

I figured today had the potential for weirdness when the bike messenger in front of me ordered a nine-shot espresso at the coffee shop. Nine shots! In one cup! I asked him if he was going to drink it or mainline it, which apparently cracked no one up but me. (Seriously, my wit is wasted on the staff of the Randolph Street Starbucks. Also, did you know it's Gingerbread Latte season again? Served in the festive red snowflake cups? Woo!)

Anyway, when I got to the office at my temp job, I started listening to talk radio and I heard all kinds of assorted foolishness. Apparently there's a movement calling for the Blue States to secede from the Red States to better reflect the nation's political leanings.

Um, yeah . . . it took six months and a multimillion-dollar advertising campaign when Chicago residents had to switch area codes, and seven years later, people are still dialing the wrong numbers.

So trying to teach citizens an entirely new currency system and national anthem?

Sure. That will happen.

As soon as my dog Loki creates a formula for cold fusion.

Later I heard John Kerry's already gearing up for a possible 2008 bid for the presidency. Excuse me, sir? A little friendly advice? *Relax*. Give yourself a minute to catch your breath. Why don't you take your wife on a nice cruise or something, you know, chill, kick back, maybe drink some banana liqueur cocktails before you make that kind of decision?

Anyway, after I returned from lunch, I heard how suicide hotlines and Canadian immigration officials have been inundated by those wanting to escape Bush's second term. Mental health professionals all over the country are working overtime to counsel those of you despondent over the election results. Apparently people are seeking postelection trauma therapy in droves.

Now I'm sorry to have to do this, but I think at this point our nation could use a little tough love and now I'm going to have to go all Dr. Phil on you guys.

Ahem.

People?

Get a fucking grip on yourselves!

Pull it together! You've had a whole week to feel sorry for yourselves—it's time to move on with your lives! Enough with the moping, wailing, and navel-gazing already! Move on! It may seem hard at first, but I know you can do it because you are *Americans*. You and your ilk are responsible for the likes of John Wayne and the Ford Mustang and Microsoft, for crying out loud! And as Americans, you were spawned from the baddest motherfuckers to ever walk this earth! Those ancestors of yours huddled inside rickety old boats to get here, battling storms, sickness, hunger, fatigue, and fear, carrying with them nothing but the will to live free.

And you know what? These people—*your people*—helped create the greatest country in the world with the best form of government known to mankind.

Does this mean our system is perfect? No. Does this mean sometimes despite your hard work, your guy or gal doesn't get elected, even though you have empirical proof he or she was the better candidate? Yes.

And it's okay to be disappointed when this happens. Because it does happen. Every election.

But please don't let your displeasure with our system cause you to lose your peace of mind, toss away your citizenship—or worse, your life—over fears about the direction this country may or may not be heading in *because your team didn't win.*

Because it's flat-fucking-ridiculous. And you're better than that.

You've had plenty of time to feel your feelings. Now it's time to organize. Get off your therapists' couches and use your pent-up energy to gather the kind of information that will change minds and perceptions. If you hate the elected officials presiding over you, then it's your duty as an American to make sure we never get stuck with them again.

Rally.

Act.

Be an agent for change.

So leather up, you nancy boys and girls, and get busy.

Because you're going to be okay.

Best,

Jen

P.S. If I could endure the fraternity party otherwise known as the Clinton administration, you can deal with President Churchy Mc-Jesus.

P.P.S. If Bush were so intent on imposing a stringent Christian lifestyle on everyone, wouldn't he have started with his kids? As it stands, the twins are but a Jell-O shot away from starring in the presidential edition of *Girls Gone Wild*.

P.P.P.S. Still, nine shots of espresso? That's just messed up.

The Neocon Express

When it comes to taking the bus, I am functionally retarded.

No, wait, I can't say "retarded" because that insults all the developmentally disabled people who manage to use public transportation to travel from Point A to Point B every day without incident. For example, I didn't see any of *them* accidentally exiting at the wrong place after getting on the wrong bus and then walking an entire mile in stupid, pointy, kitten-heel boots until they figured out where the damn Fullerton stop was already.[1]

This bus-riding phobia is an entirely new phenomenon for me,[2] and in terms of nature versus nurture, I'm confident

---

[1] And I bet it's never taken any of them two hours to go four miles either.

[2] There's no specific term for fear of riding the bus, but there totally should be, considering there are words for fear of the Pope (papaphobia), fear of poetry (metrophobia), and fear of string (linonophobia). I mean, come on, fear of *string*? WTF?

saying I'm not genetically opposed to the bus. As a kid, I adored my school bus. Our driver was a cool guy named Jim and he'd play the rock station on the radio and would occasionally pump the air brakes in time with Foreigner songs. Plus, even though the kids on my street were supposed to congregate in a couple of centrally located spots, Jim would stop in front of all our houses and pick each of us up individually. (The door-to-door service is something I cherish to this day.) For the longest time, "the bus" was equivalent with "fun," as it meant going on field trips and traveling to speech meets and, later in life, guided tours through European cities and Mexican resort towns. For most of my life I've held busses in the same esteem as ice cream trucks, which is no small feat.

Sadly, the number 56 Milwaukee Ave bus ruined me for life. My prior experiences led me to believe buses run on a schedule, yet here in Chicago posted schedules are less an "estimated arrival time" and more a "guarantee of the one moment in time the bus *won't* be here." The number 56 is supposed to pick up every ten minutes. What generally happens is the buses get stacked up along the route and then continue in a red-light-running convoy all the way downtown, which means a forty-five-minute wait at the stop instead of ten. I live an $8 cab ride away from downtown, and I much prefer taxis to the bus, but there's something intrinsically wrong with spending $8 to get to a $12/hour job.

If I do manage to trick the number 56 into showing up in a timely fashion, it's a given that people will be packed in so tightly that I end up dry-humping a stranger's briefcase all the way down Milwaukee Ave.

The real treat is when the McMuffin-eating, coffee-drinking, nail-filing, cell-phone chatting, newspaper-reading, ADD-having person up front[3] slams on the breaks for no good reason and suddenly my butt becomes an air bag for the guy looking at *Sports Illustrated* in the seat next to me.[4]

Still, even though the bus is slow, undependable, and occasionally forces me to thrust my unmentionables in a stranger's mug, it's better than taking the El. Before I moved here, I'd spent a summer in Boston and fell in love with its extensive mass-transit system. I could effortlessly get anywhere on the East Coast by simply referring to my *Car-Free in Boston* guidebook. I'd easily tool all over the city on the T and had no problem figuring out the quickest way to get from the Sam Adams Brewery[5] in Jamaica Plain to the Singing Sand Beach in Marblehead via train. Although I was from Indiana, the system was such that I could provide directions to the guests at the hotel where I was working like I'd lived my whole life on Mass Ave. I assumed the El, Chicago's elevated train system, would be equally efficient.

I assumed wrong.

The day of my first ride, my friend Greg and I were meeting some colleagues for lunch across the Loop. While we waited on the El's wooden platform, we watched a passenger toss down a burning cigarette. "Wait," I'd asked, "isn't that

---

[3] Also known as the driver.

[4] BTW, Mr. *Sports Illustrated* won't find me the least bit amusing when I suggest, "Next time you do that, you better be tipping!" in an attempt to dissipate the awkwardness.

[5] A fantastic tour—$2 admission and all the fresh beer you could drink!

flammable? If those planks catch fire, won't we all, like, die?" My friend Greg shrugged and replied, "Yeah, but what are you going to do? Chicago's a first-world city with a third-world transportation system." And it pretty much went downhill from there. Seems like every time I get on the El, the train gets delayed, the air conditioning breaks, or it turns into an *incident*, like when I try to take it to the library.

Before I discuss the *incident*, I must give some background and explain that books are my crack. I come from a family of voracious readers and books have been a crucial part of my life ever since I can remember. My second memory is of curling up next to my mother and brother on a snowy night, wearing red velvet footie pajamas and hearing her read "A Visit from St. Nicholas" ("The Night Before Christmas") from the tome with the holograph-looking cover. (My first is from Thanksgiving that year, standing in my crib drawing turkeys on the wallpaper with a Magic Marker.)

At the time, we lived in an idyllic little town in Massachusetts, physically a few miles away from Boston, but worlds away from the hustle and bustle of the city. The town had a historic bandstand and expansive green commons, nestled next to Lake Quannapowitt, and our house was only a block away. As our place was almost two hundred years old, we had no air conditioning. Most of the time it was fine, but on the hottest nights, we'd walk down to the lakeshore to cool off while listening to my mother read passages from our favorite books. Somehow a stuffy house didn't seem so bad after hearing tales of Johnny Tremain getting maimed by molten silver, and I was grateful not to sleep in a hayloft and live with a grumpy old grandfather like Heidi. Plus, no one ever tried to shuttle me off to Maine to be raised like a lady like they did in *Rebecca of Sunnybrook Farms*. From the very beginning, books made me feel better about my lot in life, hence the start of an unbreakable habit.

I'd always been a public library kind of gal, but once I moved to Chicago, I discovered bookstores had gone through a magnificent metamorphosis. Well, of sorts. Perhaps not *everyone* considers the addition of coffee shops that sell big cookies and turtle cheesecake borderline miraculous.[6] However, I loved the addition of comfortable chairs, proper lighting, and wider aisles, too. I began to buy my weight in Grisham, Hiaasen, and Goldsmith. I was in mocha-flavored, whip-topped, cinnamon-sprinkled, page-turning heaven, especially when Helen Fielding's *Bridget Jones's Diary* came out and began the onslaught of pink-jacketed, shoe-covered chick lit books I so cherish today.

Anyway, thousands of dollars and calories later, I decide I want to read Plum Sykes's *Bergdorf Blondes*, but I'm kind of broke and don't have enough money for parking *and* coffee *and* cheesecake *and* books. Unfortunately, the library branch by my apartment has closed for remodeling, so I decide to brave the journey to the big gargoyle-roofed main library downtown.

And thus I present:

---

[6] But they would be *wrong*.

Getting Bergdorf Blonde: A Sixty-Four-Step Process

- Attempt to log on to library system to see if book is available.
- System says library card is invalid when try to reserve a copy.
- Call library help desk.
- Who are no damn help at all.
- Them: "Are you sure you put your library card number in right?"
- Me: "I tried sixteen different times. Surely one of those tries should have worked?"
- Them: "You need to come in if you want it."
- Me: "Arrggh. Fine."
- Beg husband for a ride to library.
- Him: "I'm busy working. Why don't you just take the El? Or are you still afraid of it? I bet you ten dollars you end up taking a cab."
- Pfft. Am not a princess. Can figure out stupid train system if needed.
- Of course, *hate* public transportation.
- Once quoted as saying, "The thing about mass transportation is that it transports the masses."
- Famous last words?
- Take Blue Line from Chicago stop to change trains at State/Lake.
- Stare helplessly at signs because can't figure out if should

transfer to Brown or Purple Line. And why no Pink Line? Pink is *lovely* color.[7]

- Directions totally unclear.
- Have small fit.
- Decide on Purple Line. Purple is less icky color than Brown.[8]
- Wait ten minutes, no train.
- Realize am on wrong side of platform, so cross bridge to get to other side.
- Wait ten more minutes.
- Realize Orange Line goes exact same way.
- Aha! Am clever! Will take quickie shortcut Orange Line and not wait with all Purple Line chumps.
- Board Orange Line.
- Ride, ride, ride.
- Watch as library *flies* past window.
- Uh-oh.
- Realize got on express train.
- Get off at Roosevelt and double back so can catch Purple Line at Adams/Wabash.
- See big, pretty, fluffy dog and try to pet.
- Yelled at by security guards.
- "Ma'am, don't touch the dog. He's *working*."
- Wait for ten more minutes for Orange Line headed back to Loop.
- Freeze because wearing lightweight coat—thought library would be hot.

---

[7] March 30, 2006—Chicago CTA announces the creation of a new elevated train line, to be called "the Pink Line." You're welcome.

[8] Except for shoes and eye shadow, of course. Do not buy purple shoes *or* eye shadow—am not Tammy Faye Bakker.

- Catch train back to Adams/Wabash.
- Get off and wait for *right* Orange Line train.
- Notice am standing across from Art Institute.
- Feel guilty for never having visited institute.
- Except once to shop in gift shop.
- Beat self up about own vapidity and lack of fine-art knowledge.
- Freeze.
- Get on what assume is right Orange Line train, as is across tracks.
- Ride, ride, ride.
- Watch as library *flies* past window.
- Got on express train *again*.
- *What the fuck?*
- Cry a little.
- Exit train, where am openly mocked by security guards and smug, fluffy, busy dog.
- Wait for train again.
- Freeze.
- Stay on Orange Line and pray for it to wind up at Harold Washington Library.
- Yay! Am here!
- Exit train.
- Almost die when giant icicle hurtles to earth mere six inches from head.
- Enter library. Which smells like feet.
- Conduct exhaustive search.
- Seek help from surly library employees, who try to give me Candace Bushnell's *4 Blondes*.[9]

---

[9] Non-chick-lit-knowing-about philistines.

- Finally find book.
- Wait in line for fourteen minutes. Vow to hurt Sykes if isn't *Bridget Jones*–level good.
- Pay $21.90 in overdue fines because online renewal system apparently doesn't work.
- Head back to train entrance.
- Dodge yet another giant ice projectile.
- Decide "screw it" and hail taxi. Spend another $9 to get home. Husband spots self exiting taxi and mocks mercilessly.
- Total cost of the library excursion?
- $40.90,[10] two hours, and a portion of my sanity.

So taking the train to my temp job is pretty much out of the question. I'd love to drive but spending $24 on parking downtown is three times more wrong than taking a cab, so the bus it is.

I'm at the stop waiting to go to said temp assignment when the number 56 arrives *exactly when it's supposed to be here.* Not only does the bus get here on time and without incident, I actually find an open seat. Huzzah! The heavens are shining down upon me! For today *I* shall be the one who thrusts my head into someone else's crotch accidentally when the driver brakes hard for no reason! It will be *me* who curls my lip in disgust when the embarrassed straphanger makes a joke about tucking dollar bills! I claim this twelve-inch-wide carpeted-plastic throne in the name of Jen!

Delighting in the luxury, I open my canvas tote and root

---

[10] Including $10 bet.

around in it, digging past my lunch, purse, extra panty hose, hand lotion, four shades of pink-brown lipstick, and umbrella until I find my book. I feel the familiar glossy cover and I whip out *Slander* by Ann Coulter.

I know, I know . . . few authors incite the kind of passion[11] she does, but I enjoy her writing even though her politics can be too hard-core for . . . well . . . anyone. (When I gave my friends Angie, Jen, Carol, and Wendy a tour of my apartment, they made one collective gasp when they saw the book on Fletch's nightstand. To their credit, they had lunch with me anyway.) But with hair that good I figure Ann's got to be doing *something* right.[12] Anyway, as I am all about the fair and balanced, I plan to pick up Al Franken's newest soon, because I honestly believe the truth is somewhere in the middle of all the polarizing viewpoints.

I read contentedly for about five minutes until I sense someone's eyes on me. I glance up to meet the gaze of another passenger. A small, wiry woman sits across from me in some sort of yoga pose that I'm sure has a lyrical name but I only know as "Indian-style." The cut of her short, dark hair shows off jug ears and pale skin. Her natural-hewn brown sweater is bristly and appears to be in need of a shave. Big, googly sunglasses complete her ensemble, and her visage is *disturbingly* simian. This bothers me because it means even chimpanzees are more capable of riding the bus than I am.

---

[11] Read hate.

[12] Same thing goes for Nancy Pelosi—I'm not so much into her views, but I totally respect her personal style. And we should *so* nominate her colorist for president.

I notice her long, skinny limbs are all tucked inside of themselves and the overall effect is that of a monkey in a strait-jacket. I continue to read and snicker to myself. Oh, Ann, you're just *evil* sometimes. With your mean streak, I don't see why we aren't already best friends. We should have a slumber party—we could crank call Hillary Clinton and send a bunch of pizzas to Dianne Feinstein! Then we could TP Ted Kennedy's house and egg John Kerry's car before braiding each other's hair while we watch *America's Next Top Model*. I smile and nod at Ann's acerbic commentary.

The Monkey Woman clears her throat.

I continue to read and punctuate the silence of the bus with an occasional guffaw. Me-ow, Miss Thing! I am *so* sitting next to you if I'm ever invited to a big Republican fund-raiser.

The Monkey Woman clears her throat again, louder this time.

This? Right here? Is another reason I loathe the bus. I hate having to speak to perfect strangers in such close con-fines. I mean, no one on the bus ever wants to discuss interest-ing stuff, like the best way to get your pit bull to stop peeing on the rug in the hallway, or my hair. Either they're com-pelled to sell you something you don't want or to chat about your one-way ticket to hell because even though you've been baptized, you're still doomed because you weren't baptized in the Holy Name of the Evangelical Church of the Crazy Bus Zealots.

I look up and give her a quick half smile, which I hope communicates, "I'm grinning because I'd like to look friendly so you don't grab a knife with the prehensile tail I'm sure is hidden under your shaggy shirt and stab me in the neck. But if neck-stabbing is not your intention, my countenance isn't so welcoming it leads you to believe I want to buy your fundraiser M&Ms or gab about your intense personal relationship with your lord Xenu, alien ruler of the Galactic Confederacy.[13] But, um, hey, thanks for thinking about me and how 'bout I just return to my book now?"

No dice. Monkey Woman doesn't break eye contact. When she removes her sunglasses I note her small, dark, hooded eyes and sloping brow. She gestures toward the tome in my hand, declaring, "She's a fascist."

I focus on my book, replying only, "Mmmm." I don't think Ann's a fascist as much as she's someone who uses a lot of hyperbole to make a point. Yes, she's at the far end of the Michael Moore–Joe Lieberman–Pat Buchanan politicalleaning continuum, but I bet a lot of the incendiary stuff she writes is just to sell books. I'm sure when we have our slumber party she'll be totally cool. Gosh, I hope she brings Mystery Date with her! We'll set up our matching Snoopy sleeping bags by the fireplace and talk about fun stuff like potential boyfriends,[14] makeup, reality TV, whether or not our uptight old moms will *ever* let us shave our legs, and the ramifications of a flat tax. Then we'll stuff ourselves silly with Cheetos and RingDings, freeze each other's bras, and dance to my Jackson Five records until my daddy comes downstairs to tell us to stop squealing like Democrats and go to bed already.

---

[13] Seriously, if you're going to base a church on science fiction, at least base it on *good* sci-fi. Like the Holy Temple of The Men in Black with Reverend Will Smith.

[14] Sean Hannity, squee!

"Everything she says is a lie."

I'm not looking at you, I'm not looking at you, I'm not look-ing at you. "Uh-huh," I grunt, not lifting my gaze to meet hers.

"All she does is spread filthy lies and hate."

Now I know for a fact this isn't *entirely* true. It would be physically impossible for her to only spread lies and hate. Occasionally she's got to hit the salon to get her roots done, and at least once a week she's interviewed on *Fox News* because someone hurled a pie at her while she was giving a speech.[15] However, I don't feel like arguing right now so I say, "Mmph."

Monkey Woman grows agitated and begins to point at me with the kind of slender, tapered fingers that are perfect for picking nits out of those hard-to-reach places. "She *lies*! It's all *lies*! *Lies and hate!* Why are you reading *stupid lies*?"

This. Is. Getting. Old. Normally I'm all about a rousing political discussion, but only with people who I'm entirely sure won't fling poo at me. So, I simply shrug disinterestedly.

Wrong move.

Monkey Woman begins to squawk, shriek, and gesture wildly. "When you read stupid lies, you turn into a stupid liar! A dumb, unintelligent liar with *no brain cells*!! You are *stupid, stupid, stupid.*" With bated breath, she leans forward on her haunches and waits for my reply.

One nice thing about being on a bus with a bunch of city dwellers is her shouting attracts the attention of no one. We're

---

15 Ann Coulter is living proof that there's such a thing as karma, and sometimes it tastes like coconut cream!

so jaded that if we ran across a severed arm on the floor of this bus, we'd all simply step over it and debark. I look around and all I see are Yuppies enraptured by the *Red Eye* commuter newspaper or listening to music on tiny headphones. No one's even batted an eye.

Note to self: *Get iPod, like, immediately.*

"You don't say." I close the book, carefully marking my place with my bus pass. There's nothing I can do to convince her otherwise and the only way to win *this* bizarre little game is not to play.

Frustrated that I didn't pitch my book out the window in a gesture of primate solidarity, she throws her paws up in disgust and turns away from me, and . . . crisis averted.

I hate to admit the Monkey Woman rattled me, but it's true. I'm bothered greatly when people question my intelligence. I pride myself on my cognitive skills, yet when I fail at simple tasks like taking public transportation, I often wonder if my pride's based more on false bravado than actual merit.

Come to think of it, I do *a lot* of dumb stuff, like this morning when I tried to put on my pants without unzipping them first and Fletch had to get me unstuck. And then there's the second-degree burns on my right hand from last week when I forgot that pan in the oven equals hot. Or like when I fake threw the ball to the dog, only I accidentally let it go and the damn thing flew straight into the window, which then smashed into a zillion tiny shards?[16]

I sit on my plastic throne and stew. Maybe I'm not as

---

[16] That? Was expensive.

clever as I like to tell myself? What if she's right that I'm far dumber for having read Ann Coulter? I inspect my own charred paw and ruminate.

As my stop approaches, I stand and get ready to exit. Just as the brakes bring our mobile sardine can to a halt, I notice something different from my new vantage point. It's but a tiny detail, yet it gives me a shiny new perspective on my rightful place in the universe. I lean in toward Monkey Woman.

"Pardon me," I say.

Angry, dark eyes cut in my direction. "What?" she hisses.

Clutching my book to my breast so it looks like Ann's standing next to me as my "second," I whisper, "Your sweater's on inside out."

Then I gather my things and exit as Monkey Woman throws a banana at me.

Okay, the banana part's not true, but how awesome would it have been if she had?

Anyway, it probably doesn't matter; tomorrow I shall be reading Ann Coulter in a cab.

To: angie_at_home, carol_at_home, wendy_at_home, jen_at_work
From: jen@jenlancaster.com
Subject: *happy belated 4th of july*

In response to Carol's query of our respective holiday weekends . . .

Setting: The driveway of my parents' house. My sister-in-law and niece are in one car and I am in another.

Me: Where am I meeting you guys for lunch?

Mom: Well, I was thinking—why don't we go to that little Italian place by the mall?

(a beat)

(another beat while I process what my mother has just said)

(because, really, she can't possibly . . .)

Me: Do . . . do . . . do you mean *the Olive Garden?*

And . . . that pretty much sums up the past three days at my parents' house.

Please tell me your holidays were better than this.

Lie if you must.

Jen

To: angie_at_home, carol_at_home, wendy_at_home, jen_at_work
From: jen@jenlancaster.com
Subject: *adventures in gastroenterology*

Good morning,

Yet another scene from my oh-so-glamorous life.

Setting: Check-in desk for GI lab work at Northwestern Memorial Hospital. An adoring Yuppie wife with perfectly coiffed hair has her elbow linked with that of her adoring Yuppie husband. They appear to have walked right out of an Eddie Bauer ad. Fletch and I are in line behind them. I am holding part of my shirt out in front of me, trying to determine the origin of the grease stain. Bacon? Salad dressing? Not sure.

> **Yuppie Wife:** *(to Nurse, hands clasped in earnest concern)* I know an endoscopy is a routine procedure, but I'd really like to be in the recovery room to hold his hand while he comes out of the anesthesia. Can I be there? Would that be all right? Please?
>
> **Nurse:** I think it would be okay.
>
> **Yuppie Wife:** Thanks *so* much.
>
> **Nurse:** *(to Fletch)* You're also here for an endoscopy— would you like your wife to join you in the recovery room?

Me: Pfft. I'm heading to the oatmeal bar at Au Bon Pain. Good luck and see you in an hour.

Ha!

Jen

P.S. The doctor determined that Fletch is completely fine.

P.P.S. And I had grits!

P.P.P.S. What? I brought him back a muffin.

The Only Thing We Have to Fear Is Rachael Ray

lthough plagued by a number of irrational fears, I have a few that are legitimate. I've been in a couple of serious auto accidents, so the sound of squealing brakes never ceases to send chills down my spine. Whenever I hear that noise, even from the safety of my living room, I stiffen in dreaded anticipation of impact and the sickening crunch of metal on metal.

Home invasions also terrify me, since we were actually the victims of one when we lived in the supposedly-safe Yuppie enclave of Lincoln Park. Okay, so technically we were one floor up behind a locked door, the police arrived in thirty seconds, and the criminal pleaded no contest and went directly to prison.[1] Plus, our perpetrator's alias was *James Taylor*. And really, does anything say "bad to the bone" more than

---

[1] Apparently you can't call for the death penalty on a simple B&E. Also judges do not appreciate helpful suggestions.

Mr. "Sweet Baby James" Taylor? (Didn't Carly Simon even kick his ass at one point?)

To this day, we snicker about the guy "Going to Carolina *State Penitentiary* in My Mind," "Walking Down a Country Road *to Jail*," and discuss whether or not he's "Showering the People" he loves with love in his cell block.

Still, you'd think the crash of breaking glass and scraping metal in the dead of the night would be the scariest noise I'd ever heard, right? Well it's not. It's the clanging of pans coming from my kitchen because that means Fletcher is about to cook something.

♟

"Shalom, bitches!" I shout and dump my bookbag full of temping essentials—Kleenex, pens, notebook paper, spare panty hose, and enough candy to anesthetize myself—on the table next to the front door and kick off my incredibly painful shoes. Back when I used to do business there, I realized none of the chic New Yorkers sported the obnoxious sneakers-and-a-business-suit look so prevalent with the dowdy, sensible Chicago commuters, and ever since then I've sacrificed comfort for style.[2]

The dogs react to my arrival by lunging at me, the cats tacitly ignore me, and Fletch waves distractedly from the couch. I ask him, "What are you looking at so intently?" Normally in this house it's me engrossed in television, not Fletch. And at the moment, he is giving the TV an *American Idol*-worthy level of focus.

....

[2] Bone spurs and bunions? Yes. But my calves look great as I limp past you.

"Show. Busy. Cooking. Watching show," he mumbles, nodding and hastily scratching notes on a pad.

"Huh?" I sit next to him to see what's drawing him in so much. An annoyingly perky brunette is whizzing around a kitchen set in a painted-on shirt, grabbing random things from cabinets while blathering something about "Evieohoh." Fletch nods, mesmerized.

"Who's Evieohoh?" I ask. Fletch continues to stare, his jaw ever so slightly slack. I poke him in the shoulder. "*Hey!* I'm asking you a question."

"Oh, sorry. It's E.V.O.O.—extra-virgin olive oil," he mutters, concentration unbroken.

"That's dumb. Why doesn't she just use the whole name? It's only four extra syllables."[3]

We watch for a couple of minutes, not because I care what she's making but because I never see Fletch this engrossed in anything. The host continues to blather on in a language that may or may not be English.

"She said to put the scraps in a Geebee, which is a what?"

"Garbage bowl."

"Huh. Well, *yay, her* for not going all traditional and throwing junk away in a trash can," I snort. She's cooking some sort of soup, but it's kind of thick like a stew so she calls it "stoup," and she's giggling the whole time at her own cornball jokes and it's incredibly annoying. "Why's she so goddamned giddy? She whipping up hash brownies or something? Or did they pump the studio full of nitrous oxide? I hate when—"

---

[3] No one's allowed to make up cute little contractions *but me.*

"*Ssshhh!*"

So it's going to be like *that* today, is it?

I huff on the couch for another minute, which is just enough time to vow that the TV cooking chick is now my sworn enemy. *You, missy! Yes, you with the EVOO and GB and LMNOP and the rest of the stupid abbreviations. Enough with your toothy Joker smile and all the giggling. You're on television and you're teaching people to prepare a meal. Show some decorum. Also, cooking—especially when dealing with food chemistry—is one of those areas where it's nice to be specific. If you're going to chop, dice, or practically puree something, use one of those descriptive words and not "gonna run my knife through it," because that doesn't tell me anything. And how about a specific unit of measure and not just "eyeball it." Do not* make *me come on your set and take you to school with my world-famous crusted chicken, little lady. And please either turn up the heat in the studio or wear a looser shirt. 'Cause I ordered the* arugula, *not* areola, *thanks.*

Still steaming from my shushing, I stomp upstairs to change out of my work clothes. When I return, the perky brunette is gone and Fletch seems to be back to normal.

"Exactly what were you watching that led you to believe it was okay to shush your wife?"

"It's a new show called *30 Minute Meals*. The host, Rachael Ray, shows how to make a whole dinner in a half hour."

"Interesting." Not. "But what's her deal? She's so enthusiastic that I kind of want to whack her with a board full of nails."

"Really? I like her. A lot. She's all about time-saving ideas and easy, healthy, delicious meals."

"Didn't realize you were suddenly on her payroll. My apologies."

"No, no, she's totally cool and so real. She worked hard to get to this position; she wasn't some starlet who read for a part. She was knee-deep in the food-service industry and fought her way up."

"Not impressed."

"How about this, then? Did you know she has a pit bull, too?" I quickly revise my *I Dig Any Famous Pit Bull Advocate* stance, which previously gave passes to Rosie Perez, Vin Diesel, Michael J. Fox, and Jon Stewart, because I simply cannot support Fletch's interest in Miss Titter McHighbeams. "Anyway, I figured since you're working hard temping, I'd start helping out with meals."

"That's sweet, Fletch, but I wouldn't classify what I do as 'working hard.' I mean, today I handled a very important project that involved super glue, Magic Markers, and a tube of sparkles."

"Did you get high on marker fumes again?"

I flush with the shame of my secret Sharpie addiction. "A little bit. But my buzz wore off. I can still cook pork chops just fine."

"Um, Jen, about the pork chops . . . they're nice and all, and of course I like them, but I'm just saying it might be interesting to have something else once in a while. If I eat any more hog I'm going to grow hooves and a curly tail."

"Perhaps you'd prefer something with a side of nipples then?" I say out of the side of my mouth.

"What?"

"I said I also like to save nickels by making all kinds of pasta dishes."

"Yes, and each involves tomato sauce, ground beef, and Parmesan. There's not a whole lot of variety going on here, and we need to expand our repertoire. I like how Rachael takes simple ingredients and quickly cooks a great meal. Today's program gave me some ideas and I'm going to make dinner tonight. Why don't you sit down and relax?"

I grab a glass of wine and plant myself on the couch, idly scanning the channels for something slightly less breast-acular. It feels weird not to be standing around on sore feet in the kitchen right now. Correction, it feels kind of good. Like, kind of really good.

You know, I always cook and I completely hate it. If Fletch wants to help, I should probably encourage him, not stifle him. Maybe he'll want to help when we have parties, too? How awesome would it be to have a gathering where I actually get to interact with my guests rather than slave over the stove in a sweltering kitchen?

Honestly, my life would be a lot easier if I weren't tied to meal preparation five or six hours each week. That's, like, 250–300 extra hours a year. Gosh, think of all the things I could accomplish with that kind of time. I could write a screenplay or learn a foreign language. I could take up knitting. I bet by my three hundredth hour with needles and yarn, I'd be churning out kick-ass sweaters. And, really, the mayor of Chicago totally encourages small businesses, so if I knitted cool stuff, maybe the city would give me a loan and I could set up a twee little shop on Damen Avenue with all the other boutiques and sell my rocking knitwear? And I'd have books there so I could read on the job and I'd call my shop *Lit One, Purl Two*. And I'd develop such a following that all the celebrities would wear my stuff and they'd be on the red carpet telling Joan Rivers, *"Of course I'm wearing Jen Lancaster. Because she? Is totally the Cashmere Queen of Chicago."*

Wait a sec—what on earth is he making that uses oatmeal *and* sun-dried tomatoes?

Huh. So *that's* what chicken sautéed with bumblebees and paper clips tastes like.

So far this week we've had white chili that I can only describe as "pointy," a shrimp stir-fry that burned a whole layer of skin off my lips, and broiled oven mitt.[4] On the upside, I'm not dieting, but since Fletch has taken over the kitchen I've lost five pounds.

I'm probably going to hold off on the loan application for my knitting store, though.

🦞

I can't say I'm impressed with Rachael Ray yet. I believe she encourages good men to do bad things with innocent foodstuff. I confirmed this with my female friends. They all hate her, but their husbands adore her. Either it's her constant Nipplepalooza or she emits some sort of high-pitched sound

---

[4] I think it was supposed to be some sort of calzone.

that only dogs and straight men can sense? What's worse is every time I hear the opening theme to her show, the hairs on the back of my neck stand up and my gag reflex triggers a little. As for the whole thirty-minutes aspect of her meals? Yeah, in your dreams, maybe. Fletch's last thirty minutes spanned almost two hours and dirtied up every pot, pan, and plate in the joint.

Complicating matters further, my sister-in-law just gave Fletch one of Rachael's cookbooks.[5] Since he swears these recipes are foolproof I decide to give him (and her) another chance.

And then I see him pull out a Dutch oven and a hunk of . . . something.

"Honey, what is that?"

"Salt pork."

I mentally digest this for a moment.[6] "I thought they stopped making salt pork once refrigeration was invented."

"Nope." He begins to hum along to White Zombie on his iPod as he chops his vegetables. I also didn't know we owned a Dutch oven. When did we get that? Is that one of the weird things he put on our Williams-Sonoma wedding registry? I eventually deleted it because it was full of $350 toasters and $250 garbage cans when we were completely broke, but not before people bought a few of our less pricey[7] items.

Then Fletch murmurs something about "succotash" and I predict a gastronomic shipwreck of *Titanic* proportions.

----

[5] This has got to be payback for buying her kids drum sets and cap guns.
[6] Because there's no way I physically will.
[7] Read ridiculous.

Fearing local Native American tribes are going to (a) catch wind of these ingredients, (b) naturally assume such a menu is part of a Thanksgiving celebration, circa 1621, and (c) scalp us when they taste Fletch's current culinary atrocity, I err on the side of caution and sneak upstairs to call Pizza Hut.

Fletch is dicing extension cords and cotton balls to add to his vile witches' brew when the doorbell rings.

I answer the door with a couple of twenty-dollar bills in my hand, pay the all-too-familiar deliveryman, and set the boxes on our breakfast bar.

"What are you doing? I'm making dinner right now!" he exclaims.

"I know you are, sweetie. The pizzas are for just in case."

"You'll toss those pizzas in the trash when you taste this."

"Of course I will," I condescend. "Because Rachael isn't the devil *at all*. She'd never sing her siren song every night from five to five thirty p.m., making you crash against the dinner rocks since I wasn't wise enough to lash you to the mast. Or maybe she's part of a conspiracy to help devoted husbands starve a couple of pounds off their chunky wives."

"Okay, if you don't love this meal, I promise I will never watch *30 Minute Meals* again."

"Deal."

He opens the lid of the Dutch oven to show me its gelatinous contents.

"Honey," I ask, "is our supper supposed to be purple?"

Rachael Ray?
So banned in this household.

The Blue Line train isn't running this evening because some unfortunate person stepped in front of it. All the folks who normally take it from Lake Street to LaSalle are being shuttled on the number 56 bus.

After watching three full number 56s pass me at my normal stop, I realize that unless I want to wait an hour, getting home on the bus is not an option. I figure I can take a cab but then remember I gave Fletch my last $10 to get coffee on the way to his meeting, and no money equals no taxi. I call Fletch to pick me up, but he doesn't answer, so I assume he's still with clients.

So what do I do when I find myself downtown with no money?

I walk.

Twenty blocks.

Uphill.

In the rain.

With a broken umbrella.

In a pair of heeled sandals that are crippling when strolling a mere five paces to the copier.

All the way home.

When I finally get to my front door, I find Fletch sprawled out on the couch, unaware of the blinking message light, enraptured by Rachael Ray.

I don't know if the person who stepped in front of the train committed suicide.

But I guarantee you someone's going to die.

It's been a few months since Fletch went cold turkey on Rachael Ray. I'm finally at the point where I can hear him open the drawer where the pans are kept without my wanting to hide under the bed while dialing 911.

I've just finished reading two hours of Internet conspiracy theories on whether Professor Snape truly turns evil in *Harry Potter and the Half-Blood Prince*—neatly proving that given an extra three hundred hours per year, I would *not* use them wisely—when I hear excessive banging coming from the kitchen.

No.

It can't be. With much trepidation, I tiptoe down the stairs and look over the half-wall railing.

I see pans.

I see pots.

I see trouble.

Slowly, I inquire, "Whatcha doing?"

Fletch grins. "I'm making meat loaf!"

"But on the grill, right?"[8] A long pause ensues. "Fletch?" Another pause while Fletch busies himself opening multiple shrink-wrapped packages of raw meat. "Fletcher! We had a deal! After the last fiasco, you promised the fire department you'd never cook indoors again."

Sheepishly he admits, "The recipe was rated highly on FoodNetwork.com for being both delicious and easy."

"Food Network? You mean home of Rachael Ray? Have

---

[8] Fletch is still allowed to work the grill because the worst he can do out there is burn stuff.

you been watching her again? If you recall, you lost your viewing privileges after I was forced to consume Lucky Charms for seven consecutive dinners because you followed her weekly meal plan."

"This isn't her recipe."

I begin to wonder if I don't owe Rachael and her boda-cious tatas an apology. The last few things he cooked/ruined weren't her recipes, either. As an American male, Fletch is generally opposed to reading directions, so maybe his culi-nary abortions have just been user error? Then it dawns on me there's a lot of meat on the counter and I begin to add package weights in my head.

"Fletch, do you realize you have nine pounds of meat here?"

"That's what it calls for."

"And that doesn't seem excessive?"

"Nope." He drinks a Coke and bobs his head in time to some awful Ministry song.

I read the grocery store receipt. "Forty-five dollars' worth of meat? And that sounds normal to you? For one dinner?"

"Uh-huh."

"Let me see this." I grab his recipe card. "'Will make three five-pound loaves.' Sweetie, we're never going to eat fif-teen pounds of meat loaf."

"Hmm, I guess that *is* a lot. Maybe I'll just make a third of the recipe."

"Ya think?" I grab a seat because if there's going to be carnage—and there will be—I may as well have a good view. I watch as he begins to work a heaping mound of ground turkey, beef, and Italian sausage. "Whoa, you're getting it all over the counter! It's slopping out the sides! Why don't you use a bigger bowl?"

"This is the biggest one we have."

"Good thing you're not making three loaves. You'd have had to mix it in the bathtub." I feel my lips begin to pucker in distaste as he tosses in a bunch of nontraditional meat loaf components. "What are the Doritos for?"

"It's one of the ingredients."

"And the uncooked bacon? And mustard seed? And molasses? And the bottle of old Rasputin beer, which, if I recall, made you throw up?"

"All part of the Loaf, baby."

"I accidentally broke a juice glass earlier. Want me to go through the garbage and find some shards for you?"

"Respect the Loaf."

"Stop calling it that—you're making it sound all porno. Anyway, does it concern you that you have a counter full of raw meat and not one of the furry little carnivores who live here has even come near it?"

"Your taste buds will thank me."

"You are adorably delusional." I pat him on the cheek. He slaps a gigantic wad o' meat[9] into the roasting pan and glances at the recipe.

"Huh. It says here to shape this into a tube so it cooks consistently. I never knew that. That's probably why the 'meat gator'[10] I tried to make didn't turn out."

9 Hee—porno again.
10 Back in the salad days of our dating life when I thought it was funny for him to ruin our groceries by shaping them into zoo animals.

"And you wonder why your presence in my kitchen causes me to want prescription drugs?"

"Pfft. I'd stake my reputation on tonight's meat loaf."

I grab my keys off the counter. "Yes, well, best of luck with that."

"Hey, where are you going?"

"Out."

"Where?"

"To the grocery store."

"How come?"

"Because I don't have enough money for pizza and nothing scares me more than the thought of running out of Lucky Charms."

To: angie_at_home, carol_at_home, wendy_at_home, jen_at_work
From: jen@jenlancaster.com
Subject: *do you like me? circle y or n*

Settle an argument here—

Yesterday at my temp job I met a woman from one of the company's satellite offices because I'm going to assist her with a part-time project. I noticed she was wearing the exact same piece of jewelry as me.

Upon seeing her wrist, I may or may not have exclaimed, "Hey! We can be bracelet buddies!"

Fletch says no one over the age of eight would say something like this. (Like, ever.) However, I disagree. Who's right?

(And do you think this woman is going to start speaking really slowly to me?)

To: angie_at_home, carol_at_home, wendy_at_home, jen_at_work
From: jen@jenlancaster.com
Subject: *lilly pulitzer saves the day*

Hey, girls,

I can't decide if I'm xenophobic and jerky or just superobser-
vant and careful.

Observe:

A couple of Middle Eastern gentlemen got on the bus today
about halfway between my office and my house. Normally I try
to stay in my own little world on public transportation because
eye contact only encourages the crazies. However, since they
were standing right at eye level, I couldn't help but notice them
wearing big elaborate backpacks, army-surplus-type clothing, and
both messing around with what looked like cell phones in their
pockets. They appeared nervous and were holding one-day CTA
passes.

Deciding they seemed hinky, I gave them both a big smile to
gauge their reactions. Normally I'd expect grins in return, especially since I was wearing the *world's cutest* pink-and-green-
checked wrap skirt. (You can't *not* smile when you see someone
in a skirt like that, especially since it's actually reversible and
there's a darling green floral print on the other side that flaps
open and you can see it when I walk. Plus, I've lost a decent

amount of weight from Fletch's cooking and I don't look so much like a fat person anymore. Now I'm like an aging-but-still-kind-of-has-it-ex-sorority-girl-who-would-be-truly-lovely-if-only-she-could-lay-off-the-chocolate-croissants. And really? The skirt was bangin', yo.) Anyway, I smiled at them and they looked back at me with cold, hard eyes. The only expression I saw was a flicker of contempt.

So, I immediately pulled the cord and got off the bus, even though I was a mile from my house. Obviously the bus went on its merry way without incident and I had to hoof it home in ninety-degree heat and kitten heels.

Point? Here's what I'm struggling with—I hate the fact that my paranoia made me automatically assume those men were up to no good. It's unfair that a whole lot of good people in this country are being scrutinized by assholes like me just because of their ethnicity. Most likely these guys were simply tourists and I should be thanking them for visiting my fair city.

On the other hand, a bus passenger in London had this exact same feeling two weeks ago and exiting the bus early saved his life.

And I'll be damned if I was going to get exploded in that skirt.

Conflicted,

Jen

Jen Hollywood

*I*f my life were a movie, in the scene where I finish writing my book you'd see a montage of fireworks and popping champagne corks, ticker-tape parades and indigenous people all over the world leaving their mud huts and dancing up and down while cheering.[1] As I lay down my pen and switch off my computer, the score crescendos with the "Beef: It's What's for Dinner" song.[2] The skies open up and God himself beams down a golden light to illuminate the mailbox where my bundled, precious manuscript is to be deposited. As I kiss the package, wish it luck, and insert it in the slot, the "Hallelujah Chorus" sounds.

Returning home, my loving mate[3] sweeps me into his arms

---

[1] Oh, wait. That last bit is from *Independence Day* when they bring down all the aliens' ships. My bad.

[2] Some would say it's "The March of the Toreadors" from the opera *Carmen*. Whatever, you *vegans*.

[3] Played by Vince Vaughn before he got all bloated.

to congratulate me and then whisks me off somewhere fabulous to celebrate properly. When we're done dining and toasting, this would be an appropriate time for a gratuitous sex scene, unless we're being directed by Quentin Tarantino, in which case we go shoot a bunch of vampires instead.

Unfortunately my life isn't a Hollywood movie—the only thing my loving mate does upon learning of the book's completion is ask if I'm going to start cleaning the house again because the bathroom is downright hairy. And when I e-mail my manuscript to my editor, instead of turning off the computer, I log on to Monster.com because I'm going to need to work for the next nine months before the book is published, what with my overwhelming passion for living both indoors *and* in the city.[4]

Fletch reminds me if we want to move to the suburbs, we could survive nicely on his income while I attempt to get freelance writing jobs, but I'm just not ready. Someday I'd love a big rolling lawn and snappy riding mower and convenient access to strip malls with their giant parking spaces, but right now I much prefer being in the center of all the action . . . even if 99 percent of the time I'm lounging on the couch watching *Veronica Mars*.[5] Simply having the option to run off and do something urban and exotic at a moment's notice is satisfaction enough. (Plus, the average home prices in the John Hughes–movie suburbs where I'd want to live start at $1,000,000—totally out of the question.)

Resolved: I need to earn some money to help support our current rent burden.

---

[4] FYI, $4.00/word writing jobs for *Vogue* don't exist, *Carrie*.
[5] I heart you, Kristen Bell.

But what kind of job should I get? After declaring myself a writer, it seems like taking a sales job would be a big step backward. I'm experienced in a couple of other areas, like investor relations and corporate communications, but as evidenced by my almost two-year quest, not enough to land a good job doing them. Perhaps it's time to reassess my skills? I decide to brainstorm and will write down anything that comes to mind. Then when I'm done, I'll review the list and see if the perfect new career track doesn't make itself evident.

Jen's Areas of Expertise

Good at second-guessing better ways for others to do their jobs. (Generally only employed when I'm stuck standing in line due to someone else's inefficiency. I've been a cashier, so I know for a fact you don't need to ring all twelve identical cans of cat food separately.)

Proficient at choosing flattering bathroom paint colors to best enhance own features. (Asparagus green, yes. Flaming orange, no.)

Adequate written communicator. (Although wholly inept at expressing false self-deprecation about said skill.)

Have made concerted effort to stop saying everything I think. (Like when I ran into a fellow pit bull owner, I didn't remark, "This morning my bully Maisy barfed up paper towels and cat poop all over the carpet on the second floor!" And last week when I met the petite brunette with the dimples and big smile, I kept myself from exclaiming,

"Oh, my God, you look just like Laci Peterson! Except not dead!" And I've almost completely quit saying, "Shalom, motherfucker!" as my standard greeting when I enter a room anymore. Progress, I say!)

Unusually dedicated to steam-cleaning carpets. (Please see above.)

Can pick out and name every constellation in the fall sky. (Pleiades is my favorite.)

Mix a mean dirty martini and also can make delicious fruit dip using Coco Lopez and Cool Whip. (Do not serve together, though.)

Can grow lovely container gardens. (Except in the shade, where I seem to sprout more toadstools than anything.)

Would be excellent reality show contestant. (Except if competition involved touching bugs, particularly with any part of my mouth. I mean, I can't even go near a piece of chicken if I can see a vein—there's no way I could consume something still writhing.)

Able to neatly give own self a pedicure. (And the nice part is I don't have to make awkward conversation about the weather with myself while I attack my problem cuticles.)

Smart. (Except about geography. At Thanksgiving, I swore up and down that the Middle East was located partially in Africa and partially in Europe. When we got home, Fletch made me look at a map and I was proved wrong on both counts. But I don't have any desire to be a cartographer, so who cares?) (I should probably avoid any health-related fields, too. When the nurse told me my high triglyceride count wasn't that big a deal unless I had pancreatic problems, I realized I hadn't a clue what the pancreas does—is it like a Liver, Jr., or is it one of those throwaway, make-it-into-hot-dog bits like the appendix, tailbone, and little piggy toe? Who knows? Certainly not me.)

Efficient at making copies. (You'd be surprised at how complicated, expensive office machinery responds to a solid kick and mild stream of profanity.)

Anyway, it's too bad my life isn't a movie, because that'd mean I'd have a big Hollywood happy ending. I'd do my skills assessment and I'd figure out, and subsequently get, the very best non-geography-or-health-based job ever. But here in the real world the above skills will get me exactly what I deserve—another temp assignment.

One phone call to my temporary agency and I've already gotten a placement. I'm bummed that there's nothing open in the adorable Mr. James's office, but I helped him find a great permanent person when I had to quit to finish writing the book. Apparently he and his new assistant are thick as thieves, damn it.

Now I'm off to work in a nonprofit whose purpose is to help the service industry attract workers. When I hear the company description I wonder, *Is this organization really necessary? Aren't, like, millions of people shimmying over the border each year in order to get these jobs? Seems like you don't need a charitable foundation to attract them; you need some fence cutters.* Then again, I'm about to work for $11/hour, so what do I know?

I show up for my first day in a yellow twinset paired with a divine red plaid Ralph Lauren skirt, a $150 holdover from the days when my opinion used to matter. It's one of the most perfect garments known to man—lightweight so I can wear it in the summer, richly colored so it's appropriate for the fall, and it has a wrap closure to accommodate those ten[6] extra pounds. This outfit merits its own one-paragraph description not because even at five years old it's still fabulous, but because by so wearing it, when I arrive everyone mistakes me for the brand-new vice president of fund-raising, who's also scheduled to start today. The receptionist actually places me in the VP's private office until she realizes her mistake.

As I follow the receptionist down the long, beige-carpeted corridor to my new workspace, I notice the people here take "business casual" to a whole new level. I've already seen an embroidered Mickey Mouse sweatshirt and I spied someone wearing flannel pajama bottoms. However, I've been advised the nonprofit world is very different from the for-profit world, so I guess I shouldn't be surprised the dress code is relaxed. I try not to judge, but God, I do it so well.[7]

I spend my first day wandering around the office asking if anyone has anything they'd like me to do and it's painfully boring. I report to the EVP of Communications, but she's

---

[6] Fifty.

[7] Note to self: Add "sit in judgment" to skills list.

away on a fund-raising trip. Until she returns, her twenty-two-year-old, St. Louis Cardinals–ball-cap-wearing staff member is in charge of me. He's five feet four with freckles and child-bearing hips and is a dead ringer for Jimmy Neutron. After my effusive greeting, I'm relatively sure I terrify him. Jimmy has exactly nothing for me to work on so I wile away the day Google-stalking old high school classmates.[8]

In the movie version of this experience, I'd excel at my work so much I'd be placed in the fund-raising VP's position. But the reality is I spend three more days doing exactly nothing and I really begin to question why I'm here. This place is a nonprofit and relies on corporate donations to keep going. So isn't having me doing nothing but reading *Veronica Mars* recaps on TelevisionWithoutPity.com's Web site a criminal waste of resources?

I keep encouraging Jimmy Neutron to take advantage of my writing experience. I offer my proofreading skills and try to sell myself, asking where else he could get his stuff professionally edited for $11/hour? Tired of having me hover over him with an anticipatory grin on my face, he finally finds me a project. Only instead of editing, I'm presented with a stack of paper six feet high and a home-office-grade shredder.[9]

Anyway, Jimmy's boss returns from her trip and pops into the office for a couple of minutes. The EVP is about to attend an off-site seminar for the day, but before she goes we have a

---

[8] Sure, I could have caught up with them at the reunion this year, but (a) I had a zit on my neck and (b) I'd gained a ton of weight since my size-five Jordache jeans days. And I wasn't nice enough in high school for either the blemish or the cellulite to be forgiven, so I stayed home.

[9] Which is why I fail to see how it's my fault when the shredder catches on fire.

chance to powwow. She's delighted to know about my writing experience[10] and promises she'll assign more challenging work upon her return. Until then, she gives me a stack of expenses to file and a pile of Jimmy's work to edit. I finish both projects in less than an hour.

The next morning I'm at my cube with nothing to do, so I decide to keep an activity log to amuse myself, backtracking to cover all aspects of my day.

6:25 a.m.—Out of bed. Would be nice if I could have one morning where I didn't wake up and immediately step in a pile of something cold, wet, and having squirted out of one of the pets.

7:48 a.m.—All out of heart-healthy canola oil margarine from Trader Joe's, so I put triple cream Brie on my bagel instead. Consume, then have intermittent chest pains.

8:26 a.m.—Get ride to work. No bus today—yay!

Me: What does that magnetic ribbon say on that car over there?

Fletch: *(squinting)* Powered by Jesus.

Me: Yeah? Not powerful enough in my opinion. *(rolls down window)* Hey, Jesus, learn to accelerate! *(screeches to halt)* Whoa! Jesus just turned that light from green to red with no yellow in between!

Fletch: Maybe it wasn't Jesus. Maybe it was Karma.

Me: What? Is my name Earl or something? Karma's punishing me for letting a dawdling Baptist know she needs to use her gas pedal?

---

[10] *I told you so, Jimmy Neutron.*

Fletch: Just sayin'.

Me: What a great show that is—and I love Jason Lee. I just wish he weren't a Scientologist.

Fletch: I don't fault Jason for his belief system. I bet he's actually a closet Episcopalian and Scientology is just to advance his career. Besides, is their theory on Theatans so much more far-fetched than the Christian belief that Jesus turned water to wine?

Me: I'd say no, but if Jesus turns one more light red, I'm going to be late for work.

8:29 a.m.—Arrive. Am best-dressed person here again. It is a sad state of affairs when my stupid poplin khakis make me appear "all fancy."

8:37 a.m.—Already booored. Jimmy says he has nothing for me to do.

8:38 a.m.—Girl next to me needs to blow her nose.

8:46 a.m.—Girl next to me really needs to blow her nose.

8:51 a.m.—Girl next to me needs to blow her nose before something bad happens.

9:12 a.m.—Asked to work on Very Important Project involving stapler. But at least I will be away from Sinus Queen.

10:00 a.m.—Admire self in bathroom mirror. Wearing stupid, pointy shoes[11] today because oh, so cute! Glad Fletch dropped me off and will pick me up and I won't have to do any walking.

10:09 a.m.—*Alarm bells! Fire! Fire!! Fire?* Oh. No fire. It's just a fire drill. Must walk down fifteen flights of stairs in stupid pointy shoes.[12] Lumber along behind two dumb guys drinking

---

[11] From Target! I heart you, Isaac Mizrahi.

[12] Do not heart you now, Isaac Mizrahi. Would a little bit of cushioning have killed you?

coffee and chatting about Cubs' chances this year. Naturally if this were a real emergency, I would *stomp all over their flaming carcasses in stupid pointy shoes* to get to the bottom first. Because for $11/hour? I could give a shit about *your* safety.

10:09 a.m.—Jesus? Did that on purpose.

10:31 a.m.—Duck out of fire drill to buy a certain permanent employee some Kleenex.

10:44 a.m.—Snort.

10:45 a.m.—Snuffle.

10:46 a.m.—Oh, yes. Jesus taunting me.

10:47 a.m.—Sniiiiiffff.

10:48 a.m.—*"Blow your freaking nose!"*

10:49 a.m.—Apologize.

10:50 a.m.—Profusely.

10:53 a.m.—Totally not sorry.

11:54 a.m.—Called into EVP's office to discuss expense report. Found over $300 in missing receipts from last trip. Am *rock star*—which will hopefully make up for flaming shredder foolishness last week.

12:14 p.m.—EVP does not think my idea of sending out a Save the Date e-mail with the title "I Have an STD with Your Name on It!" is funny. Regardless, I laugh myself into an asthma attack.

12:15 p.m.—Am no longer a rock star. It's still funny, though.

12:30 p.m.—Attempt to eat lunch in cafeteria while reading new Marian Keyes book. Am accosted by Disney-sweatshirt-wearing permanent employee who thinks "nobody should eat alone." I reply, "Unless of course you have a good book and enjoy quiet time." (Hold up book to emphasize point.) Pretend to read, but Big Fucking Mouse Shirt will not be dissuaded. Spend rest of meal hearing pitch for Discovery Toys interspersed with stories about Big Fucking Mouse Shirt's own toddler, Little Fucking Mouse Shirt. Added bonus? Stories told in baby talk! Vow to eat lunch at desk. For rest of life.

1:42 p.m.—Given press release to write. Finish in fifteen minutes.

1:57 p.m.—EVP's socks? Completely knocked off. Rock star again!

2:30 p.m.—Given presentation written by Jimmy Neutron to proofread.

2:55 p.m.—Explain to Jimmy that he should avoid using made-up words like "mandation" when asking donors for money.

2:56 p.m.—Jimmy may possibly want to kick me 'til I'm dead.

3:00 p.m.—Whatever. Tell Jimmy I must leave for important medical appointment.

3:01 p.m.—What? Hair is body part. Is totally considered medical.

3:10 p.m.—Ahhh, bleach? Is good.

5:24 p.m.—Arrive home. Voice mail from temp agent. Says I am fired from job because Jimmy claims I said "filing is *not* part of my job description."

5:25 p.m.—Lies! Such lies! I would never say such a thing!

5:26 p.m.—Bitch? Sure! But never slacker.

5:27 p.m.—Well played, Jimmy Neutron. And Jesus? Obviously still pissed.

So that's the nice thing about temping—I'm just that—temporary. No matter how good or bad the job is, it's going to be over relatively quickly. I enjoy being able to slip in and out of the shadows and not be noticed, because the last thing I want is to get embroiled in someone else's corporate culture. For example, it's United Way Week here on my newest job, meaning this particular company is doing all sorts of "cute" things in the name of fund-raising. They're having a balloon drive, and for a dollar donation you can send one to someone in the office. Overjoyed employee volunteers[13] dance up and down the cube farms distributing balloons to delighted recipients with cheery notes attached stating sentiments like "You're the very bestest boss!"

Yeah, you'd line up and pay $10 US to see *that* film, right?

The company must be raising a shitload of money because when I walk out for the evening, each cube has at least five to seven balloons.

Except mine—exactly my intent.

On the way home from work, I laugh about my balloon-free cube. Frankly, I'm delighted to have avoided the whole socially awkward aspect of it. I just don't enjoy everything that goes along with the politics of working in an office; it's a lot of the reason I became a writer. I don't always play well with others, but by temping I can make a few bucks while avoiding foolishness like Secret Santa drawings, obligatory employee outings, departmental baby showers, retirement parties, and all the other small-talk-making, not-getting-my-work-done distractions that used to make me want to take a hostage.

---

[13]Who obviously do not have enough work to do.

Naturally, I'm greeted with a desk full of balloons and happy notes when I arrive this morning because I am so irony's bitch.

Yes, I should be flattered. But, here's the problem: in the course of this assignment, I accomplish very little that a helper monkey couldn't do once he learned to work the copy machine. So there's no need to thank me for my hard work with a bunch of balloons because it's *not hard*. Knowing how easy this job is means that I got balloons because *people pitied me*.

Now I'm faced with the dilemma of how to thank the people who thanked me. Should I send them balloons? Because then they'd thank me for the thanks of thanking them for thanking me and then what happens? I'd get more balloons? And then I'd have to send more? Would they then react in kind? When does it stop?

This has the potential to turn into a helium-based arms race.

Or a fucking Dilbert cartoon.

Of course, no movie, no matter how dramatic, is without comic relief. But in the Hollywood version of my life, I'd always be right and everyone around me would be the ones to look foolish. But the unfortunate reality is sometimes the dumbass in the office? Is me.

I'm working at a lovely hospitality company where I'm given an easy project. Although the task is basic, I have a couple of niggling questions, so I leave my workspace to ask the project manager. He's an easygoing, funny guy named Matt and sort of reminds me of Jim on *The Office*. I've been here about a month and we've become friendly, so I feel like I can let my guard down around him.

"What's up, Jen? You need something?"

"Yes," I reply. "I understand I have to upload the spreadsheet and save it to the new directory, but I don't have a copy of it."

"You do," he explains patiently. "It's in the archives."

"Oh. But where are the archives? I didn't see them. How will I know which ones they are?"

He sighs. "Because they're labeled *Archives*." He starts to say something else when I spy a little figurine on his desk. It's a man in a light suit with a weird little black bow tie, wavy white hair, black glasses, and a white goatee.

"Oh, my God! You have a *Colonel Sanders* action figure! That's so cool—where did you get it? eBay?"

He shakes his head. "Ah, no. This is Sigmund Freud."

"No, it can't be. He looks just like the colonel. Are you sure?"

"Yes, I'm sure."

"Are you super-sure?"

"Yeah. Now, about the archives—"

"Are you extra-crispy, eleven-herbs-and-spices sure?"

"Yes."

"Then why is he clutching a chicken leg in his kung fu grip?" Ha! Touché!

"Jen, it's a *cigar*."

"Oh."

"Yeah. So, once you grab your document from the archives, you—"

I explode with laughter. "Ha! I thought *Freud* was *the colonel*! That's hysterical! No, better yet, it's *Freudian*! Sometimes a cigar's not a cigar; sometimes it's a drumstick! *Ha!* So, would my KFC obsession be considered an oral fixation? Or maybe my unconscious is telling me I want poultry for lunch?"

The conversation deteriorates from here because I sort of go off on a tangent about Kentucky Fried coleslaw. By the time I walk back to my cubicle, I'm pretty sure I hear Matt thunking his head against his desk.

Perhaps I should probably cross "Makes a concerted effort to stop saying everything I think" off my skills assessment?

I've been temping a few months now and the whole business is starting to wear on me. It's not that I mind the work—I quite like being helpful, actually. I'm just so tired of staying in an office all day. Back when I had a "real" job, I was in sales and was perpetually on the road. Coming into the office was practically a treat; it meant I wasn't carting my suitcases through O'Hare for the umpteenth time, nor was I being grilled in the boardroom by a client angry at items outside of my control.

But now that I'm in-house all day, every day, little things are grating on me. Take, for example, the microwave. I generally bring my lunch to the office, as do many. The floor I work on has only one microwave for about a hundred employees. This shouldn't be an issue because the lunchroom has an entire bank of microwaves. However, it is apparently *far too difficult* to take the elevator up two floors to use one of the many spare microwaves. So, starting at eleven a.m., people begin jockeying for position in the heat-my-lunch line. Some days there are ten frozen Lean Cuisines in a row slowly defrosting on the counter waiting their turn.

But this is not what annoys me. If there's a line, I eat later or take my food upstairs.

What makes me want to go all Russell Crowe is the stupid bimbo who brings in a gigantic raw potato every day and then nukes it for fifteen minutes. And since my desk is closest to the kitchen, people stand and whine about it *right next to me*. This happens *every single day*. This means fifteen minutes of potato-complaining times five times a week times the six weeks I'm to be on this assignment equals 450 minutes of my life I will never get back. That's seven and a half hours. I could fly to Las Vegas round-trip and people would still be bitching about the potato in the microwave.

The state of being annoyed is like a cancer. My aggravation spreads and begins to encompass everything around me. Like right now, I'm bugged by what I'm wearing to the point I want to tear it off and stomp all over it. I'm wearing one of my dozen similar Ralph Lauren wrap skirts; this particular variation has been hanging in my closet for years. It's a pastel madras plaid and it's very long and very straight—practically to the ankle—and it's greatly limiting my range of motion. If I don't take tiny steps like a geisha, I'll totally bite it as I scurry off to the copy machine. I guess I could pull the wrap apart so I can run better, but it might be nice if I stop accidentally flashing my support garments to the rest of the secretarial pool for once. (This has been the Summer of the Flippy

Skirt. Which, I learned too late, tends to fly up at the slightest breeze, like from when someone sneezes. Achoo and voilà—your nonstop ticket to Girdle City!)

Anyway, when I got dressed this morning, I couldn't remember why I never wear this skirt. With its lavender, pink, green, and turquoise stripes, it matches almost everything in my closet. But as I bunny-hop over to the Xerox machine, I suddenly remember Fletch used to call it *The Hobbler*. I flash back to the last time I wore this skirt—it's summer of 2001 and I'm in Orlando for a big investor relations conference. The New York Stock Exchange has rented out a large portion of Universal Studios to host a party. I spend the evening woofing down top-shelf scotch, networking with other corporate executives, and, when not movementally challenged, admiring my place among the financial glitterati.

Which causes me to glance at the stack of paper in my hand and grow more annoyed. And even though I already know the answer, I can't help but wonder how I've gone from making million-dollar decisions to making copies.

I collate and glower, and when I finish I stop into yet another new boss's office with a stack of warm-from-the-machine papers. He looks up at me with a big grin and nary an ounce of condescension to say, "Thanks, Jen! You're a lifesaver!"

This stops me in my tracks.

When I used to wear this skirt, no one said thank you. Ever. Back when I made the kind of decisions that impacted stock prices—positively, of course—no one verbalized appreciation. Ever. Nobody valued my fourteen-hour days. No one cared when I sacrificed my weekends to tweak proposals and prepare RFPs. I was barely ever congratulated for projects implemented, deals closed, agreements struck, and when I was, it was in a backhanded, what-have-you-done-for-me-lately sense. Even though I gave my company my all, nothing I did was ever good enough.

Yet for the act of making a simple stack of copies, something any child could do, I receive the kind of accolade I used to dream about. At this moment, I realize I never had a professional job I didn't loathe on some level. NYSE parties not withstanding, I despised almost every aspect of all the real jobs I ever had—the backstabbing, the premeeting meetings, the protracted "mission statement" discussions. I detested the bullshit conference calls, the ridiculous panty hose–mandatory meetings even in hundred-degree August humidity, redundant results reporting. Although I was unaware of it at the time, getting up every morning and facing chaotic day after chaotic day managing people and products I hated was an exercise in futility. In short, I despised every bit of Corporate America and now it makes sense why I was so mean to people and why I tried to bolster my happiness with multiple $150 Ralph Lauren skirt purchases.

I realize now as a temp I get to work when I want, where I want. And if Jimmy Neutron and his childbearing hips annoy me, we can part ways without incident. I can stroll out of whatever office I'm in that day at 4:30 on the dot and take my dogs for a leisurely walk without bringing a cell phone and pager, just in case San Francisco clients need to contact me. I can chat about goofy reality TV over the watercooler without stressing over my loss of productivity. I can make friends who, despite thinking I'm an idiot just because I've mistaken Sigmund Freud for Colonel Sanders, won't take that information and use it against me in order to jockey for position. I can make mistakes without the unspoken threat of being replaced by someone a bit younger and hungrier than me. And the best part? I get to pursue my dream of being an author *and* still afford to pay rent in the city that inspires me.

And if that means an occasional trip to the copy machine? That's just fine with me.

I hand my boss his copy and hobble back to my desk, smiling the whole way.

Hey, what do you know?

I actually do get my Hollywood happy ending.

To: angie_at_home, carol_at_home, wendy_at_home, jen_at_work
From: jen@jenlancaster.com
Subject: *instances where i have annoyed my sainted husband in the past few days*

Monday

12:25 a.m.

Me: Of course I'll get up with you tomorrow. I know your mornings go much more smoothly when we rise at the same time.

6:45 a.m.

Fletch: Jen, it's time to get up.

Me: Piss off. Zzzz . . .

8:57 a.m.

Me: (opening the front door, dogs in tow, announcing in my out-side voice) No poopies this morning!

Fletch: (gesturing toward the phone with one hand and making "shh" motions with the other) Absolutely, I'll get that spread-sheet to you by this afternoon.

(Okay, that wasn't completely my fault. He wasn't on the phone when I left and it *does* have a mute button. The man has lived with me for ten-plus years. He should know better by now.)

6:05 p.m.

Fletch: (*on our way to Home Depot for more plants*) Ha!

Me: What's so funny?

Fletch: The guy next to us has a Morrissey bumper sticker and he's driving an Escort. He may as well put on a bumper sticker that reads "Kick me."

Me: I don't get it.

Fletch: Jen, the sticker says *Morrissey*. You know, Morrissey? It's funny.

Me: I don't get it.

Fletch: Morrissey? An Escort? A little tiny guy driving it wearing big Drew Carey glasses? He's practically begging for someone to beat him up.

Me: I don't get it.

Fletch: (*sighs*) Never mind.

6:07 p.m.

Fletch: Promise me you're going to make this quick and that you'll only spend what you've got on your Home Depot gift certificate.

Me: I promise.

Cashier: *(fifty-two minutes later)* Your total is $70.46.

Me: *(to Fletch)* Can I have $45.46, please?

7:37 p.m.

Fletch: Jen, I just remembered, can you please pick up my prescription at—

Me: There is no talking during *America's Next Top Model!*

11:39 p.m.

Me: Of course I'll get up with you tomorrow. I know your mornings go much more smoothly when we rise at the same time.

Tuesday

7:01 a.m.

Fletch: Jen, it's time to get up.

Me: Piss off. Zzzz . . .

4:58 p.m.

Fletch: If you're watering plants on the second-floor deck, please don't toss the hose off when you're done. Leave it and I'll take care of it later. You've already broken three nozzles this year doing that and it's only May fifth.

5:26 p.m.

Me: *(only remembering after tossing hose off second-floor deck and watching it clatter and shatter on the bricks)* Uh-oh.

(Okay, this one wasn't as bad as it sounds, either. Nozzle three was a high-pressure model and it left my plants cowering in their pots because it must have felt like being sprayed down by the Gestapo.)

7:36 p.m.

Fletch: *(motioning toward our cinnamon apples and dilled red potatoes on the prep line, waiting to be bagged with our chicken at Boston Market)* I feel like a little kid because I see those containers and want to say to everyone, "That's our food." *(He puts a childlike expression on his face and points earnestly.)*

Me: Bah ha ha!

(Who doesn't enjoy the tinkling of their wife's laugher at an amusing little scenario? If I'd simply giggled at Fletch's joke, it wouldn't have been annoying. But because I snorted and guffawed like a 'tard *the entire ride home*, it was.)

10:49 p.m.

Fletch: I'm really exhausted. I'm hitting the hay. Are you coming?

Me: No, I'm going to read a few blogs and take a bath first. You'll be asleep by the time I'm done.

Fletch: Okay, but don't forget, I've already set the house alarm.

Me: Alrighty, perimeter is armed. I won't forget. Good night.

11:14 p.m.

Me: (running into the bedroom to turn off the blaring alarm, which has woken up Fletch, the neighbors, and their dogs on either side of our apartment because I wanted to spy on the people loitering by the complex's front gate) Sorry about that!

11:58 p.m.

Me: *(wildly waving the* Glamour *magazine with Mischa Barton on the cover at the clanging smoke alarm that has gone off because of the steam from my bath)* Sorry about that!

Wednesday

12:07 a.m.

Me: I'm going downstairs to send a few e-mails now, but of course I'll get up with you tomorrow. I know your mornings go much more smoothly when we rise at the same time.

I think we all know how this is going to end.

To: angie_at_home, carol_at_home, wendy_at_home, jen_at_work
From: jen@jenlancaster.com
Subject: *pots and kettles*

Why the hell don't we have our own sitcom?

Setting: Our living room, ten minutes ago, drinking coffee, watching a Lysol commercial about how germy cutting boards and sinks are.

Me: *(seeing fruit served on a toilet seat)* Eeew!

(Fletch rolls his eyes)

Me: *(seeing a sink full of stinky, wet garbage)* Eeewww!!

(Fletch rolls his eyes again)

Me: *(commercial ends)* Whoa, that *totally* squicked me out.

Fletch: *(going for the eye-rolling trifecta)* Oh, *please*. The commercial told you nothing you didn't already know. Leather up, nancy girl.

Me: Advice to toughen up might be more credible if you weren't taking a sick day because *you hurt yourself with dental floss.*

To: angie_at_home, carol_at_home, wendy_at_home, jen_at_work

From: jen@jenlancaster.com

Subject: *pots and kettles, part 2*

Apparently Fletch has to have gum surgery.

(But it's still a little funny.)

Lovin', Touchin', Squeezin' (and Bruisin')

Ever see those blissfully happy couples at the supermarket? They dress all matchy-matchy in brightly colored North Face jackets and have that weird twin-speak shared dialogue? You know the ones—she says, "Hey, did you?" and he replies, "Yeah, Thursday," and then she goes, "But what about?" and he's all, "Covered," and then when they walk past a display of Cheez Whiz they exclaim in perfect unison, "Monterey!" before dying over their private joke?[1] And because of their whole mind-meld, they're, like, so *into* their romance they can't seem to keep their paws off each other? And you'd be happy they were both able to find the lid to their pot, as it were, but they've started making out *directly* in front of the ice cream, and all you want to do is grab a pint a Phish Food and go home to watch *Project Runway*, but you can't because their damn *love* is blocking the cooler?

---

[1] Thus rendering satisfying eavesdropping completely impossible.

Well, Fletch and I are that couple. As long as you substitute "hitting" for "making out" and "fists" for "paws." (We'd prefer DOA over PDA, thank you very much.) One of the reasons we mesh so well is we're both insanely competitive. Back in the dot-com era, we used to spur each other on professionally. He made $24,000 at his first job, so I had to find one that paid $24,500. Then when he became a manager, I had to try for director. When he was promoted to director, I strove to make it to VP level, which was great, until we both got laid off and had to find a different way to compete.

Were either of us athletic, I'm sure one would start speed-walking and the other jogging. Then I'd enter a 5K, so he'd have to top me with a 10K and our athletic arms race would eventually escalate to the point that we'd swim, bike, and run to our deaths in Kona's Ironman competition. Fortunately, we consider ourselves stand-and-fight people, rather than run-away people, and our current physical exertion generally manifests itself in twelve-ounce curls.[2]

As an outlet for our misplaced professional aggression, Fletch and I make bets and play games. One night at dinner he wagers $5 I won't eat the chunk of rock salt from our clams casino serving platter. Not to be deterred by a bit of sodium chloride the size of a bottle cap, I take that bet. Sure, I spend the next three days trying to slake my unquenchable thirst with gallons and gallons of water, but still . . . *I win, I win, I win!!* We carry on with culinary challenges until our blissfully married mealtime resembles an episode of *Fear Factor*, and

[2] Thank God we don't do triathlons—Fletch's legs would look *so* much better than mine if he shaved them.

we call a truce. Incidentally, this competitive drive is why we try to avoid fighting with each other—too much potential for mutually assured destruction.[3]

Eventually we channel our competitiveness into Slug Bug, a game we play whenever we get in the car. If you aren't familiar, you're allowed to punch your friend in the arm when you see a Volkswagen Beetle as long as you shout "Slug bug!" first. Fletch normally wins these rounds because as the driver his attention is more focused on the traffic around us. He almost always drives, what with my tendency to drift onto the sidewalk when behind the wheel. We've found we're much happier if I'm not in control of the little bit of metal standing between our living long, healthy lives and being smashed to bloody bits.[4] However, when the new-school VW Bugs come out, my arm is perpetually sore from being hit so much since everyone in Chicago owns one now. Stupid safe, economical city car.

Luckily, the only thing Fletch likes less than losing is listening to me whine, so the game morphs into Slug Pug. Same rules, only the object in question is my favorite kind of dog. In this version, I'm the far superior player. The best day of my life is when we're sitting in an outdoor coffee shop as hundreds of black-and-tan pugs dressed in tiny bee suits and tu-

---

[3] We teetered precariously on the edge that time I wrote "asshole" on his arm in self-tanner and he had to wear long-sleeve shirts for a whole week in the middle of summer, prompting him to retaliate by shaving off most of my eyebrow. We called a truce after that, too—no one wanted to lose a tooth. Or worse.

[4] Although if you have a trick for putting on lipstick *and* not steering into a mailbox, I'd certainly like to hear it.

tus parade past, and I pound Fletch so many times the waitress threatens to separate us.

Being the better sport, Fletch allows the game to continue until it proves too dangerous. We're on our way to the grocery store, having a perfectly lovely conversation about Jennifer Garner, when it happens.

"Hey, guess what?" I ask.

"What?" he replies.

"I did it!"

He glances over at me from the driver's seat. "You did what?"

"I can't just tell you, you have to guess!"

He clicks on his turn signal and we drive up Racine on the way to Webster so we can cut up to the Jewel on Ashland. "Is this one of those situations where I'm never going to guess correctly because what you've accomplished is so esoteric?"

Curses, foiled again! "Okay, probably, so I'll just tell you. I finally finished watching the first three seasons of *Alias* on DVD—that's sixty-six episodes."

"The show wasn't just Jennifer Garner wearing a variety of wigs? It was actually well done?"

"Yes. Except for all the implausible situations they resolved by using satellites. Or having Sydney kick people while wearing stompy shoes."

"Then how come every time I've walked in while you're watching it's nothing but satellites and roundhouse kicks?" He brakes rather suddenly so a woman with an SUV stroller can cross the street in front of us, against the light. God, I hate Lincoln Park. It's the epicenter of Yuppie living in the city, with nothing but outdoor dining and dog bakeries as far as the eye can see. The junk-bond traders began migrating up here from the Gold Coast in the eighties, snapping up cheap real estate and filling their new pads with art deco Nagle prints and Duran Duran albums. Due to its proximity to the lake and public transportation, it's been on the rise ever since then and homes that sold for $75,000 at the time are now worth $2,000,000. Which is criminal.

"Sure, sometimes the plot holes make my brain hurt, so I always drink wine while watching. Whenever Sydney gets released from a Chinese prison because Marshall makes a couple of keystrokes thousands of miles away, I take a sip of Zinfandel and it suddenly makes perfect sense."

We turn onto Webster, right in the heart of Lincoln Park. "Let's see, that's sixty-six episodes times three servings per hour equals one hundred ninety-eight glasses of wine. Congratulations. You're an inspiration to us all."

Before I can come up with a snappy retort, I spy a Lincoln Park Trixie[5] walking her pug on a harness in front of a trendy bistro, so I instead shriek, *"Slug pug! Slug pug! Pug, pug, pug! I win, I win! Aiiieee!!!"* and wildly flail my fists in his line of vision,[6] which causes Fletch to jerk the wheel and almost plow into the entire crowd of al fresco diners. The Yuppies drop their cloth napkins and shoot us smoldering glances.

"Never do that again!" he shouts. "I practically drove into all those people! God!"

....

[5] A Trixie is a Jetta-driving, PR-job-having, overpaid, Kate Spade–carrying, bleached-toned-and-clueless girl who shares a $2,000 apartment with five of her sorority sisters. (And yes, I used to be one.) (Shut up.)

[6] Have I ever mentioned what a poor winner I am?

"Oh. I'm sorry. But still, I did win. Yay, me!"

He shakes his head and purses his lips. "That's it. This is the third time you've almost caused an accident in Lincoln Park alone. We need a new game, because you know what goes well with foie gras and Sauternes?"

"Um, not dying?"

"Exactly. Start thinking."

Once we get to the store, we grab a cart, pull out our Oreo-centric shopping list, and begin to debate the new game while strolling down the aisles.

"Whatever we choose, I think the name should rhyme," I tell him. "Maybe we could play Slug Chug? I'd get to hit you every time you take a drink."

"No way." Oh, boy, would I win *that* one.

I snicker. "But it would be fun for me."

"No."

"Okay, how about Slug Lug?"

"What the hell is Slug Lug?" he asks, loading a big bag of Arm & Hammer Fresh Step into our cart.

"That's when we hit each other if we see someone carrying something heavy, like . . . cat litter!" I whack him on the shoulder and inadvertently let out a squeal of glee.

"Do it again and you'll lose a hand. We need to agree before we play." He rubs his shoulder. Don't let the pearls fool you—I pack a mean right hook.

"Oh. I'm sorry.[7] Let me think. How about Slug Jug? Wait, that makes no sense. How often do we see marauding bands of jugs out on Ashland Avenue? Maybe Slug Shag Rug?"

---

[7] Not.

"Dumb."

"Slug Beer Mug?"

"Dumber."

"Slug Prescription Drug?"

"Dumbest. Hey, Jen, why do we need three packages of Oreos?"

"Because our town house is three stories tall. *Duh.*"

He rolls his eyes. "What was I thinking?" Fletch insists we grocery shop together ever since the time I bought three mini birthday cakes and a *Star* magazine for dinner. What? It was a balanced meal—I added ice cream.

"Ooh, I've got it!" I exclaim. "Whenever we see someone decked out in gang colors, Starter jackets, and bling, we'll play Slug Thug! That? Would be hilarious."

Instead of responding to my brilliant idea, Fletch looks at the speaker in the ceiling, head cocked to the side like our pit bull Maisy when we say "Doggie Park." "Do you hear that?"

"I hear a lot of stuff, Fletch. Cash registers, squeaky shopping carts, ridiculous girls so busy barking into their cell phones about their hookups they don't notice they *keep cutting in front of us.*" Glaring, I address the stupid blonde with a phone glued to her head, totally blocking access to the Frankenberry cereal and utterly oblivious to our presence. "BTW, sweetie? Bob's not calling you back because you 'did' him on your first date. He thinks you're way too easy." No reaction. I turn back to Fletch. "See? Nothing. For God's sake, I'm a loud, fat girl in a black-and-yellow rugby shirt—I look like a school bus. How does she *not* see or hear me? Do you think I'd get in trouble if I 'accidentally' smashed into her with a shopping cart? She wouldn't know it was us."

"Shh—listen!" he hisses.

"To who? Slutty McGabsalot? I've heard about three separate dalliances since we've been behind her. She practically hosted her own personal Fleet Week last Saturday. If she tells her friend she has chlamydia, we're so out of here."

"No, listen to the song that's playing—it's Whitesnake!" He points at the ceiling.

"Pardon?"

"Whitesnake."

As a New Wave eighties girl, I was all about Madness, the Clash, and the like,[8] so I never learned which hair-band was which. In my mind, the metal groups are all stuck together in a viscous cloud of Aqua Net, groupies, and bourbon. "Help me out here, Fletcher. Whitesnake—were those the we-thought-fireworks-indoors-were-a-good-idea guys?"

"Nope, that was Great White."

"Tragic. Okay, so they were the look-at-my-pretty-face-and-teased-bouffant-and-bare-chest-lead-singer folks?"

"That was Kip Winger of Winger."

"He was lovely, wasn't he? Fabulous hair. So, do you mean the single-entendre-she's-my-cherry-pie-and-here's-a-fire-hose-just-in-case-you-didn't-get-the-symbolism jackasses?"

"You're thinking of Warrant."

Wow. Fletch is a repository of shitty eighties music. I take one final guess. "Whitesnake, were they the Tawny-Kitaen-writhing-on-the-car-hood-and-making-me-feel-like-a-fat-chick-even-though-I-was-borderline-anorexic gentlemen?"

---

[8] Fine—I mostly listened to Wham! and the Go-Gos, but I totally appreciated the good stuff, too.

"Yeah." He continues to listen and nod his head in time with the song.

"Did you know years later Tawny got arrested for assault? She kicked her husband in the junk with pointy shoes and then he divorced her. I guess they didn't have their own Slug Nuts game. Too bad. Also? She's totally not hot anymore. I saw her mug shot. Ha! Serves her right for getting ass-prints all over that lovely Jaguar. And ruining my nineteen-year-old self-esteem. Anyway, Whitesnake's playing at Jewel Foods, what's the big deal?"

Fletch shrugged. "For a brief moment in the eighties, those guys were rock gods. I saw them open for Mötley Crüe in 1987, and they were Led Zeppelin meets Deep Purple."

"Hmm, fascinating." I examine the fat content on a jar of Alfredo sauce and place it in my cart anyway.

"Whitesnake put on an incredible show—I thought they'd become legends like their predecessors. But where are they now? They've vanished, leaving nothing but eyeliner and acid-wash in their wake."

"Number one, I can't believe I married someone who'd pay to see Mötley Crüe—they're more like Mötley Eeew." I explode into a fit of giggles while Fletch patiently waits for me to compose myself.[9] "And number two, according to all the episodes of VH1's *Behind the Music* I've seen, the metal guys manage to hold on to their money, unlike poor bankrupt MC Hammer.[10] What's the big deal?"

---

[9] The upside of a narcissistic personality disorder is you think your own jokes are the funniest in the world.

[10] We should totally hold a telathon for him.

"I just feel bad for David Coverdale. I bet he never expected the anthems of his youth to echo through the produce aisle."

"Unless David Coverdale's working the register here tonight, I wouldn't waste your sympathy. After all, he got to nail Tawny Kitaen."

He laughs and grabs a couple of cans of refried beans. "You know that most women don't say stuff like that, don't you?"

"And that's why you're with me." Because I? Am all about the locker-room humor.

We continue to shop, one ear cocked toward the sound system. While we wait in line for deli-sliced roast beef, we hear a Journey song. While we thump melons, we hear another. While we inspect eggs for cracks, we hear a third.

"Why does this place play so damn much Journey? I feel like I'm at a high school dance. Makes me want to feather my hair, yank the zipper up on my skintight Chic jeans with a rat-tail comb, and be mean to the cute boys because I've yet to master the fine art of flirting," I say.

Fletch exclaims, "That's it! Journey! *Steve Perry!!*" And then he punches me in the arm. Hard.

"*Ow!* What the *hell*, Fletcher?" I rub my throbbing triceps.

"I figured out our new game! Every time we hear Journey, you have to say '*Steeeve Perry!*' the way Matt and Trey did in *BASEketball*.[11] Whoever says it first gets to take one shot."

"I don't really recall most Journey songs because I didn't

----

[11] Years from now, monuments will be built to recognize the genius of Matt Stone and Trey Parker.

listen to them. Remember? I was all about Belinda Carlisle and Madonna, back before she lost her mind."

"Then I guess you're going to get hit a lot."

Wrong answer. "I hate this idea."

"Because you're going to lose more often than not?"

Yes. "No."

"Would you prefer I run over a crowd of casual diners next time we play Slug Pug because you're such a terrible winner?"

Yes. "No."

"I'll make you a deal—how about we keep a log? If you're getting creamed, I'd be willing to reconsider."

I mull over his proposition, finally deciding, "That sounds fair."

Jen's Steeeve Perry Victory Log

May 26, Stanley's Fruit Market on Elston—Fletch scores with "I'll Be Alright Without You." I resist the urge to throw a bunch of plantains at him. (Barely.) Fletch 1, Jen 0.

May 30, Trader Joe's on Clybourn—Fletch scores with "Wheel in the Sky." Arrrgggh! Fletch 2, Jen 0.

June 2, Best Buy on North—Fletch three-peats with "Faithfully," "Who's Crying Now," and "Separate Ways."[12] I am starting to feel a bit stabby. Fletch 3, Jen 0.

---

[12] Also? We grocery shop a lot. No wonder we're fat.

June 9, Jewel on Ashland Ave—Fletch *again* with "Oh Sherrie." I actually notice it before he does but can't tell if it's Steve singing. *"Is this him or another guy?"* I ask. *"Didn't Journey have a couple of vocalists?"* Fletch responds with a blow to the biceps and a jovial, *"It's Steeeve Perry!"* I demand a rule change and decree that I can punch first and ask questions later when in doubt. He grudgingly acquiesces. Fletch 4, Jen 0.

That same night, Jewel on Ashland Ave—I hear a familiar song and strike an unsuspecting Fletch right in his breadbasket. *"Steeeve Perry!"* As he leans over the frozen vegetable bin, gasping for breath and clutching his stomach, he sputters, *"That was Pearl Jam, you asshat."* Then he gets to punch me back because I'm wrong and I forfeit my win. Fletch 5, Jen still 0.

June 14, en route to post office—Fletch scores with "Lovin', Touchin', Squeezin'" (and divorcin' if I don't get a legitimate hit soon). Fletch 6, Jen 0.

June 17, our living room, at the end of *The Simpsons* episode guest-starring Rodney Dangerfield as Mr. Burns's son—When Fletch doesn't realize "Any Way You Want It" is playing during the credits, I nail him in the thigh and shriek, *"Steeeve Perry! Steeeve Perry! Steeeve Perry! Aiiiieeee!!"*

While jumping around crowing about my great victory, I trip on the coffee table, spill my glass of wine, twist my ankle, and collapse in a puddle of Riesling. I spend the rest of the night in damp sweatpants, icing my ankle with a bag of frozen cauliflower.

And you know what? It's totally worth it.

Jen 1.

I win! I win! I win!!

To: angie_at_home, carol_at_home, wendy_at_home, jen_at_work
From: jen@jenlancaster.com
Subject: *jen equals glenn close? not so much.*

Hey, all,

The driver of the number 56 Milwaukee/Blue Line bus thinks he has a stalker now.

Specifically?

Me.

A variety of errands too banal to explain here—yes, even I have my limits—put me on the number 56 a total of five times over the course of the day. Since I've taken a lot of cabs lately, I've become accustomed to giving salutations upon entering and exiting the vehicle.

Apparently, this small politeness is *not* de rigueur on public transportation and speaking to the bus driver is frowned upon.

So, when the vagaries of the Chicago transit system put me on the same driver's bus that many times in a row, I couldn't help laughing and exclaiming to the driver, "Hey, it's me *again!* I must be following you!" as I fed my card into the slot for the fourth time.

That motherfucker had the gall to look at me as though I'd just boiled his bunny.

Okay, not to blow my own horn or anything, but if I were to:

A) completely shit-can my happy marriage, and

B) start stalking a desirable member of the opposite sex, I'm pretty sure he wouldn't be

C) a sixty-year-old bus driver named Jesus.

Jesus, indeed.

Jen

Loathe Thy Neighbor

*M*y track record of befriending neighbors leaves some room for improvement. Like, Aaron Spelling's house complete with bowling alley, discotheque, and gift-wrap-area-sized room for improvement.

I'm not really sure how this happened; I used to be great at making friends with those around me. Growing up, I was buddies with almost everyone on my street,[1] and once I got to college things didn't change much. My pals were those who lived on the same dorm floor as me,[2] and my very best girl-friend was my roommate, although I'm sure had Joanna and I been paired differently, the girls we may have lived with

---

[1] Except stupid Brenda Mitchell. But more on that bitch in a minute.

[2] Except for Jen H., who accused me of sleeping with her boyfriend, which for the record *I never, ever did, not once, not even close.* Sure, of course I made out with him—he looked just like Christopher Atkins! How do you *not* kiss Mr. Blue Lagoon, given the opportunity? But no s-e-x. That's for damn sure.

would have fit that bill, too. And when I pledged my sorority, suddenly everyone under that roof became my BFFs.[3]

The fast and easy friendships from those days make sense because by residing in a college dorm or on a cul-de-sac in a subdivision, circumstances are fairly homogeneous. Whether it was having lunch in the same dining hall or playing on the same swing set, we were living similar circumstances and therefore intrinsically knew a CliffsNotes version of each other's lives. We didn't have to share long backstories to get a bead on our histories because they were pretty much the same. Maybe they watched *Happy Days* instead of *Good Times*,[4] or they pledged Kappa instead of Pi Phi, but overall we had a real understanding of one another because we *were* one another.

I guess things changed after college when I moved into my first Chicago-area apartment. Suddenly I found myself living around people very different from me. We were diverse not due to ethnicity, race, or age, but because we didn't come from a shared past; our jobs, hometowns, educations, and experiences were all vastly different and we had no instant commonalities. Proximity was no longer the pool from which I drew friends; *those* I made at work. Plus? Our neighbors were weirdos.

Fletch and I lived in a suburb called Palatine[5] for the first few months before we worked up the nerve to move to the city

---

[3] Until I made out with their boyfriends. What can I say? I was very friendly in college.

[4] We were a *Good Times* household.

[5] An Indian word for "Land of Many Strip Malls."

proper. We had a one-bedroom place on the top floor of a decent building. Our apartment was small but well laid out and brand-new, so it felt very grown-up. One wild night we were watching *The X Files* and playing Scrabble[6] when there was a knock at our door.

"Who could that be?" I asked. Ours was a security building and we'd yet to meet anyone who'd be comfortable enough to drop by unannounced at nine p.m. on a Friday night.

"Dunno. I'll get it." He rose from his spot on the floor and looked out the peephole while I surreptitiously swapped out my X tile for one with a vowel.[7] He turned and shrugged at me before opening it. "Hi, can I help you?" he asked the guy standing at our door.

I recognized the man by the excess body fur creeping out of his shirt and up to his ears, as I believe he was half Sasquatch. I'd learned he was our downstairs neighbor because he introduced himself the day I moved in. He told me if I heard thumping, not to worry. His daughter wore a helmet to bed and sometimes she hit her head on the wall, and also, his wife had night terrors. So . . . yeah. I figured there were more details as to why *Follicle Man and the Family Helmet Head* opted for the tiny one-bedroom place, but I was pretty sure I didn't want to know what they might be. (I guess circus folk have to live somewhere, right?)

"You need to keep it down. My daughter is asleep."

---

[6] I wish this were a euphemism for something really dirty so we don't sound like tremendous nerds. Unfortunately, it's not.

[7] Scully and Mulder said I could, so it's not cheating.

"Excuse me?" Fletch and I shot confused glances at each other.

"You're making too much noise."

"Are you sure you mean us?" *Do you think he washes himself with soap or shampoo? Really, it could go either way.*

"Yes, I'm sure. The noise was coming from directly above me."

I rose to join Fletch at the door. "Dude, are you kidding? We're playing *Scrabble*. We couldn't make less noise unless we were asleep. Or, like, dead." *God, look at all the fur on his hands. You can't even see his skin. He's Robin Williams hairy.*

"Well, you're too loud."

Fletch crossed his arms and folded them against his chest. "No, we're really not. If you hear us moving around, sorry, but you chose to live on the first floor." *I saw him once at the pool with his shirt off and I had to pretend I'd stubbed my toe because of how I'd screamed. And then when he'd dived in, the water slicked everything back and I swear to God his hairline started half an inch above his eyebrows. Correction, eyebrow.*

"Are you saying you're not going to keep it down?"

"Yes, because there's nothing *to* keep down." *Is it that hard to manscape? You know, get an electric razor, trim up your shrubbery, blow out your front yard a bit? Maybe he's overheating because he's too well insulated?*

The neighbor began to nod quickly. "So—so—that's how you're going to be, huh? There's a child downstairs and *you* can't knock off all the racket? Really? Really. And what if I called the police?"

"Listen, pal, I've got a right to have a conversation with my girlfriend here in our apartment. We're not partying, we're not listening to loud music, we're playing a motherfucking board game on a Friday night at nine p.m. If you don't like it, call the police and get yourself a citation for falsely reporting a noise violation. Good night." Fletch closed the door on the neighbor, who at that point had begun to vibrate with agitation, and I loved that he was able to resolve the situation without violence or intimidation.

"And maybe you should buy yourself a helmet while you're at it, you hairy jackass!" I shouted through the closed door. What can I say? Fletch is a better man than I.

Fletch sat back down in front of our game board. "Was that necessary?"

I thought about it for a moment. "You know what? It was."

Yadda, yadda, yadda, the guy swore revenge on us, prompting me to purchase and stomp around the house in an ungainly pair of clogs. He and his family moved out a month later, leaving a lovely L-shaped couch in the Dumpster, which we immediately claimed for our own. Yes, he certainly showed *us*. However, our exchange skewed the way I looked at those living around me, and started me on the road from passive to aggressive neighbor relations.

The longer we've lived in the city, the less tolerant I've grown of sharing my space with other people. Sometimes I get so tired of existing a wall, floor, or ceiling away from strangers. I hate having no choice but to smell what they're cooking for dinner or to hear what they're viewing on TV. (Plus they never watch good stuff like *24*, as I wouldn't mind hearing my boyfriend Kiefer Sutherland in stereo.) The only way to not let it get to me is to act like I'm in an elevator, tuning out everything but what's happening in my square foot of personal buffer zone, but in neighborhoods—like in elevators—there's always some ass-clapper snapping her gum or cutting his lawn at six thirty a.m. and I can't ignore it. What Fletch and I need to do is move ourselves to a desolate, windswept mountaintop somewhere in Wyoming, but then I'd probably bitch about how long it took me to drive to Target. 'Til then? It's Sweet Home Chicago.

When Fletch and I lived in the sketchy area during our unemployment, most of our neighbors were immigrants more intent on fostering the rodent population than assimilation, so we weren't exactly a hit at the block parties. Chasing them down with steamy sacks of their dogs' abandoned poop, saying, *"Ja pomyśleć ty zapominal twój drugie śniadanie u mój polana!"* also did nothing to improve our popularity.[8]

The hippie vegans who lived downstairs were American, but I managed to inadvertently alienate them when the female half of the couple told me she was a poet. Apparently it is *not* flattering to blow Dr Pepper out your nose and yelp, "Oh, sweetie, it's okay if you're unemployed! All the cool kids are," and then ask if she knows any words that rhyme with "severance." Couple that with their anything but noise-proofed ceilings and we had the recipe for an Israel-Palestine level of hostility. And it probably didn't help when I'd hear said hippie vegans having organically grown sex and would shout through the floorboards the male half of the couple might last longer if he added some meat to his diet.[9]

The thing is, I accept responsibility for the problems I

---

[8] Polish for "I think you left your lunch on my lawn."
[9] I can see how he'd be pissed, but, really, *she* should have thanked me.

created for myself in previous living arrangements. I never should have admonished the hippies about smoking so much pot that *my* kids would be born with webbed feet. In Lincoln Park, maybe the college kids around us would have liked me more had I not thrown their beer cans back at them. And when we lived in the Bucktown penthouse, things may have gone better with the cool people next door if during our evening of *The Big Lebowski* and White Russians I didn't drink so much I lost my shirt. And my dinner.[10]

Upon moving into this condo complex, I feel like we've been given a second chance and I want to do everything differently. (If you've ever gone from being a six-figure-earning asshole to begging your parents for grocery money in less than two years, you'll know what I mean.) I can't change my past, but I can avoid making the same mistakes going forward. I'm going to try making some friends . . . or at least not creating more enemies. Somehow the idea of passing from home to car without danger of being pelted with rotten tomatoes appeals to me. To be a good neighbor, I needed to change my M.O., which means no more spying, no more booby traps, and no more throwing things. Hence, I put away my Gladys Kravitz–model binoculars and little catapult and folded up my *Don't Tread on Me* yard flag.

Now, instead of my prior policy of glaring and mocking, I smile and wave. I make small talk. I compliment new outfits, hairstyles, and patio furniture. I hold the parking lot gate and allow everyone to pull in ahead of me. Honest to God, I've

---

[10] No bonus points were awarded for gaining a dorsal fin, either.

been on my very best behavior and have made every effort to be nice even though almost no one responds in kind. For example, despite the fact I'd like to tear down and pee on the Socialist Party campaign signs posted on every square inch of unit C's patio,[11] instead I call a cheery hello whenever I see him hauling in hemp sacks of pesticide-free groceries from the local food co-op, even though he's yet to acknowledge me with a nod.

When the anachronism otherwise known as Greg and Maggie dance out of their corner unit in their tennis togs with their eighties hairstyles after hosting one of their eighties Jacuzzi parties in their eighties black-lacquered, polished-chrome, glass-tabled, leopard-printed travesty of a domicile, I attempt to start a weather-based conversation while they scuttle off to their jobs as junk-bond dealers.

Honestly, I could catalog each respective snub from the gay guys I call the Giggler, Poo Diary, the Pitcher, and the Catcher, the mean woman across from us also known as My Big, Fat Manic Mommy, and Queen of the Harpies in the center unit, but I think you get the point. (Ahem, people? Maybe if you introduced yourselves to me I wouldn't have to nickname you.) In an entire year I've made no progress, causing me to exclaim more than once, *"Damn it, why don't you jack-asses like me?"*

It's not like we've crapped up the joint; our yard is freaking immaculate and beautifully landscaped. I've spent every single penny I've touched in the past two months creating a garden paradise in the front of our town house. There are

---

[11] And the bumper of his hybrid electric car.

twenty-eight different types of budding plants between the patio and balcony alone, not counting all the vines and ferns. Big variegated violet and white petunias spill over the sides of the window boxes, nestled among white phlox and multihued vincas and dotted with velvety fuchsia geraniums, the blooms the size of fists that I'm not presently using to shake at neighbors. Because of careful pruning, dinner-plate-sized hibiscus flowers blossom daily with coral-colored petals surrounding their borderline obscene pink and yellow stamens. My gardenias make the yard smell like paradise itself and the area around my spotlighted tree where the red and white tulips grew after first frost is now covered in rich green climbing ivy and burnt sienna mulch, perfectly matching my well-grouped terra-cotta pots. Each flower was planted with my striped teak patio umbrella in mind and all the shades of yellow, orange, pink, green, and purple have been strategically placed around the property in perfect harmony.

But are we appreciated for my sweat equity, which has done nothing but improve their property values? Hell, no. From the way we're tacitly ignored, you'd have thought we'd adorned out patio with old auto parts and a clothesline full of pit-stained undershirts, not cascading sprays of wave petunias and lush asparagus fern.

Why?

Because we—*pearls clutched, gasp, the horror!*—are renters. Even though we pay the same amount of rent as their mortgages for the privilege of living around these awful people, we're shunned for not being our townhome's rightful owners.

Making matters worse, we're the only family who rents at

the moment. Another renter lived in the unit next door, but she moved out earlier this spring when the owners sold her place. She was a sweet young widow and occasionally we'd exchange pleasantries. She was great—friendly but not intrusive, enthusiastic without being overbearing, and blissfully quiet . . . until she bought the drum set. For nine long months she played *thump* the *thump* same *thump* damn *thump* riff *thump* for *thump* hours *thump* on *thump* end *thump*. Previously such behavior would have led me to plot her painful demise, but I've really committed myself to being a better person. Plus, I couldn't be mean to a widow. I gritted my teeth and listened to her bang away, not improving even one iota despite constant *thump* resounding *thump* soul-rattling *thump* practice. When her movers showed up last month, I hugged her good-bye and told her to take care of herself. And then I cracked open a bottle of the finest $8 champagne I could find.

Anyway, I've been scheming to get my neighbors' attention for the past few weeks, figuring that if they'd just *talk* with me they'd like me. *I am likable, damn it.* Sure, I told Fletch I hate these folks, but that's only because they show no interest in me. Truthfully, their rebukes hurt my delicate little feelings and have driven me to distraction. They can't really *not* want to meet me simply because I write a check to my landlord instead of my lender, *can they?* According to the gal next door, my landlord was an exhibitionist and used to *do it* every day, blinds open, lights on, and generally wearing a role-playing costume.[12] I imagine not seeing my bare butt flying around the living room

---

[12] I don't pay our rent in person anymore—I can't keep a straight face.

in a Red Riding Hood cape would be a huge selling point, so how are we worse neighbors than *that*?

Maybe that's just how life is in the city? When I was a kid, my family knew everyone in a four-block radius. We celebrated holidays with them and attended their children's weddings. If they were young, we sent casseroles over when they had babies. If they were old, we shoveled their driveways without asking. But, here? I have no idea how to interact and it's hard to connect—no roles have been established.

The old me would have said, "Fuck 'em," and I'd have found a nice sawed-off bathtub and placed a figure of the Virgin Mary next to my baby pool and pink flamingos right in the center of the patio. And despite my almost crippling modesty, those bedroom curtains would be open 24/7 for the *All Jen's Naked White Ass, All the Time Show*. But the new Slightly Kinder, Slightly Gentler Jen instead creates a foolproof turn-neighbors-into-friends scheme.

I'm outside executing said plan when Fletch comes home.

"What on earth are you doing?"

In our household, Fletch asks this question a lot. "What do you mean?" is my stock response. Generally whatever I'm doing is patently obvious, whether it's having the dog try on my niece's birthday tutu[13] or painting the room earmarked for Fletch's den cotton-candy pink after we'd agreed on taupe. (Oh, come on, who wouldn't like to work in Barbie's Dream Office? I mean, except for Fletcher?)

"Clarification; what on earth are you doing *out here*?"

---

[13] My dog Maisy and niece Sarah appear to be the same size—what better way to check the fit?

Fletch sits next to me in one of our teak chairs and places his briefcase on the slatted table.

"I'm reading. *Duh*." I wave a stack of papers at him. A writer friend asked me to look at a manuscript and possibly give a quote for the book's jacket, so I'm out on our patio perusing its pages. I take a slug of my Pinot Noir and attempt to get back to work.

Fletch lights a cigarette, grabs a sip of my wine, and continues. "You're going to make me spell this out, aren't you? Why are you reading out here *in the dark*?"

I close my manuscript with a thud. "Because the people across the parking lot are having a party and I want to be invited. I figure if I sit here with my glass of wine, two things will happen. One, they'll ask what I'm reading. Then I'll get to imply how cool I am, what with reviewing this manuscript and all. And two, when they see the wine they'll ascertain I'm in the mood for a cocktail and they'll insist I join them, *again*, what with me being so cool and all. Then they'll be my best friends and I will be the most popular girl in the neighborhood. After all, who doesn't want a soon-to-be-famous author at their soiree?"[14]

Fletch takes a moment to digest what I've just said, fortifying himself with yet more of my wine. "*Posing* is your master plan? This is what you've been scheming about behind closed doors for a month? And you're expecting success? By just sitting here with paper in front of you? You're a bucket of black

---

[14] And current-day temp. Also, I have no idea on the pending fame bit. But since my book doesn't come out 'til next spring, it's not outside the realm of the possible, right?

paint shy of turning into Wile E. Coyote. Hmm, perhaps you could drop Acme-brand anvils on all their heads if posing doesn't work. Meep, meep."

"Honey, what you fail to realize is I perfected my 'get invited' strategy thirty years ago and I can't believe I didn't think of it sooner. The simplicity is the key to its brilliance! See, when I was in second grade, my neighbor Brenda Mitchell used to swim with her friends every day at noon. Because she was an older kid with no time for 'babies,' she never wanted to hang out with me. And yet I managed to swim with her whenever I wanted."

Fletch looks skeptical, so I continue.

"See, Mrs. Mitchell was really nice. So I'd knock on the door to ask if Brenda could come out and play, knowing full well she was in the water. Mrs. Mitchell would insist I run home, put my suit on, and join them, never once suspecting I was a seven-year-old Machiavelli. Lather, rinse, repeat, once a day, every day, for the entire summer. The end."

"Did Brenda ever try to drown you?"

"Oh, sure, on a daily basis. But hey, you can't be drowned if you're not in a pool!"

"I knew you were a master manipulator; I didn't realize you'd started so early. But back to the matter at hand—you hate those guys across the street. Why are you so desperate to join them?"

"They have banana daiquiris. With drink umbrellas! I'd sell state secrets to the Taliban for a good banana daiquiri."[15]

---

[15] Or possibly for a piña colada, but only if it's made with sweet coconut milk. If I'm going to commit treason, it had better be delicious.

"Then make your own instead of sucking up to people you don't like. We've got rum, bananas, and some mix in the freezer—we may even have a few umbrellas left in the junk drawer. Come on inside; we'll try out the new blender."

"Yeah, I could . . ." I trail off.

"What? You have a big 'but' in your voice."

"It's just that . . ." I sigh.

"It's just that what?"

I nod and gaze longingly across our brick, U-shaped parking lot. "Honey, everyone over there is either a fat chick or a gay guy."

"What's the problem? I thought those were your kind of people."

"Yes, exactly! They totally *are* my kind of people. But those guys are ignoring me, when by all rights *I should be their queen.*"

Speechless, Fletch stubs out his cigarette, collects his bag, and retreats into the brightness of the house. The sun has long since set and the mosquitoes are biting in earnest. I watch as the people across from me gather up daiquiri glasses and bottles, extinguishing torches and citronella candles, and file inside. The last one closes the front door and with nary a wave or nod in my direction turns off the porch light. I'm left alone in the dark with an empty wineglass, a stack of paper, and my thoughts. Considering I live within walking distance of the Sears Tower, it's eerie how quiet it is out here.

Generally I prefer the anonymity the city offers, which is why I've yet to take off for the 'burbs or that Wyoming mountaintop. I like not being defined by silly incidents that happened in the neighborhood ages before. Case in point, twenty-one years later, Kim from across the street still teases me about the time my brother flew out of the car and kissed the ground after taking me for a driving lesson. It's nice to dash out for a gallon of milk wearing no makeup and glasses, knowing you won't run into anyone. I relish the fluidity of up-grading apartments by moving and never once mourning the place I just left. Residing in the middle of this big, beautiful city gives me the sense of freedom and independence I never had growing up in Huntington, Indiana. Yet once in a while, it would be nice to be offered a damn banana daiquiri.

Looks like I'm never going to be able to join these neighbors, so I resign myself to beating them.

Now, where did I put those binoculars?

To: angie_at_home, carol_at_home, wendy_at_home, jen_at_work
From: jen@jenlancaster.com
Subject: *greetings from the job*

What up, bitches?

I've been working a decent temp gig for the past few weeks, hence the sporadic contact. At first I thought I'd get some really fantastic material out of the job because the administrative assistant who was training me hated the other admin with a passion and spoke at length about their whole East Coast–West Coast gangsta level of animosity and I was sure caps would be placed in respective asses, except by "caps" I mean dirty looks and snide comments about the craftsmanship of the other's shoes whispered at a barely perceptible level over by the Diet Coke machine. Alas, the first admin went to her new job once I was trained and the admin who is left is really pleasant, incredibly competent, helpful, and professional. So I guess she wasn't the bad guy.

Anyway, I'm not going to bitch about the company because, again, I landed somewhere nice. They have free flavored coffee creamers in the lunchroom—which, by the way, is as nice as a restaurant—plus they stock Splenda *and* NutraSweet. Also, they have a crushed-ice machine and real silverware for the employees to use when they eat their lunch. You could say that having been jobless for so long I appreciate the little things. The more likely explanation is that I'm easily impressed.

The only downside is the executives I support are out of town and I'm *bored*. Unfortunately, it's not the kind of place where I can just blatantly work on personal stuff. Today to kill a half hour, I looked up all the doctors the old assistant had written on the calendar she left behind. She went to a number of different gynecologists. Apparently she had a problem with her girly bits.

Tomorrow I plan to swap out my chair.

Jen

To: angie_at_home, carol_at_home, wendy_at_home, jen_at_work
From: jen@jenlancaster.com
Subject: *except for all the sailing, it's a really hard job*

Poor Fletch—he's under a lot of pressure right now because he started a job at a new company. However, before you feel too sorry for him, I should mention (a) this is his dream job, (b) much of the pressure is self-imposed, and (c) he has to go sailing with clients and a full cooler of beverages every Friday. His tan is better than mine right now and don't think I'm not a tad resentful.

Regardless, my point is whenever he gets stressed, he talks in his sleep. After a whole week of waking up to hearing him say some whacky shit, I've started to write it down.

From last night:

"Who's the douchebag that threw the grenade?"

and

"So everyone gets a new fucking watch?"

I am more than a little awed at how coherent and profane these thoughts are, but I'm also conflicted. On the one hand, I want his stress level to decrease because I love him and don't want him feeling undue pressure. But on the other, I hate to mess with the funny.

What to do?

Jen

If the Werewolves
Are in London . . .

L ive in an urban area long enough and eventually you're going to find yourself desensitized to the un-expected.[1] On a stroll down Michigan Ave, I'm likely to see a man dressed in nothing but burlap sacks whizzing on Ralph Lauren's display window while a fishnet-and-cashmere-clad fashionista[2] languidly finishes her Perrier in the outdoor RL Café a mere six feet away. Across the street a person covered in head-to-toe silver paint strikes a perfectly motionless Tin-Man pose while an-other holding an old-fashioned sandwich board shouts into

---

[1] I'm reminded of this each time my small-town mother visits and wants to call the police when she hears a car alarm. Although for someone so concerned about grand theft auto, you'd think she wouldn't make a habit of keeping her keys in her unlocked car.

[2] Her sweater-wearing teacup terrier, Donatella, shivers in her thousand-dollar carrying bag—strategically placed in its own chair—dying for a bite of the chocolate chip muffin his owner has no intention of ingesting.

a megaphone about the Microsoft/General Mills–sponsored end of the world.[3]

While this scene isn't exactly Main Street USA, it's business as usual to those of us who live here. Every day I see the atypical—a woman with a stroller who's just as likely to be pushing aluminum cans as she is a baby. Pierced and tattooed runaways stand on the El platform right next to the guy in the $1,500 suit, smiling at each other while discussing the Cubs' chances this year. Garbage pirates steer their trucks full of scrap metal past the sex shops down the rainbow-flag-adorned Pride Parade route. Immigrants who just finished swimming in their underpants sun themselves on a blanket just feet away from the PR girl with the brand-new boob job at the Fullerton Ave beach. In a world where I share a dry cleaner with drag queens and a Target with crackheads and heiresses, I often think I've seen it all and tend to assume nothing can surprise me anymore.

And that's where I'd be wrong.

We're about to pull into our parking lot when I learn exactly how wrong I can be.

Fresh from a Target run, Fletch and I drive into our gated parking lot, in the middle of our ten thousandth daily debate about nothing. "How can you say that? He was brilliant! Groundbreaking, even! I mean, he *made* the whole *Andy*

---

[3] But I ask you, how could the company who created Lucky Charms be evil? Impossible! And magically delicious!

Griffith Show. I'm telling you no one gave a shit about Mayberry after he left."

Fletch shrugs. "I just never found him that funny."

"Even on *Three's Company*?" I am incredulous. "The man wore a neckerchief! With a leisure suit! And was homophobic about someone who wasn't even homosexual! Plus he, like, practically *invented* physical comedy."

"Nope, don't see it. Not even on *Three's Company*," he argues.

"Okay, if you say you fell for the hackneyed, hayseed antics of Jim Nabors, or worse, Howard Morris, the guy who played Ernest T. Bass, you are *so* sleeping on the couch tonight. Plus, ten bucks says if Ernest T. Bass were around today, Sheriff Andy would pull him in for being a pedophile. Seriously, with his greasy hair, cutoff coveralls, and shifty eyes, doesn't he look like every child molester you see on the news these days?"

Fletch backs up the car and angles the steering wheel so our cargo is closer to the sidewalk before cutting the lights. "I didn't hate Ernest. He was always throwing bricks through windows, and on many levels I appreciate that. He was unapologetically bad. However, I was mostly a Floyd Lawson fan."

"*Gah!* The barber? Your favorite character was *Floyd the barber*? How can that be, you philistine? That's like saying your favorite flavor of yogurt is plain. Floyd was Wonder Bread with a side of fat-free mayo. He was diet Sprite and Freedent gum, all rolled into one. No flavor, so very boring! Seriously, when my boy Barney bugged his eyes, pursed his lips, and pulled out his single bullet, the heavens opened up and God himself laughed his ass off. Years from now, scholars and holy men are going to study *The Tao of Fife*."

"So your thesis statement is the Lord God Almighty had a direct hand in guiding Don Knotts's career?"

"Um, *yeah*."

"Care to defend that statement?"

"Yes. I have four words for you. *The. Incredible. Mr. Limpet*."

Fletch locks the front of the car and opens the hatch, pausing first to rub a bit of dirt off the taillight. Fletch is beyond meticulous when it comes to keeping his car clean and sort of hates when I drive it out of town to visit my parents for the weekend. Something about me losing French fries like the dogs shed fur?

"Come again?" he asks.

"*The Incredible Mr. Limpet* is only the best movie ever to exist in the entire world and I am not exaggerating. You know, it's the one where Don Knotts turns into a cartoon fish and he helps the navy bomb Japanese ships in the Pacific and thus allows us to win World War Two."

He rolls his eyes. "Sounds like a classic."

"It *is*. Although I never got the part why he had to wear glasses once he turned into a fish. I thought fish oil was supposed to improve your vision? Plus, he had no problem leaving his wife for Lady Fish. He was all, *'Later,'* and then just swam away after the Widow Limpet gave him his spare set of glasses. That was kind of cold, but in no way do these troublesome plot points detract from his genius. I'll put it in our Netflix queue so you can see for yourself."

Fletch dryly agrees, "Yeah, still not convinced he wasn't a hack. Name me one film he was actually good in."

"*No Deposit, No Return? Herbie Goes to Monte Carlo? The Apple Dumpling Gang?*"

"Never saw it, never saw it, never saw it."

"What the *hell?* Did you not touch down on this planet until the eighties or something? How did you have a childhood without having seen these film classics?"

"My family never went to the movies. Oh, wait, that's not true. My psychotic sister took me to see *The Bad News Bears* once. Instead of helping me practice pitching, catching, or hitting, she thought this movie would improve my Pee Wee baseball skills. And before you ask—no, it didn't."

I gawp at him in the blue glow cast by the parking lot's sodium lights and I shake my head. "Worst. Childhood. Ever." Although I could debate the brilliance of Don Knotts all night, I decide to let this topic slide. I have neither the time nor the inclination to explain myself to a man who rises and sleeps under the blanket of the very freedom that the Incredible Mr. Limpet provided and then questions the manner in which he provided it.[4] Instead, I start lifting bags in the hatch to see which weigh the least, gravitating toward those containing paper towels. "Anyway, sweetie, I've got these here, so maybe you can haul in the kitty litter?"

"Yeah, I've got it," he replies, gingerly hoisting a giant bag of sweetly scented clay onto his shoulder. "Do you need me to—*oh my God!!*"

....

[4] Oh, Mr. Knotts. If only you could have lived long enough to make *A Few Good Fish*—it surely would have been your swan song.

Fletch immediately drops his bag of cat litter, runs to the front of the complex, punches the electronic gate's code, and hurls the door open, at which point I see the orange of his polar fleece jacket dissolve into the darkness as he dashes down the street.

How very odd, I think. *Fletch doesn't normally shriek like a scalded ape and run away in the middle of conversations about Don Knotts. Indeed, that is strange. I wonder why he did that? Yes, he's mentioned improving our commitment to physical fitness, but* this very moment *seems like an odd time to take up jogging.*

I finish grabbing the light bags out of the back of the car and head down the sidewalk to our unit. Everyone's got their drapes closed so I can't do any spying, which is a darn shame.[5] I unlock the door and am greeted far too enthusiastically by our dogs. Loki begins to howl and Maisy launches herself from the floor to up around my shoulders so she can lick my face. Yes, I understand they miss us when we leave, but we've only been gone forty-five minutes; there's no reason to throw us the canine version of a ticker-tape parade.

I pet them both, toss them a couple of big chewies, disperse cat treats, and begin to unpack. Our front hall closet spans almost the entire length of our first floor. Since we don't have twenty-five feet worth of coats to hang, Fletch got some lumber and turned half of the space into a walk-in pantry, allowing us to buy and store bulk items. His handiwork is nothing short of California Closets worthy. I'm perpetually amazed

---

[5] I like to keep tabs on what's happening so I can catalog suspicious doings on the Internet.

at the kind of home-improvement stuff he can do, considering I come from a long line of people who consider butter knives and shoes to be tools. I admire the shelves once more and begin to stow tins of pet food and cleaning products in between all the boxes of cookies and bags of snack food.

Minutes later, Fletch has still not returned. *How very, very peculiar,* I think. *Perhaps he's having an acid flashback from when he was a roadie for* Jefferson Airplane *at Woodstock?[6] Or maybe the genetic insanity in his family has finally caught up with him? I knew he'd eventually go bat-shit crazy, but I'd hoped for at least one more lucid decade.[7]*

I wait another minute before going out to retrieve the cat litter and dog food cans myself. As I load up, I notice my husband[8] running up and down the street, flailing his arms and gesturing wildly but silently, trying to get me to join him. I shake my head and sigh. *Oh, honey. You're really not physically fit enough for* this *kind of crazy.*

Once upon a time Fletch would have been fit enough to run up and down the street all night. When we met in college ten-plus years ago, he was a perfect V shape. His broad shoulders tapered down to an almost Scarlett O'Hara–like twenty-nine-inch waist and his healthy eating habits and overall dietary discipline were beyond reproach; *he* certainly wasn't going to gorge himself at the Twelve Oaks barbecue. He was lean and lithe and used to brag about how his Army

---

[6] No, scratch that. He was only a year old at the time and likely not yet strong enough to carry heavy amplifiers.

[7] Or at least long enough for him to carry in the cat litter.

[8] Henceforth known as Captain Whackypants.

Reserve uniform looked as though it had been custom-tailored just for him.

And that was great.

Until I saw that he had a waterbed in his apartment.

Afraid that the first time I stayed there'd be a mortifying seesaw effect and I'd displace more water than he would because I was heavier, I started him on a clandestine weight-gaining program. I introduced him to a world of butter-drenched crab legs and prime rib with thick horse-radish sauce and white chocolate raspberry mousse cake. I schooled him in the world of all things fried and con queso and taught him donuts aren't just for breakfast anymore. Shortly thereafter he began to fill out, and in the span of two years he went from a whippet-waisted 145 pounds to a much more huggable 215.[9] (Unfortunately, I was so devoted to this program that I gained right along with him.)

I catch another flash of orange dashing past me. Yep. He's certifiable. But now that Fletch has lost his mind, who am I going to banter with about classic TV moments? Although we've been together ten years, we haven't even gotten to eighties programming yet. *Magnum, PI*, *Miami Vice*, *Perfect Strangers*, *Joanie Loves Chachi*—so many conversations left unsaid. I'm devastated we'll never have the chance to discuss Blair, Tootie, or Sheriff Lobo. With which Duke boy did he most identify? What was his favorite catchphrase from *The A-Team*? I guess I'll never know.

I return to the house, set down the cat litter, and contemplate what my life is going to be like now that I'm single.

---

[9] But he's almost six feet three and I swear it looks good.

Chances are good I'm not going to find another "I love you just the way you are" kind of guy. I survey myself in the mirror by the front door. After a quick and brutally honest assessment, I determine I'm not nice enough to attract a man based on my personality. Sure I'm still relatively cute now with my decent tan and good haircut, but I'm going to *have* to lose weight if I ever want to find someone who'll carry the heavy bags again. I mean, look at all the famous bitches in history—Leona Helmsley, Joan Crawford, Joan Rivers, Alexis Carrington, Cruella DeVille—not a porker in the bunch and they all managed to land a man, despite their acid wits.[10]

I gaze longingly at the brand-new box of Hostess Cup-Cakes on the counter. Tears well in my eyes as I place their chocolate-coated, cream-filled goodness in the garbage can. *Au revoir, my sweet.* The Hershey's Symphony bar meets a similar fate. *I'll miss you and your bonus toffee-flavored chips.* A quick scan of the fridge reveals a whole wedge of Brie en croute, heavy cream, and leftover kung pao chicken, all which must go. *Good-bye, old friends. My life will be less rich without you in it. But I simply can't carry the groceries by myself.*

I'm on the Internet researching the dating sites that only show photos from the neck up when Fletch finally huffs into the house. He stands doubled over, hands on his thighs, and attempts to catch his breath. The sweat from his brow drips all over the hardwood.[11]

---

[10] Actually, I'm not 100 percent sure about Cruella, but she was always surrounded by her toadies, and one of them must have played cabana-boy when the cameras were off, yes?

[11] Good thing we got paper towels!

He points toward the street and attempts to speak. "Coyote . . . coyote . . . coyote out there . . . puffy tail . . . black glowing eyes!!"

"I have no idea what you're trying to tell me," I reply.

He takes a couple more deep breaths and straightens up, saying, "I just saw a coyote! On the street! I chased after it but it was too fast for me. I couldn't catch up to it."

I decide to humor him because I can't be sure if *this* brand of crazy comes with or without a side of violence. "Of course you did, sweetie! Chicago is well known for coyotes, especially within walking distance of the Sears Tower. You know, our forefathers had a hell of a time deciding whether to nickname Chicago 'the Windy City' or 'the Coyote City.' They eventually had to toss a coin." *Hmm, do they still make ephedrine-based diet pills? And what about those meds they pulled off the market? What were they called, Phen-Fen? Redux? Yeah, they gave people holes in their hearts, but wasn't the weight loss pretty significant, too?*

He exclaims, "I'm not kidding! He went to the bathroom right out in the middle of the street."

"Really, I'm sure he did. But I wonder what brought him to River West? I thought coyotes preferred Bucktown."[12] *Maybe I should start power walking the dogs? Except it looks so goofy that I'm not sure I could do it with a straight face. Power walkers all hustle around like they've got a load in their shorts. I can't look at them without cracking up. Although, isn't laughter supposed to tone your abs?*

----

[12] Coyotes hate the Gold Coast, a.k.a. "the Viagra Triangle." Too plastic, too much of a "scene."

"Wait, don't you believe me?" he asks.

"Um, honey? The coyote didn't mention anything about having you burn things, right? Because that would be wrong," I tell him gently. *Salads don't count as low-calorie if you drown them in cheese and ranch dressing, do they?*

Flabbergasted, Fletch takes a step back. "You think I'm making this up."

"No, sweetie. I don't think you're making this up. I think you've lost your fucking mind. Do you understand the difference?" *How about doing Tae Bo? I imagine I'd excel at anything where punching and kicking was involved. And we do have that nice lake here in town. (Some might even call it "great.") What if I were to propel myself around it in some manner, perhaps on a bike or Rollerblades, rather than just eating fried chicken and salt-and-vinegar chips while I sit baking in a lawn chair next to it?*

"Come outside and see where he went to the bathroom— *then* you'll believe me."

Grudgingly, I follow him to the door, grabbing the only weapon within reach on my way out—the broom I used a couple of hours ago to sweep the patio, back in the good old days when my husband hadn't yet gone all rubber room and white strappy jacket on me. We wind down the walkway, out the front gate, and into the street.

"See?" he crows. "There! It's *right there*." He points to a pile of what's obviously dog poop.

I poke at the pile of scat with the tip of my broom. "Yep. No doubt about it. That sure looks like coyote dookie to me." I nod gravely.

"Holy shit, there he is again!" Fletch bolts down the street, leaving me alone again.

So what do people wear on dates nowadays? I wonder. *Last time I was on the market it was little jeans and big hair.*[13] *And do people even say stuff like "nowadays" anymore? Am I going to have to buy thongs?*[14] *Or be all slutty like the* Sex and the City *women? (Way to set a precedent, you dirty girls.) And learn to dance? The Macarena—that's still popular with the kids, yes?*

I'm trying to figure out where my arms should go when I get to the part about the boy named Nicorino when my new next-door neighbor Holly strolls up with her dog.

"Hey, Jen. What's up? Why are you standing in the street? And are you—are you doing *the Macarena*?" Holly asks.

"Um, no. No! Heh, heh. Don't be silly. Why would I be doing the Macarena? Heh." I giggle nervously. So busted. "I'm standing out here because Fletch has gone crazy Vegas-style."

"Oh, sorry to hear that."

"Yeah, we had a good run, but he's suddenly become unhinged so it's over. A shame, really. Now I'm going to have to lose a ton of weight if I ever want to talk to anyone about *Fantasy Island* again."

"Hmm, I guess you've got to do what you've got to do. But might I ask what happened? He seemed sane earlier when he

---

[13]Now I have big jeans and little hair. And that's bad.
[14]Also a problem considering I get skeeved out just flossing my *teeth*.

was watering your plants. I'd hate for you to spend all that time on the StairMaster if he's not really lost his mind."

"He thinks he's out here, um, this is *insane*, um, *chasing a coyote*." I burst into nervous, husband-committing laughter.

I expect Holly to concur with my diagnosis and help me find a nice institution and a sensible but satisfying diet plan that includes chocolate at least a couple days a week. And real butter—not that yellow cardboard-paste stuff. Instead, she replies, "I saw one earlier, too. There's a couple of them over by where they're tearing down the factory next to the north branch of the river."

"No way." Surely she can't be telling me the truth. (But if so, I have a whole trash can full of cupcakes to rescue.)

"Seriously, Jen, the coyotes follow the path of the water and they come down here looking for food."

"But why would they come to Chicago? The shows? The shopping? I've got to tell you, I've yet to see one at Bloomingdale's," I respond knowingly. I imagine if the coyotes did hit Bloomie's, they'd go for the sheepskin stuff first.

"As we encroach on the wilderness, wild animals are forced into increasingly urban areas. It's really sad."

Oh.

So the coyotes leave their habitat because they're hungry. Having gone to the Cub Foods in the 'hood more than once at twelve thirty a.m. simply to buy their house-brand big, yummy muffins, I totally get it. Yet I suddenly feel sorry these wild creatures have been driven from their woods and meadows in search of nourishment, only to be stalked down Racine

Avenue by a porky phone-company executive in a bright orange fleece pullover.

The good news is Fletch isn't crazy.

I'm still increasing his meds, though, because I *really* hate doing sit-ups and I haven't the strength to school a new guy on the genius of Don Knotts.

To: angie_at_home, carol_at_home, wendy_at_home, jen_at_work
From: jen@jenlancaster.com
Subject: *pieces of me*

Four hours and $256.00 later, I now have Ashlee Simpson's exact hairstyle.

Fuck.

To: angie_at_home, carol_at_home, wendy_at_home,
jen_at_work
From: jen@jenlancaster.com
Subject: *trout pout*

Shalom, ladies!

So, I never quite understood the allure of injecting collagen in
one's lips . . .

. . . until I went to Sephora.

While Fletch perused the men's section for upscale shaving gel, I
amused myself at the "lip plumping station." (I know, it totally
sounds dirty.) I brushed a variety of potions with clever names
like Pout and Plump and Lipscription on my hand . . . and nothing happened.

I wasn't surprised because I didn't believe for one minute they'd
actually *do* anything. If I've learned anything about cosmetics, it's
that manufacturers *lie*. Nothing will eliminate your wrinkles or
eradicate your pores, yet the industry thrives on these beauty
myths. The best you can hope for is decent camouflage. So I
knew the lip stuff was a farce.

Bored with the display, I worked my way through the shampoos
and on to the perfume wall. While examining an incredibly
phallic-looking bottle of Jessica Simpson's Dessert Treats
fragrance, I realized my left hand hurt. Had I bumped into

something? Glancing down to see my distended digits, I briefly wondered when I'd shut my hand in a car door.

And then it hit me—that's where I'd applied the Too Faced Lip Injection.

Oh, my God, this shit actually works!

I pushed through a pack of tourists from Cleveland while rushing to the register to purchase my prize. Out of the way, you slack-jawed yokels . . . Baby needs a new beak!

Promising Fletch I'd meet him at Nordstrom in fifteen minutes, I dashed off to the ladies' room to apply my miracle potion. I smoothed on the glossy substance with care and gazed at my reflection, waiting for magic to happen.

Waiting . . .

. . . waiting . . .

. . . and waiting . . . for nothing.

Perhaps the capsicum in Lip Injection only worked on the skin of my hand? Damn it, that meant I'd just wasted $16.50. I waited a bit more and finally trudged defeated to Nordstrom's entrance.

A couple of minutes later, Fletch appeared. As he approached, I noticed an odd look on his face. He peered intensely at the area right above my chin. My hand flew to my mouth, where a change had magically taken place at some point between the bathroom mirror and the shoe department.

With a tentative touch, I prodded my newly lush lips . . .

. . . and they were glorious! Thick, pouty, and gorgeous! I felt like a movie star! Move over, Lara Flynn Boyle, there's a new sheriff in town! Step aside, Meg Ryan, for I laugh at your shriveled little pucker!

Grinning madly with my newly magnificent smile, I waited for Fletch to tell me how much prettier I'd become. As he inched nearer to me, I twitched with anticipation, anxious to receive my oh-so-deserved kudos.

After what seemed like an eternity, he finally stood before me. And leaning in to the point where we were almost touching, I could feel his soft breath on my face as he whispered those magical words . . .

"Did somebody just punch you in the mouth?"

Nice.

Jen

P.S. Sephora has a liberal return policy.

My So-Called (Superficial) Life

Fifteen years ago, I had an epiphany that deeply disturbed me. Really? It rocked me to my very core. However, because I was twenty-one years old, I had just enough self-awareness to understand that possibly every idea I had wasn't "epiphany" grade. I mean, did I *really* believe it was the Hand of the Divine that inspired me to combine cranberry juice and Southern Comfort? Or that the same Being who created our universe also led me to look on the sale rack where I discovered those low-waisted, boy-cut Forenza jeans that gave me tiny hips, a flat stomach, and the kind of exquisitely rounded butt that inspired a thousand rap songs?[1]

As I wasn't fully confident in my own callow thought process, I decided to query the most responsible, respected, impartial source I could find—my own spiritual leader, if you will.

---

[1] Baby got back, indeed.

Heidi, my sorority's president, seemed to best fit this bill.

Heidi was helping me carry sorority rush materials from my car because I was on crutches at the time. (In an effort to show the entire Sigma Phi Epsilon house *exactly* how good my Forenza-clad booty looked walking away, I made my grand exit, thus forgetting to actually watch where I was going, and fell down a bunch of stairs, twisting my ankle—not really the impression with which I wanted to leave them.[2])

As we made our way to the Pi Phi common room, Heidi hauling our super-secret sorority rush tools—poster board and spools of burgundy and blue ribbon—I approached her with my dilemma.

"Heidi, do you think—oh, this is so silly, and I just know you're going to disagree—but, do think that I might be . . ." I paused to allow the gravity of my question to sink in, ". . . vapid? I know I talk a lot about my Forenza jeans and *Beverly Hills, 90210* and how I want a job creating names for nail polish colors, but that doesn't make me shallow, right?"

It took Heidi a moment to stop choking on a Diet Coke before she could answer. "Um, well, Jen, let's just say talking to you doesn't exactly require hip waders."

Ouch.

What made this opinion particularly painful was that Heidi once insisted our chapter vote on which shade of red she should dye her hair.

Anyway, ever since I had the epiphany of being shallow, I've fought against my natural propensity for the puerile and superficial. I changed my major from interior design to political

---

[2] Alcohol may have been involved.

science. I subscribed to the *New Yorker*. I actually talked to the grad students I met in campus bars instead of just laughing at their earnestness and flannel shirts.[3] I dipped into classics by Dostoyevsky, Steinbeck, and Hemingway for personal edification and not just class assignments. (And I actually read my class assignments and not just the CliffsNotes.) I actively sought out Ibsen's plays and Verdi's operas. In short, I tried to smarten up my life, and since then I have been more or less successful. So it was at the height of my de-stupid-ification that I met Fletch, and his first impression was that I was kind of deep because we had a profoundly philosophical talk the night of our first date. (In truth, I was so hungover I simply nodded at most of his complex notions because I was trying not to barf.)

Fifteen years later, there are days when I wake up, watch the Sunday morning political shows, read three newspapers, and discuss Kierkegaard with Fletch over steamy demitasses of espresso at a smart European coffeehouse.

But today is not one of those days.

With a mouth crammed full of Froot Loops, I try to engage Fletch in casual conversation about the new issue of *Star* magazine I'm reading while he's engrossed in a documentary about the history of unconventional warfare.

"I'm concerned about Nick and Jessica," I begin.

"Hmm?" he asks.

"I said I'm worried about Nick and Jessica. They have everything going for them but I'm concerned her father's constant interference in her marriage is going to bite them all in the ass. And what's the deal with Daddy Joe being so proud

---

[3] Slurring may have been involved. And possibly making out.

of the size of her cans? I read that he's always mentioning her cup size to reporters. Gross. Five bucks says my dad doesn't even remember my middle name. Also, having cameras follow them around nonstop isn't going to help them either. No one stays that cute together forever."

"Mmm-hmm." He turns up the volume and moves farther away from me on the couch.

"And you know her little sister Ashlee? With the overbite and the bad haircut? I don't trust her. I bet she's brewing up some stunt to gain Daddy's attention.[4] I don't care how close you claim to be to your sister, sibling rivalry's a bitch."

He sets down his coffee cup and turns to look at me. "You mean she's come up with yet another evil new plan after all those you so neatly detailed for me last night when we discussed the topic?"

"We already talked about this?"

"Yes. Twice. And you drew me a chart. This conversation makes it three times."

"What are you saying? That you'd probably like to watch your little show in peace?"

"Hey, that's a novel idea—why don't we give it a whirl to see if it works."

The quiet lasts about five minutes, even though I'm dying to discuss Brad and Jen and how Christina Aguilera is suddenly super glam. I don't know if she changed stylists or colorists but now she's a modern-day Marilyn Monroe and it

---

[4] FYI, currently there are over nine million Google entries on Ashlee Simpson. Nietzsche was right: God is dead. And we killed him with all our Ashlee Freakin' Simpson Google entries.

218 · Jen Lancaster

totally works for her. Regardless, out of respect I keep my piehole closed until the show's host describes how the Mongols perpetrated the first biological weapon attack back in the twelfth century by catapulting plague-ridden bodies into villages, causing me to share my most erudite thoughts.

"Dude! That's fucked up!" I squeal.

"I think you might be happier reading your magazine upstairs, Jen."

"Nah, I'm cool." Then I notice the expression on his face. "You mean *you* might be happier. I just turned into my mom for a second with the running commentary, didn't I?" No one likes watching TV with my mother because of her urge to narrate the whole program, as though you're blind and require blow-by-blow descriptions. Plus, since she's busy telling you what she sees, she isn't paying attention to what's said and then you have to explain what just happened.

Every. Thirty. Seconds.

On the annoyance scale, this is on par with gum snapping and driving thirty-five miles per hour in the fast lane.[5] He nods. "Okay, okay, I'm going." Banished from our TV room, I head upstairs, chastened for having lapsed into the Vapid Zone yet again.

When I said I'd been more or less successful in fighting my shallow nature, I guess I meant less. But I fully intend to rectify the situation by picking up my well-thumbed copy of Thomas Friedman's *From Beirut to Jerusalem*.[6] I plan to read

----

[5] Two of her other habits. (Which are fine because she is a beautiful and loving woman who has never charged me interest on the money I still owe her.)

[6] Well-thumbed because it took me two years of carrying it around in my beach bag to finally finish it.

quietly and contemplate how thoroughly Israel's victory in the Six-Day War humiliated the Jordanians, Egyptians, and Syrians. Before I do that, I want to go online and order one of those cerebrally badass T-shirts with the Israeli flag and SIX DAYS, BITCH logo on it like I've been meaning to do for so long. Because you know who would appreciate that shirt? Smart people like Fletcher.

Inexplicably, my fingers have a mind of their own, and suddenly I find them typing in the URL for Television-WithoutPity, and pulling up the *Amish in the City* message boards.

As I log my deeply trenchant and thought-provoking opinions about the house,[7] the city kids,[8] and the Amish,[9] I'm filled with self-loathing for yet again getting sucked into the candy-coated, skin-deep programming otherwise known as reality TV.

Post-epiphany, one of the tactics I employed was to eschew television. Granted, I was busy out drinking, but still, I was most certainly not planted in front of the tube. I watched almost nothing from 1991 to 1996 except for glancing at the TV while at the Wabash Yacht Club bar when the Blackhawks were playing. (And that's only because I had a crush on player Chris Chelios.)

However, I did make an exception for the show *The Real World*. The concept was groundbreaking—take seven diverse strangers, stick them in a loft, and watch how their lives

[7] Ugly.
[8] Annoying.
[9] Darling!

unfold. What *did* happen when people stopped being polite and started getting real? I, for one, wanted to know. Would Heather B. make it as a rapper? And what of Norman and his art career? I was hooked from the very first second sweet, naïve Julie from Alabama drawled her way into my voyeuristic little heart. But other than that, TV's sole purpose was to tell me the weather and to display the numbers to dial psychic hotlines when I came home drunk.

However, when I moved to the Chicago suburbs with Fletch after graduation, we made very little money in proportion to our expenses and found ourselves broke and planted in front of the television more often than not. He had a penchant for the highbrow, so we watched a lot of educational programming together, although I found myself switching over to *Friends* whenever he wasn't around. When our lease expired, we both moved to the city proper—I got a one-bedroom by myself and Fletch took an apartment with friends.[10] I started leaving the television on to drown out the street noise and to keep me company. I learned something about myself back then—if the TV's on, I'm going to watch.

At the time I was a contract negotiator for an HMO and was under a lot of pressure, as my job entailed convincing some of the best physicians in the country to accept less money for their services. When I wasn't on appointments, I worked out of my home, and having trashy daytime talk

_____

[10] No, I didn't try to stop him. I figured after living with stupid boys he'd be begging to live in a clean, pretty apartment where the seat was always down and the fridge was always full. (Also, I was a lot cuter than his friend Greg.) He moved in with me a few short months later.

shows on in the background helped alleviate my stress. Sure, doctors still called and screamed at me, but watching toothless people wrestle in a tub of chocolate pudding over a paternity test result somehow gave me perspective. *Of course, Doctor,* I'd think, *yell all you want. But until you throw a chair at me, we don't have a problem we can't resolve.*

The higher I rose up the corporate food chain, the less I watched, but once I lost my job, I was right back on the box full-time. Between frantically sending out resumes and calling employers, I took breaks to view TLC's daytime lineup and dreamed of the day they'd feature the same person as he or she progressed from *A Makeover Story* to *A Dating Story* to *A Wedding Story* to *A Baby Story*, and God willing, to *Trading Spaces*.

I was addicted to the trashiest reality shows—no *Amazing Race* for me because I might accidentally learn something about geography. Since my life was so chaotic and out of control, it comforted me to see a bunch of people dumber than me willingly subject their relationships to the allure of guilt-free cheating on *Temptation Island*. I delighted in observing contestants slowly go stir-crazy locked in their multi-pooled mansion at *Paradise Hotel*, especially as the show's tag line was "Hook Up or Go Home." Disgusted, Fletch would leave me on my own to watch most of this crap, holing up in his office with Sun Tzu.

Bob Barker became my ad hoc salvation when things were their darkest when Fletch and I were both out of work. No matter how sad I was or how desperate our situation, I knew for an hour I could tune in to *The Price Is Right* and see people so happy about winning the prizes that hadn't changed an iota since my childhood. A new Betamax player, woo-hoo! My best days were the ones when the grandma or the person in the military uniform won their showcases.

I finally recognized the extent of my television obsession when I learned the reality show featuring Paris Hilton and Nicole Richie had beaten a live interview with President Bush in the ratings. So, essentially, more Americans chose to watch the antics of a whore and ex-junkie than the leader of the free world.

And why was this problematic?

Because I was one of them.

Granted, I wasn't aware Bush was competing against *The Simple Life*. But had I known, I still wouldn't have made the appropriate choice.[11] There I was—a college graduate with a degree in political science (with an emphasis on the study of terrorism and genocide, mind you)—and I chose to watch a couple of idiots with hair extensions run a kissing booth over a wartime interview with the president.

The worst part was I realized I was far more likely to vote for an *American Idol* contestant than a government official, as evidenced by my not walking next door to vote in the last local election because it was raining.

After this realization, I was far more conscientious about what I put in my brain—I chose smarter books, read news and information Web sites, and watched a whole lot of PBS, much to Fletcher's delight. Yet the day an *Us Weekly* accidentally fell into our shopping cart, I started to backslide yet again, espe-

---

[11] I mean, come on—Paris thought they sold *walls* at Wal-Mart. How do you *not* watch?

cially when I discovered shows like *America's Next Top Model*, *Sorority Life*, and *My Big Fat Obnoxious Fiancé*. And at the present moment, I can't think of the last time he and I discussed Kierkegaard. We've been back to the trendy Euro coffeehouse, but I spent the whole time sniggering about the bull ring in our waitress's nose.

I log off the *Amish in the City* message boards and vow to take action. Maybe if I keep track of what I do with my day tomorrow, I can find areas where I can improve myself.

Jen's Daily Log

8:45 a.m.—Remind self it's brother's birthday, and make mental note to call him later. Shower and do hair to get ready for hair appointment.[12]

9:50 a.m.—En route for hair appointment.

10:00 a.m.—Get hair cut and highlighted and have extensive conversation about whether or not Renée Zellweger has had Botox in between reading new *People* magazine.

12:46 p.m.—Admire snappy new haircut in mirror in second-floor bathroom. Turn on TLC and leave on all day.

12:51 p.m.—Scan all friends' Web sites to see if they mentioned me in any of today's posts. Nobody does. Bastards.

1:25 p.m.—Admire snappy new haircut, only this time in mirror in third-floor bathroom. Want to see hair contrasted against green walls. Congratulate self on scoring a free cut and

---

[12] If you show up with bad hair, it sets the bar too low. Tress to impress, people.

$15 color job on Training Day at the ultra-hip Art + Science salon in Wicker Park.

1:30 p.m.—Wonder briefly if the $300 per visit spent each time at Molto Bene is worth it, considering that for $285 less, current coif looks *exactly* the same.

1:31 p.m.—Cease line of thinking immediately for fear that brain may explode.

1:59 p.m.—Admire snappy new haircut in mirror by front door. Is not vain because I *had* to pass by this mirror on way in the door.

2:00 p.m.—Remind self to call brother. Watch few minutes of *Fox News* headlines. Briefly mourn George's vote-off on *Idol* while on phone with Shayla.

2:43 p.m.—Go to Costco. Vow to never hit Costco midday again due to being only person there not holding some variety of toddler. Renew previous vow to remain child-free as do not like to carry heavy things.

3:59 p.m.—Remind self to call brother. Admire snappy new haircut in rearview mirror. Not vain or shallow because had not yet seen the color in daylight.

4:00 p.m.—Unable to resist siren song of plant department at Home Depot. Feel compelled to spend the $12 skimmed off of household budget by buying cheap dog food at Costco on more flowers.

4:15 p.m.—Unload car and plant purchases. Compulsively scrub dirt from under nails. Since can't keep promise to not buy any more plants, must at least attempt to hide the evidence.

4:30 p.m.—Remind self to call brother.

4:31 p.m.—Pick Fletch up at work. Get busted when he detects smell of fresh soil in backseat. Shit, what is this, *CSI* or something?

5:04 p.m.—Notice that while on patio, can see reflection of snappy new haircut *and* pretty, pretty container garden in glass doors.

5:05 p.m.—Preen and admire.

5:50 p.m.—Notice Vesuvius-like growth on cheek below eye due to clogged pore created by use of cheap wrinkle cream. Non-comedogenic, my ass. Take ibuprofen to stop throbbing. Remind self to call brother when done poking and prodding pitcher's-mound-sized bump.

5:58 p.m.—Boil hands and scrub off first two layers of skin.

5:59 p.m.—Create lavish stir-fry dinner with seven kinds of vegetables and the carnivore's version of tofu. (Also known as chicken.)

6:18 p.m.—Eat dinner while watching *Cops*. Notice central theme in each segment that woman is willing to put up with domestic abuse because "he pays my bills." Decide (a) paying bills is overrated and (b) most women on *Cops* are big dummies.

6:49 p.m.—Wonder what ever happened to Ione Skye . . . she was a good actress.

6:50 p.m.—Wonder if "Ione Skye" was her given name, or something she created.

6:51 p.m.—Remembered that when in junior high and wanted to be an actress, decided stage name would be Shea

Fields. Now realize would be better name for ballpark. Remind self to call brother.

6:52 p.m. to 10:30 p.m.—Slip into apparent black hole, as cannot remember what happened. Maybe played with cats and dogs? Admired self? Ogled flower boxes? Oh, yes, watched reality TV. Is like catnip to me. Watching strangers yell at each other while competing for mystery prizes? Six beautiful girls stand before me but I only have five photographs? Will you accept this rose? Hell, yes, I'm there.

10:31 p.m. to 10:59 p.m.—Watch *Family Guy*. During commercial breaks, try to badger husband into going out to buy me a Hostess Fruit Pie. Unsuccessful. (Prefer apple, but would have accepted cherry or chocolate.)

11:00 p.m.—Kiss husband good night. Dig through basket to find clean nightgown. Prefer yellow nightgown with coffee cups on it, but is dirty. Settle for lavender cotton with puffy clouds and little slivers of moon. Question usefulness of breast pocket, as do not customarily carry pens around in nightgown. Guess is nice to have the option, though.

11:01 p.m. to 11:56 p.m.—Catch up on the latest celebrity news on ten bookmarked sites.

11:57 p.m. to 12:17 a.m.— Record activity log.

I'm having coffee and reviewing my daily activity log and I cringe at the vapidity of the previous day. In addition, I realize I never called my brother to wish him a happy birthday. Now I'm a bad sister *and* a shallow person.[13]

I yearn to be a woman of more depth, but I'm not so fond of the path I'd need to follow to get there. Yet I don't want to always be the girl everyone looks at when they can't remember the name of the chick who replaced Suzanne Somers on *Three's Company*,[14] hence my dilemma. Fletch is kind of an intellectual and I often wonder if he deserves to be with someone who's more into the magazine *Time* and less *Time Out*. When there's breaking news and I turn on *Fox News*, my first comment should not be *"OMG, I love Juliet Huddy's outfit today!"* Given the choice, I'm always going to prefer *Cosmopolitan* over the *Utne Reader*, and even though I can discuss the Tax Reform Act of 1986, I'd rather talk about my hair.

As I berate myself I hear Fletch moving around in the living room. He switches on the television, and moments later I hear the theme song to the cartoon show *Super Friends*. And suddenly I feel better.

[13] Although my hair still looks really good.
[14] Jenilee Harrison.

To: angie_at_home, carol_at_home, wendy_at_home,
jen_at_work
From: jen@jenlancaster.com
Subject: *keep your laws off my pigment*

Hey, ladies,

First, perhaps y'all can save the "I told you sos" 'til the end of
the story.

Setting: My snappy new tanning salon on Clybourn Ave, last week.

Annoyingly Perky Desk Clerk: Hi, your name?

Me: Lancaster—comma—Jen.

APDC: *(taps away at the computer, high blonde ponytail swinging back and forth)* And . . . okey-dokey, there you are! Finger,
please.

My snappy new tanning salon employs a fingerprint recognition system, nice because it ensures no one else can sneak
in on my membership. (BTW? If you own a place on
Milwaukee Ave and you decide to cheap out and buy bed
management software from your native country Poland?
And you tell me my $100 worth of remaining tanning ses-
sions are gone because the computer "makes approximate"
and "sometimes she round off" and then when I politely
show you tangible, irrefutable proof that I didn't use them,

that your software is flawed, and that I should be credited, you point a stubby Slavic finger in my face and declare, "No, ees jewoo who ees wrong!"? Well, don't be surprised when my head *fucking explodes*.)

(Also, should I be concerned that my snappy new tanning salon provides better fraud protection than my bank?)

APDC: Alrighty, which bed?

Me: I want the ergonomic one with the water misters and aromatherapy. *(Oh, yeah, it's that kind of nice.)*

APDC: *(tappity, tappity)* Whoopsie! It's 8:17!

Me: Um . . . and?

APDC: Well, I'm super sorry, but you can't tan until 9:01.

Me: What? I have unlimited tanning, so what's with the wait?

APDC: There's an annoying state law that says you have to have twenty-four hours between tanning sessions and—

Me: Whoa, hold the phone. Are you trying to tell me that the *state* is now actively involved with the tanning industry? Are you kidding me? What business do a bunch of pasty bureaucrats have dictating what I do or don't do to my skin?

APDC: I'm sorry, ma'am, but—

Me: *(growing agitated)* You know what? I'm an adult with a college degree and I'm familiar with the dangers of UV rays, so I don't need Big Brother sticking his nose in my personal business in a ham-handed attempt to keep me safe.

APDC: It's just that—

Me: Sure, the twenty-four-hour waiting period is okay in theory, but the reality is that it's incredibly inconvenient and inefficient for me to have to either sit here or drive home and back. What difference will forty-three minutes make? As long as it's the next day, what's the big deal?

APDC: Maybe you'd be, like, more comfortable if you—

Me: You know, if I want to do something stupid, destructive, and potentially cancer-causing to my body, *that's my decision.* How dare the government spend time and money orchestrating laws which restrict my freedoms. *My body, my choice.* . . .

(pause as a lightbulb goes off in my dim little Republican brain)

. . . oh. Wait a minute. *This* is why everyone's up in arms about the new Supreme Court nominee, isn't it?

APDC: *(cocks her head to the side)* I don't understand.

Me: Never mind. I'll see you in an hour.

APDC: Bye-bye!

So I thought you guys should be the first to know I get it now.

Finally.

Later,

Jen

To: angie_at_home, carol_at_home, wendy_at_home, jen_at_work
From: jen@jenlancaster.com
Subject: *i don't like mike*

What is it with the crazy people e-mailing me? I hope you all enjoy this message from today's in-box as much as I did:

hi there:
very very sexy person i am older 47 live in the city i am still married looking for a friend/lover i am gng thru a pinfull divorce.
I am 6* 200 brwn hair and brwn (bedroom) eyes I work out 5-6 times a week and I love golf-boating
I own my business so if you want to see what happens let me know
I know I am not for eveyone still being married.
srry no pics until i am divorced shhhhhhhhhhh
mike

Like I'm *not* going to respond to this before blocking him from contacting me?

Dear Mike,

Thanks for your thoughtful offer. However, I will have to politely decline for the following reasons:

1) I hate golf-boating. So hard to get the ball to stay on the tee with all the waves.

2) Sorry to hear about your "pinfull" divorce. Perhaps if you weren't busy trawling for sex with strangers first thing in the morning, it may have worked out better for you?

3) Were I to cheat on my spouse (which is never going to happen, BTW) it certainly wouldn't be with someone who should be cited by the Grammar Police.

I do not want to see what happens. And I am letting you know.

Best,

Jen

Loser? Yes, but Not the Biggest

I'm a loser.

Or, at least I'm hoping to be.

I'm scheduled to go on a casting call for NBC's *The Biggest Loser* program. This is the reality show where a bunch of overweight folks compete with each other to drop the flab and gain $250-large. But since everyone on the show sheds a ton of weight, there are no losers. Or, um, they're all losers. Just not in the pejorative sense.

So, I've been watching the show and each week I scream[1] epithets at those I don't think are working hard enough. For example, during a competition that involves climbing ninety flights of stairs, a contestant has a panic attack around floor thirty-four and has to be carted off in an ambulance. As I shout, "You big pussy!" at her image on the screen, Fletch re-

[1] Sometimes with a mouth crammed full of Oreos.

minds me I've been sitting with my legs crossed for half an hour since I'm too lazy to climb the stairs to my bathroom.

Oh, yes. *That.*

For as faithfully as I watch the show, it's surprising I'd never considered auditioning before, especially since I'd be an awesome reality show contestant. I'd be the one to stir up trouble over some already-simmering issue and then neatly step away from it while I watched the other contestants implode. And then at the height of the crisis, in the midst of all the yelling and producer intervention, I'd say something so witty and sardonic, yet showing my humanity, that the message boards would explode with "Oh, my God, I can't believe she *went* there" commentary and yet another battle would ensue between those who loved and those who hated me.

The seed to audition was planted about a month ago after my last physical. My internist advised me to lose thirty pounds, even though my blood pressure was "outstanding"[2] and my cholesterol was good, which is interesting considering the fact I've thought about adding butter to my coffee more than once. He instructed me to start logging what I ate, saying if I charted fat grams and calories, I'd make better choices and thus shed those pounds.

I smiled and nodded, but inwardly rolled my eyes. The poor, deluded soul thought I didn't know that lack of exercise and abundance of calories were making me heavy. I wanted to tell him, "Doctor, I'm an ex–sorority girl. There's nothing you can tell a sorority girl about fat and calories she

[2] His words, not mine. But I like the idea that even my blood kicks ass.

doesn't already know. Shoot, half my sisters had some variety of eating disorder and the other half majored in dietetics. So great was our obsession with nutrition that any one of us could have taught the ADA a thing or two." But I didn't because I was trying to angle a way to get him to prescribe me some recreational Xanax and figured he wouldn't if I acted like a jerk.

Although people lose weight for a lot of reasons, my dilemma to this point has been that I haven't been able to come up with one compelling enough to change my habits. Sure, the idea of being healthier sounds nice, but that's an abstract concept and certainly not enough to get me off the cake and on the bike. And, yeah, the idea of living longer appeals, but by denying myself now, I rationalize I might simply be prolonging the adult diaper years. Plus, if Fletch doesn't stop smoking he's not going to be around to keep me company anyway.

And speaking of Fletch, I'd never be one who was swayed by the whole "do it for him" argument. I truly despise the men I see on daytime talk shows who get Dr. Phil to intervene because "my wife ain't skinny like she used to be." Seems like if your marriage can't withstand a couple of pounds, you may need more help than Jenny Craig offers.

I'll admit the idea of being thinner isn't all bad. Perhaps I'd enjoy not sweating when I eat? If I weren't plus-sized, I bet I'd be more likely to take advantage of some of the perks the city has to offer, like ice skating in Millennium Park. I just hate the idea of engaging in any public physical activity that makes me look foolish, and I've found myself avoiding things I used to like because I'm heavy now.[3] For example, Chicago has dozens of cool gyms with pools and juice bars and climbing walls, and yet I can't quite bring myself to join one of them because I'm vaguely embarrassed. I want to become a member, but, you know, not 'til I'm a little thinner. (This is the same specious logic that makes people clean their homes the day before the maid comes.)

I talk over my weight-loss aversion with Fletch and we try to figure out what might motivate me. His theory is the only way people lose weight is because something clicks inside them and they decide it's time. He calls the impetus for the click "the X-factor" and claims the X-factor is what coaxes you out of bed to walk briskly with the dogs on a chilly morning and convinces you that an orange is a better snack than half a box of Twinkies. According to Fletch, the X-factor is more important than exercising or eating right because it's what drives people to do so in the first place. The X-factor? Is all powerful.

As we discuss what might inspire my X-factor, Fletch mentions what a good article this would make. He says a magazine might be interested if I were to document my weight-loss story from month to month, discussing the healthy changes I'd made. I could include pictures and some sort of table depicting how close I was to getting to my goal weight. A smaller waistline and a modicum of notoriety? The more I think about it, the better it sounds.

---

[3] I will still swim in Lake Michigan, but I'm generally submerged 90 percent of the time I'm at the beach, so that doesn't count.

And thus the beginnings of an X-factor form.

Shortly after this epiphany, I see a notice for a local casting call on Craigslist and decide it's fate, even though the idea of parading around on television in all my rotund glory terrifies me. Generally, death is a more attractive option for me than humiliation. I mean, when my mother answers her cell phone in a restaurant, I want to slip through the floorboards and disappear. And that's nothing compared to the sheer mortification of 10 million Americans seeing my real weight projected on the big screen.[4] However, I also think the only way to conquer fear is to face it head-on, and if it means seeing my big ass on the television, so be it. I pick up the phone and wrangle my way into a face-to-face interview.

I'm now tasked with preparing for this interview. I download an application form, even though they'll be available at the casting call tomorrow. But fussy as I am about my words, I'm better off getting a jump-start on the competition. I crack open a chilled bottle of Gewurztraminer and start writing.

Okay, *name*, easy. *Address*, simple. *Phone*, there you go. *Height*, five feet seven. *Weight*.

Oh, God.

This is one of those numbers I've never spoken out loud. Because if I were to verbalize it, that would mean it was actually true.

---

[4] Fletch? When I tell you I weigh 150 pounds? I lie.

I take a long drink of the cool wine and feel the liquid travel all the way down my esophagus. After having a few more sips of grape-flavored courage, I fill in a truly frightening sum. But I'm comforted in the knowledge that if I can answer that question honestly, the rest of the application questions will be easy. I move on to the first essay question.

> **How would someone describe your best/worst qualities?**

Dunno. My mother thinks I'm pretty and my husband says I make a mean Parmesan-crusted chicken breast. But that's not the kind of answer that will land me on the *Today* show, now is it?

I polish off my first glass of wine in hopes it will make me more creative. Mmm, that's better. Now concentrate. Think of Matt Lauer. What would he want to read? *"Katie, we've all grown tired of your shtick?"* No, that won't work. How about:

I'm best known for my humility. (Ha!) No, seriously, my ex-employees would describe me as smart, driven, and tenacious, sometimes to the point of bringing them to tears.[5] But I expect 100 percent from everyone, all the time, and it makes me crazy when others slack.

Let's segue into my worst qualities. . . . I'm incredibly impatient and I don't tolerate excuses or poor work ethics. Whatever I do, I give it my all and I tend to win. Because of this, I can be arrogant, and on occasion, condescending. However, if you're on

---

[5] Which equals bitch.

my team and are also putting forth your best effort, I will be supportive, motivational, kind, and fiercely loyal. You mess with my friends and I will cut you. (I'm kidding, of course.[6])

> **Have you tried to lose weight? How?**

C'mon, are you fucking kidding me? Who hasn't?

Nope, nope, family show. No f-bombs. Remember the FCC. Viewers want to hear my profanity as much as they wanted to see Janet Jackson's nipple. Which is not at all.

I have a tad more thinking juice.

Okay. Here we go:

Yes, about a million times. I've had success on Atkins but it's so unnatural. No one can eat that way for a prolonged period. And every time I do Atkins, I find myself wanting to wrestle people in the lunchroom for their half-eaten peaches. I know fruit is not evil, nor is bread the Devil. Atkins just doesn't make sense. The only healthy way to lose is to eat less (of a balanced diet) and exercise more. So easy in theory; it's the execution where I falter.

> **What's your biggest obstacle to losing weight?**

Absolute narcissism manifesting in obscene self-indulgence?

Or perhaps just an open mouth?

I'm my own biggest obstacle. The problem is my self-esteem;

---

[6] Sort of.

it's too high. Even at (redacted)[7] pounds, I look at myself in the mirror and think, "Damn, girl. You fiiiiine." I have a hard time with self-denial because I love me, so why wouldn't I treat my fabulous self to anything I wanted?

In addition, I've been through some hard times over the past few years. I went from having a ridiculously high household income to practically being evicted from a ghetto apartment, due to the vagaries of the post-9/11 economy. As well, I had to prop up my formerly successful husband because he was deeply depressed after losing his job. I was the strong one for both of us, and because I was too proud to share my feelings, my only comfort was food. I told myself it was okay to eat whatever I wanted, and I'd address my ever-growing ass only once I'd gotten us through everything.

I successfully navigated the storms and, in so doing, landed representation with a literary agency, and subsequently, a publishing contract. So I also indulged myself while working on the book, with the caveat that as soon as I was done with the proposal, I'd start taking better care of myself. (Again, if you'd like to know more of my story, please buy my book.) Now that it's sold, my behavior hasn't changed, and at this point my biggest concerns aren't those of vanity; they're health-related. By weighing what I weigh, I'm prescribing myself an early death sentence. (Even if this does mean missing the adult diaper years.)

And, frankly?

I'm not ready to renegotiate my own mortality. This excess baggage needs to go!

---

[7] Unless you want to provide me with a ten-week spa pass, I'm not giving out that number.

What do you want to do when you lose the weight?

Wear a bikini to my twentieth class reunion and yell into the crowd, "You all sucked in high school and you all still suck!" No. I sound like a psycho. Have some delicious wine and try again.

For all my bravado, I'm actually thin-skinned. My greatest fear is someone making fun of how I look, and sometimes this causes me to avoid things I enjoy. For example, although I like figure skating, I won't go to Millennium Park because I worry that people will giggle and point and say, "Hey, look! It's Jamie Salé! And she's apparently swallowed David Pelletier! Bah, ha, ha!!" I love to ride horses, but I won't because at my favorite stable, there's a weight limit and I don't want to be questioned. And I adore designer clothing, but so few designers make plus-sized garb. I try to make myself feel better, saying it's their loss, but every time I walk Michigan Ave with a Lane Bryant bag instead of one from Bebe, I feel like I'm advertising my own failure.

How competitive are you?

I have bloodlust.

Nope.

Psycho again.

I don't know; how do you judge? How about on a scale from one to ten, I'm somewhere around a million. I'm one of the most competitive people on the face of the earth. And yes, I know you're going to talk to a bazillion fame whores who will proudly march in and proclaim, "I'm the biggest loser!" However, when I say it, it will actually be true. *I am as relentless as my pit bull Maisy when it comes to pursuing what I want. For example, at my last job there was a competition that involved the company's entire sales force. My boss looked at me and said, "I expect you to win this thing." So I worked like never before, and you know what? I did win. I trounced more than five hundred salespeople to take the National Marketplace Leadership Award. And like a West Point cadet, I didn't lie, cheat, or steal to get there. I just worked harder than anyone else. I'd do the same on* The Biggest Loser, *should NBC allow me the chance.*

Besides, I've watched enough *American Idol* auditions to know simply pointing to oneself and announcing one is *"the next American Idol"* is no real indicator of success. See? I just said it to myself a second ago, but in no way, shape, or form is it reality. What I've got going for me is a track record of over-achievement and I hope I can convey this to the casting people.

What is the most outrageous thing you've ever done?

Excuse me, I didn't realize this was the elimiDATE application. And what do they consider outrageous? Should it be a time when I was brave? Took a risk? Made a stupid decision? Do they want to hear about my vacationing alone for the first time? Moving to a city fifteen hundred miles away from home with $30 in my pocket? Or do they want dirty? I bet they want dirty. Arrgghh.

You're looking for a sex-in-a-public-place, everybody-gets-naked kind of answer, aren't you, you perverts! Well, I'm only PG-

13 *and that's because of language—there's no one without pants on around here. Instead, I'll tell you that my most outrageous story involves a homeless guy and the world's most perfect Coach briefcase. Let's just say I convinced him that my lunch for his gorgeous—but almost definitely hot—Coach briefcase would be an even trade. (Is telling a homeless person that wasabi peas are crack rocks actually a crime? If so, then, um, that may or may not have happened.[8])*

Here's the thing, in this competition I won't lie, cheat, or steal, nor tolerate those who do. But I didn't say anything about manipulation. People, I am the puppet master *in regard to making others do my bidding. And my plotting would make for some damn fine reality TV.*

How much weight do you want to lose?

A metric ton. And if I lost a metric ton, how much of it would be wine? I decide I'd be interested to know as I drain glass number three.

If I lost (redacted), I'd be the exact same weight I was when I competed in pageants. Although I never won a crown, I was Miss Photogenic on many an occasion. Never Miss Congeniality, though. Hmm . . .

Bottom line? Cast me on The Biggest Loser *and I will concurrently be the most loved and hated person on reality TV.*

Whew! That took *forever*. So, now I'll add a couple of recent snapshots, and an old one from when I was So Very Cute

---

[8] It totally did.

and I'll title them **Jen + NBC = The New Hotness, 2005.** Yes, NBC should definitely be made aware of my HP.[9]

Okay, I'm a bit drunkety now with all the drinky-drinky wine. Must sleep. Zzzzzzz.

In retrospect, chugging an entire bottle of wine while working on my application was not the best plan. I wake up this morning with cotton mouth and a slight case of the spins, causing me to shriek down the stairs, "Fletch! Coffee! *Now!*"

Why do I suddenly think he might not mind if I went away for ten weeks?

I take special care applying makeup and straightening my hair, banking on the casting people appreciating good grooming. I put on my favorite Sigrid Olsen sweater, which is a pink plaid with a scoop neck surrounded by a kind of hairy fringe. I pile on the jewelry and practically bathe in Dior J'adore. After a little more coffee, I slide my application into a leather pad-folio and Fletch drives me to the audition.

The casting offices are in a cool loft building directly west of Michigan Ave. I ease myself into the tiny elevator and punch the button for the second floor. As the doors open, I notice my hands are trembling. I can't determine if it's nerves or all the sweet, sweet booze.

As I enter the office a gorgeous plus-sized woman exits. We smile as we pass and wish each other luck while I say a silent prayer about her not also being funny. I peer around the

---

[9] Hotness Potential.

office and am sorely disappointed to discover no donuts lying in wait.[10]

Seven other women are hunkered over the wooden benches, efficiently filling in their applications. I congratulate myself on my foresight to type out my answers and place them in the snappy plastic binder.[11]

Unfortunately, the other women are also pretty and vivacious. I'd kind of hoped my competition would be straight off the short bus. I toss my hair and concentrate on determining what might set me apart.

When three of the ladies finish their applications, a casting agent invites us back to the interview area. My first thought is, *Young man, does your mother know you're skipping school?* In truth, he's likely mid to late twenties, but ever since I hit my late thirties, I think everyone in trendy jeans is a high school student. (What the hell do I know?)

Slightly disappointed I won't be interviewed alone, I proceed down the short hallway to a conference room where a female casting agent, also in trendy jeans, waits at a long table. Upon entering, I attempt to shake her hand, but she refuses. She says she's nursing a terrible cold and doesn't want to infect me.

I try not to take this as a bad omen.

The applicants gather in a semicircle, the vantage point allowing me to size up[12] my competition. On the far left, a young blonde girl perches in her chair. *(Okay, she obviously*

---

[10] Damn. There goes my lurid donut-eating contest audition fantasy.
[11] Indeed I shall be the Biggest Loser for I have been to Office Depot!
[12] Rim shot!

hasn't had her roots done in six months. Score one point for Jen.) Next to her sits a forty-something soccer mom who was very helpful to the other applicants back in the waiting room. *(Damn. Friendlier than me. Minus one point for Jen.)* Her pal sits between us and her brown ponytail is pulled so tight it's making her eyes slant upward. *(Good skin but what's up with the ponytail face-lift? Plus one point.)*

Head Cold Girl welcomes us and the other applicants launch into a diatribe about finding a parking space. *(Shit, I've got nothing to add to this inane conversation! Damn it, why didn't I drive so I could bitch, too? That way they could see how much funnier I am when I'm complaining. Minus three points for Jen!)* So I attempt to smile, sparkle, and radiate while feigning interest. Questions are posed about our marital status and the girl on the end is the only single ("but looking!") person in the group. The middle two have a pack of kids each and call themselves Baseball Moms, whatever that means.

Casting Guy asks Miss Roots why she'd be good on the show. She replies she's funny and competitive. To punctuate these facts, she giggles at herself. I roll my eyes at the agents, hoping this communicates our (assumed) shared "show, don't tell" philosophy. Head Cold Girl follows up by saying, "Uh-huh. And how, exactly, does this set you apart from everyone else?" *Oooh, snap! I think I just developed a nonsexual crush on Head Cold Girl!* Miss Roots answers something utterly forgettable. *You're done. Thanks for playing.*

Same question goes to Baseball Mom One. Before she can reply, Casting Guy interjects that he "loves her application essays." Looks like she filled in one- and two-word answers.

Heh. Add Casting Guy to my new crush list. We catch each other's eyes and smile. I am *so* in.

Having learned from her friend's nonanswers, Baseball Mom Two puts on her game face. She explains she'd be good on the show because she's funny, smart, and could get along with any race, sex, or creed. *And how exactly is that good television? One more point for Jen by default.* Head Cold Girl probes more and Mom Two admits she can't stomach bad parents. *Oh, like the kind who'd leave their kids for ten weeks to appear on a reality show? Swing and a miss.* Then Mom Two launches into a diatribe about child abuse, completely losing her audience.

And then they get to me.

When posed with the "Why you?" question, I answer I want to be on the show because I intend to win it. I back up my statement with many examples of prior successes and I give them the Brief History of Jennsylvania. I tell them about the book and elaborate on my application answers. I do my steamroller-talking thing and no one gets a word in edgewise until Head Cold Girl asks me if I'm doing this just to promote my book.

Fuck.

I mean, yes, I was. I totally was. I wanted to get on the show so I could sell books and magazine articles. But somewhere between the first glass of wine and now, I've discovered some truths about myself and I realize how much I want this. I've already started planning my life as a thin person, mentally shopping for Rollerblades and the kind of sports bra I can wear when I skate by the lake. So it's with complete honesty that I answer, "No. I'm here because I want to be thin again." I imagine if I make it onto the show, I won't be allowed to discuss the book. And you know what? No problem! Being trim and being published can be mutually exclusive.

Our interview ends and the casting people tell us if we're to be called back, they'll phone us within the week. If we don't get a call, thanks and good luck. I head back down the teeny elevator and go home.

So, will I make it to the next round? I have no clue. I guess it all depends on what kind of "types" they are casting. By being a wholly self-assured borderline arrogant person, I may be just the gal to fill the "villain" role and they'll ask me back. But if they want touchy-squeezy, let's-all-hug-and-talk-about-food-issues-and-feelings people, I am so out it's not even funny.

I come home and immediately check out the message boards to see if anyone else had a casting experience like mine. I expect to read posts from others who'd been to the calls and are equally obsessed with rehashing their auditions. Because I'm a perfectionist, I ruminate about my performance all day. Did I say the right things? Did I come across as cocky instead of confident? Did they think my sweater was cute?[13]

Instead, I find a pack of losers. And yes, *this* time I mean in the pejorative sense. Granted, a few of the people are there to exchange information, such as "What time should I show

---

[13] Wait, what am I asking? Of course they thought my sweater was cute.

up for the open call?" and "How long is the audition process—should I take a whole day off of work?" but the majority of the posts can be divided into a couple of categories.

First, the **It's Not Fair** folks:

> *"I'm fourteen and I really need to be on the show because I weigh four hundred pounds. It's not fair you have to be a legal adult to participate."* (And not to be insensitive, but this is what happens when school districts decide gym class is unnecessary.)

> *"I'm Canadian and it's not fair you have to be a U.S. citizen to be on the show."* Likely this has more to do with work visas than discrimination.

More insidious are the **I've Done Nothing and I'm All Out of Ideas** people:

> *"I want to be on the show but I don't own a video recorder to make an audition tape. Please make an exception for me."*

> *"I have to work late and I can't make the casting call. I know I'd be good on the show,[14] so please make an exception for me."*

---

[14] Despite providing no empirical evidence.

"I'm overweight, unhappy, and unhealthy. But the show lasts ten weeks and I'd miss my dog. Please make an exception for us and allow me to bring him."

These people really make me sad. Getting on this show is an opportunity of a lifetime. I can't even guess how much ten weeks of room and board at a luxury spa with round-the-clock personal trainers would cost. And not only is the stay free, but NBC pays the participants a stipend while they do nothing but take care of themselves. Best of all, they have a chance to win fabulous prizes and the big winner takes home a cool quarter of a mil. Yet the people on the message boards are letting relatively tiny obstacles stand between them and the promise of a fit future and I find it so frustrating. I know how easy it is to make excuses rather than changes, and I feel for them.

I want to shake all of them and convince them fighting for themselves is worth it. I want to say, listen, I understand procuring a video camera might be difficult. And maybe it's embarrassing to have to borrow one and explain why you need it. Driving ten hours to a casting call is probably no one's idea of a good time. And personally, imagining my sweet little Maisy dog sitting by the front door for ten weeks while I'm gone makes me want to cry, but it's a sacrifice I'm willing to make. Just being able to take her for a proper run down the street would make the experience worth it for both of us. I want them to understand if they want something badly enough, they have to find a way to fight for it.

Unfortunately, from what I'm reading on the boards, the

majority of posters have decided to simply half-ass the application, sending in no tape and a passel of excuses, while spouting the platitude "I'll be selected if it's meant to be." They honestly believe NBC is going to cast them and spend millions to produce and publicize a show about people who aren't even willing to put forth the bare minimum for participation. And when they aren't selected, they'll be overwhelmed by self-loathing at failing another of life's little tests and will be resigned to the fact that they're meant to be fat.

And this completely breaks my heart.

The requisite week passes, as does the next, and it's becoming abundantly clear I've not been selected to move on to the next round of casting.

Regardless, the experience helps me find my real X-factor and I'm inspired not only to join a gym but to actually go. I know if I finally commit myself, the weight will come off regardless of the presence of nutritionists, Beta cams, and gaffers.

So even if I'm not *The Biggest Loser*?

I can still be a loser.

Which is just fine with me.

To: angie_at_home, carol_at_home, wendy_at_home, jen_at_work
From: jen@jenlancaster.com
Subject: *hurricane season*

WTF, ladies?

Is this making any of the rest of you sensible gals crazy? I just saw yet another interview with the parents of a couple honey-mooning in Cancun. I empathize with the families' concern; not knowing if their kids are safe has to be devastating. However, this empathy is overshadowed by annoyance.

Um, hello, people? This is *hurricane season.*

Which means conditions are favorable for *hurricanes.*

Which are *bad.*

So people might want to *reconsider heading directly to the places they are most likely to hit during the time they are most likely to occur.*

A $25 Cancun hotel room is not a bargain if you have to spend the week hunkered down in the basement of a third-world city government building with six hundred other people precisely as stupid as you. (If you want a cheap room, why not head to Vegas off-season? It's supa-fun in any weather.)

And if your dumb ass accidentally gets killed because you're down there voluntarily vacationing during hurricane season? That's not bad luck; it's social Darwinism.

The kicker is that these particular honeymooners are from Alabama. Not Urbana, Illinois, or Fargo, North Dakota, or Las Vegas, Nevada, or anyplace else where hurricanes are nothing but exciting weekend television viewing. They come directly from Storm Country, USA. Um, aren't they probably still bailing out their basements from Katrina and Rita? What the fuck were they thinking going to Cancun in October? How do they live in this world and still make the decision to go down there? Do they not have access to television? Or a newspaper? Or the Internet? Or a Farmer's Almanac?

If the couple was cognizant of the risk but decided to roll the dice anyway, why didn't they just go to Vegas? They could see the Chihuly glass display in the Bellagio and venture over to the Liberace museum. They could go from Paris to Venice to the Middle East to the Orient *without ever crossing the street!* They could dance in trendy clubs, watch shows, and attend concerts, each event more exciting than the last. Plus they could drink *all the tap water they want and never get sick!* In addition, the weather's totally perfect at least nine months out of the year, the dining and shopping are second to none, the accommodations are world-class, and everyone speaks English. Plus, if you gamble and lose there, you'd still get free shrimp cocktails.

Call me callous, but I just don't get it.

This e-mail brought to you by the Las Vegas tourism board.

I Love the Smell of Cardboard in the Morning

"Yo? Fletch?" I call up the stairs to where he's installing my new antivirus program.[1] "It's raining again."

"Yeah, I know. It's been sprinkling off and on all day."

Normally this would be an innocuous conversation, except for the fact that the rain is coming down *on our breakfast bar* from a gaping hole in the ceiling.

About a month ago something happened to the wax seal on our second-floor toilet and it began leaking sewage into our kitchen.[2] After a few days of frantic phone calls, our landlord finally sent someone to cut a hole in the Sheetrock and remove the most offensive bits. Since then, neither the toilet nor ceiling have been touched. I'd worry our landlord was hurt or

---

[1] I kind of wiped out my whole hard drive when I downloaded a bottlecap-matching game. Whoops.

[2] I cannot even begin to describe the horror of this situation so I shall spare you my attempts to do so.

perhaps trapped under something heavy, but apparently he's been well enough to cash our rent checks. (Our landlord is Fletch's colleague and friend, but ever since *Operation Brown Rain*, not so much on the friend part.)

The worst part isn't the very real possibility of catching cholera in my own damn home; it's going up to the third floor to use the bathroom. Even though I've been religiously working out at the gym and doing up to eighty minutes of cardio at a time, there's something about navigating our stairs that just knocks me on my ass. (And no, Fletch won't let me pee in the second-floor bathtub, and, yes, I asked.)

Disconnecting the toilet has stopped about 90 percent of the water but our kitchen ceiling still leaks intermittently. I say this is God's way of telling us we should stop cooking and start eating more McDonald's, but Fletch disagrees. *He* says it's God's way of telling us we need a new grill. Regardless, we both agree if something doesn't change and soon, we're not renewing our lease.

We're outside cooking the most gorgeous dill and butter-brushed tuna steaks on our rickety old grill when our next-door neighbor Holly comes home. She's one of two friends we've made in this sixteen-unit complex. Tommy is the other, and he lives two doors down in the extravagant corner unit with the $50,000 kitchen upgrade and hot tub, although I can't imagine why he likes us after I kind of accidentally reported him to Homeland Security. (What? He dresses like a thug, acts shifty, has no discernible source of income, and is always rolling into the parking lot in a variety of luxury cars— Ferraris, Mercedeses, Lamborghinis, etc. What was I supposed to think? Big time X dealer? Club promoter? Polish mafia? *Terrorist*, perhaps? Eventually, I found out that if you actually *talk* to your neighbor instead of just spying on him you'll learn all sorts of interesting stuff . . . like real estate developers often wear casual clothes and keep strange hours . . . and parents who own luxury car dealerships often let their adult children borrow various vehicles . . . and sometimes "aloof" is another word for "shy." The kicker is he actually went to the same college as Fletch and I. Tommy's a *Boilermaker*, not a *terrorist*.[3])

Anyway, Holly's struggling to unload her groceries and manage her giant Rottweiler, so I run over to help. Yeah, yeah, I know—since when am I helpful? But Fletch and I have both gotten tight with Holly over the past couple of months. She's always so upbeat and silly and she reminds us of our friend Suz[4] from college. If I ever want an adventure—taking the dogs to the lake, climbing over the side of the rail on the expressway to get an unobstructed photo of the harvest moon, breaking into the construction site across the street to see if the new condos are *really* worth their $600,000[5] asking price—Holly's up for it.

"Hey, baby, what's happening?" she calls by way of greeting. Her swingy black bob shines in the sunlight. (Note to self: Ask what kind of conditioner she uses.)

I grab Vaughn's leash. "You look like you're struggling. Thought I'd lend a hand." Vaughn couldn't be happier to see

---

[3] And we? Are *dicks*.

[4] The first time Fletch met Suz was when she showed up at my place early one morning and needed me to help her find her car. And her pants. God, I miss her.

[5] They aren't.

me and practically lunges at me. His enormous tongue reaches me a good fifteen seconds before the rest of him. Holly claims he's in love with me, and a lot of times he'll sit in the corner of her yard and stare wistfully in at me through our giant glass wall of windows, wagging his stub of a tail the whole time. When he stands on his hind legs he can reach my face, so I let him give me a couple of sloppy kisses and a big doggie hug before I pull on his leash. He immediately collapses at my feet and shows me his downy belly.

After I wipe off my face with my shirttail, I notice ten Trader Joe's bags in the trunk of Holly's tiny car. She's single, fit, and lives alone, so this seems like an awful lot of food. "Wow, are you having a party or are you developing an eating disorder?"

She replies, "None of the above. I have a girlfriend coming to stay with me for a while."

Fletch covers the grill and comes over to join us on the sidewalk that runs in front of our apartments. "That sounds like fun. Maybe you guys want to join us tomorrow? We're going to be grilling out again. We're having Coronas and margaritas and I'm cooking carne asada. Come over—we can make some noise and piss off all the assholes on the condo board." Behind Fletch's back, I'm shaking my head, mouthing "No!" and "Run!" while pantomiming vomiting, gagging, and jogging. He sees me reflected in our windows and swats me with a fishy set of tongs.

Holly sucks air in through her teeth. "Oh, you're sweet to offer, but no."

"You probably want to get your shots before you eat Fletch's cooking again?" I nod knowingly.

"Oh, give me a break, little *Miss Fry a Pork Chop within an Inch of Its Life and then Cover It with Sweet Baby Ray's Barbecue Sauce to Make them 'Exotic.'*[6] At least I try new stuff."

"Mmm, yes. New stuff. Last week he made some Ethiopian dish with spinach and peanut butter. You know what? There's a reason they're all so skinny over there." BTW, there is not enough chocolate cake *in the world* to wash the taste of that culinary abomination out of your mouth. "Anyway, do you have other plans? With *boys*, perhaps?" I ask, my voice tinged with excitement.

Holly is not only vivacious and lovely but also at the top of her game professionally. However, she's just turned forty-two, which apparently in this city means social suicide. Why is that? There are plenty of unattached men here in their forties, but they seem to go for the twenty-something girls and I have no idea why. I mean, wouldn't they get tired of having to explain cultural references over and over? It scares me to think that there are whole generations of people who have no idea *The Love Boat* ever existed. *Excuse me, middle-aged single gentlemen of Chicago? Yes, you there, with the Porsche and the hair plugs, hanging out in the Viagra Triangle in Diesels when you should be in Dockers. Listen up—I don't care how young, hot, or untouched by gravity your current plaything is— at some point, you're going to grow really weary of having to explain your joke about Adrienne Barbeau. The little girl you're with has no idea that Paul Newman isn't just "the salad dressing guy," and when you and your grown-up friends argue*

---

[6] My pork chops *kick ass* and everyone knows it, so I'm having no part of his slanderous accusations.

about whether David Hasselhoff was the talking-car guy or the monkey in the truck and the Two Dads dude, or they bring up the age-old Ginger or Mary Ann debate, she'll be of no help. Anyway, even if the men in Chicago don't appreciate Holly, we certainly do. But if there's a possibility of a date, we're going to be psyched for her.

"Nope, no hot new romances, nothing like that. The woman that's coming, she's an old buddy from college. We were best friends twenty years ago, but she was still such a huge partier after graduation that we eventually lost touch. I couldn't take her drunken four a.m. calls when I had to be up a couple of hours later."

"So, how'd she end up coming here?" Fletch asks. I notice the grill is getting particularly smoky, but I assume[7] Fletch knows what he's doing.

"You see, my friend Tracy's had kind of a rough time of it and she's coming here to dry out. She's been in and out of rehab facilities for years and her family's had it with her. I guess I was her last hope. When she called, I probably hadn't spoken to her in five years—I've no idea how she got my new number. Anyway, we have such a long, shared history that I couldn't say no. So, she's going to stay with me until she can transition back into a normal life. She'll be here later today."

"Oh, my God. You're, like, the best friend in the world." *Shoot,* I think, *you can't even count on me for a ride to the airport.*

She looks out at the horizon and sighs. "Yeah, well, I try.

---

[7] Mistake.

Listen, I've got to put this stuff away before it melts, so I'll see you later, okay?"

I lead Vaughn up to her yard, giving him one last scratch behind the ears. "Hey, good luck. Let us know if we can help." Holly enters her house and through her giant wall of glass I can see her loading groceries into the fridge. I turn to Fletch and tell him, "I've got a feeling this isn't going to end well. There's a reason people rehab in actual facilities."

Fletch nods. "Maybe, but I thought after the *Tommy Terrorist* foolishness you were going to start minding your own business."

"I will, I will. My bad. I'm just saying Holly's really nice and I hope her friend isn't here to take advantage of her."

"As do I." He turns his attention to the fish-shaped lumps of carbon on the grill. "So, who likes tuna?"

Tracy has arrived and I'm doing my best not to be annoyed. She has a tendency to glom onto us and spew copious amounts of highly inappropriate self-disclosure whenever we cross paths. I mean, when did saying *Hi, how are you?* become an invitation to tell me about your daddy issues?[8]

Tracy must have the hearing of a bat because every time we try to sit on our patio or second-floor balcony, she's out within seconds to join us. She hangs over the iron gate or wooden lattice and starts spilling all her problems. We're trying to be kind because we figure the poor thing is probably

---

[8] Ma'am, I don't even know your last name. Do *not* share your bad-touch stories.

just talking to keep the spiders from crawling all over her. So, we smile, nod, and grudgingly listen until we can escape back indoors without seeming rude. As charter members of the Jerk Club, neither of us is used to being terribly tolerant. However, Holly seems so strained that I want to do something to ease her burden. I'd never seen her without a smile until this week. She normally looks like she's about twenty-five, but lately every line on her face is showing. Even poor, laid-back Vaughn is stressed, evidenced by the giant bald patch he's licked on his leg. But I realize sobering up is the kind of struggle I can't fathom,[9] so I put on my polite face any time Tracy wants to chat.

I try not to be skeeved out when she gives me a bouquet of dead flowers she's picked, nor do Fletch and I make disparaging remarks to each other when she asks if we'd like her to wash our car. And we don't close our blinds when she takes Vaughn's spot, positioning her lawn chair so it faces directly into our living room.[10] Instead, we give her mad props for trying.

That is, until today.

I'm opening the blinds in the living room when I see Holly pulling a suitcase down our walkway. I pop out to say hello and learn that she's got a cab waiting. She's off to San Francisco for business and Tracy's going to dog-sit. I tell her to have a good time and watch her leave through the gate. "Hey, Fletch?" I call up the stairs.

---

[9] Obviously.

[10] But if there's anything creepier than someone watching you watch TV, I've yet to experience it.

"Yeah?"

"Holly's leaving Tracy alone. Ten bucks says the shit's about to hit the fan."

Half an hour later, we're still in our jammies, drinking coffee, eating Lucky Charms, and watching *SpongeBob*[11] when Tracy comes over. Being the consummate adult, I haul ass up the stairs and leave Fletch to answer the door. I'm crouched behind the wall, doing my best to eavesdrop, but I can't hear anything. As soon as the door closes, I'm back down the stairs as fast as my footie-pajama'd feet can carry me.

"Thanks a lot, asshole," he says.

"Yeah, yeah, whatever. What'd she want?"

"She wanted to prove you right, apparently."

"Meaning?"

"She asked for money."

"No way!" I predicted this, but I'd hoped I was wrong. I try to think the best of people yet I'm constantly disappointed.

"Tracy said Holly was supposed to leave some money for her but 'forgot.'"

"You believe that?"

Fletch gives me the weary, raised-eyebrow, tilted-chin look my father perfected many years ago when I tried to convince him $50 designer jeans were an investment in my future.[12] "She told me an elaborate story about a check getting lost in the hurricane and she wanted to know if she could borrow one hundred dollars to tide her over 'til it arrives."

---

[11] The breakfast of champions!
[12] You know what comes between me and my Calvins? My dad.

264 · *Jen Lancaster*

I contemplate for a moment. "The truth generally requires very little backstory."

"Exactly."

"And you said?"

"I was honest. Told her we're broke, but we're happy to send her over a plate of whatever we have for dinner if she doesn't have any groceries."

"This is *so* not going to end well."

"You've mentioned that."

We watch as Tracy goes from door to door in the complex. I should note the only person the neighbors hate more than us? Is Holly. She's nice as can be, but everyone here is terrified of Vaughn. He wouldn't hurt a kitten, even if he looks like a tremendous brute. However, he's a barker and she lets him hang out in her little gated front yard, woofing his head off every morning at six a.m. I sleep with earplugs, so I'm not bothered, but the fat girls and gay boys are totally up in arms. I've tried to warn her they've been banding against her, but to this point she's ignored my advice. She's of the "people are basically good" school of thought and has no idea how vituperative these shrews are.

From our panoramic view on the couch, we observe the fat girls and gay boys shake their heads with pinched expressions. It's almost painful to watch, yet I can't stop. Fletch could, but if he did, he'd have to put up with my running commentary, so it's easier just to witness this himself. Tracy is summarily rejected until she gets to Tommy's house. He nods and opens his wallet and from fifty feet away we see her eyes light up.[13]

---

[13] When we ask him about this later he says it was worth $50 to get her to stop talking.

In the time it takes me to shower and play a few rounds of my bottlecap game,[14] Tracy has not only stocked up on liquor but also managed to get drunk as a monkey and lock herself out of Holly's apartment. We help her get back in by having her go up to the second floor, through the office, out onto our balcony, over the lattice dividing our properties, and into her open glass door. Fortunately we have an early-afternoon wedding to attend and we leave for a while, but not before bolting and bracing our own doors in the office. When we return a few hours later, we assume Tracy will be passed out and that I can water my flowers unmolested.

Um, no.

Not only does Tracy decide to come out and visit with me, she chooses to do so naked.

Naked.

Nude.

In the buff.

Birthday suit.

Clothes-o a no-no.

I wish I were kidding.

I convince her to get dressed, and while she does I run inside the house and close the blinds. Unfortunately, we've already started the grill so we're stuck going back out, where we find we're not alone.

She is, mercifully, dressed this time.

Fletch is just about to get his shout on, but before he can she begins weeping hysterically about a family issue. Call us wusses, but we simply can't yell at a crying person. Then she

---

[14] Shh, don't tell Fletch.

offers to wash our car again. We decide trichinosis be damned; we tear the steaks off the grill and hurry back inside to eat them raw.

Over the next four hours, I watch her sit in Holly's car, running down the battery by listening to the same song over and over on the CD player. She sobs while the car's flashers blink and the windshield wipers run and poor Vaughn howls from the patio. I go out and comfort the dog, but he's having none of it. And when I tap on the car's window, Tracy ignores me.

I'm recounting this not to be funny because, really? It's heartrending. This girl is obviously in tremendous pain to act out like this. What I don't understand is *what the hell am I supposed to do here?* I try to call and e-mail Holly, telling her there's weirdness afoot, but I haven't heard back from her. I consider contacting the police, but I don't think Tracy is violating any laws. Technically the car isn't on, so she's not actually driving while intoxicated. In the meantime, what do I do?[15]

I'd like to be compassionate, but now Tracy isn't even *trying* to straighten herself out and that makes me angry. I'm also mad because she made our already hostile neighbors even more agitated at Holly by hitting them up for drinkin' money. I reflect on the days of our combined unemployment when we ate nothing but egg salad and little pizzas made out of leftover hamburger buns, and I still waited a whole week before I approached my parents for a loan to buy food.[16] Yet Tracy has no problem asking complete strangers for money to feed

---

[15] All the crazy to be found in New York and Carrie Bradshaw never encountered anything like this? I don't buy it.
[16] Which I have since paid back in full, thank you very much.

her habit and that irks me. And I'm pissed off she's essentially spit in the face of our lovely neighbor who was only trying to help.

I don't want to be blatantly mean next time she comes out to hover over us, but I'm really exasperated that I can't use my yard or deck unaccompanied.[17] And then I'm annoyed at myself because I feel like a terrible person for not being more compassionate. But I'm most concerned about Tracy hurting herself or others, and I'll be damned if I let her start the car and try to drive, so I stay up to keep an eye on her, trying not to wonder where my responsibility as a decent person ends and hers begins.

I'm totally at a loss.

I run into the gay boys and fat girls when I go out to get my paper this morning. I'm exhausted because I watched Tracy until she staggered into the house around three a.m. I learn that while we were at the wedding, Tracy offered to blow some of our gay neighbors for cash. I'm greatly upset because this is *not the way a healthy person acts.*[18] What gets me is we're only a few blocks from the projects in Cabrini Green. What's to stop her from going over there to peddle her wares, as it were? She's engaging in behavior that could get her killed and I hate that there's not a damn thing I can do to stop it. I voice my concerns to the gay boys and fat girls, hoping somehow we can come to a compassionate consensus.

---

[17] And the Calcutta of our kitchen is no prize, either.
[18] I'll take *A Cry for Help* for $200, Alex.

Instead of helping me problem-solve, the head fat girl starts to bitch about what this poor wretch is doing to her property value. The others concur. I stand there, mouth agape, unbelieving that anyone could be so cold.

You know what?

That's it.

We're moving.

Why do we put ourselves through this?

It's not as though we enjoy gathering up our shit every couple of years. We get no thrill from seeing all the nail holes we've made in our walls or the dirt paths we've beaten into the Berber, nor do we get off on the smell of cardboard boxes and packing tape. We don't delight in handing out a week's pay to a group of thick-necked gentlemen because we've grown too old and fat to carry our own stuff . . . and yet we're looking at moving to our *sixth* new apartment in less than a decade.

God help us.

The worst part isn't even the physical logistics of a move.[19] The nadir of Operation Unearthing a Chicago Home (a.k.a. OUCH) is going through the apartment-finding process.

To find a new apartment in my city, there are a handful of options. You can check out the *Chicago Reader*, our weekly hipster newspaper. Granted, there are a ton of listings, but every ad reads the same—"Beautiful apartment! Must see! Call 555-1212." So, if you want to know any details, like if

---

[19] See also *Paycheck, Parting With.*

there's central AC or the building is dog-friendly, you have to call the number listed, only to reach the landlord's voice mail (on which he'll leave *no* apartment specifics), the landlord will try to call you back and get your voice mail, and then the two of you will end up playing phone tag until your lease expires and you and your dogs have to go live in a van down by the river.

You can also stroll the neighborhood you like in search of FOR RENT signs. The occasional clever landlord will actually list some of the unit's features on the sign, but most will simply put a phone number and all of a sudden it's you and the dogs in a van again.

Craigslist posts ads and they're actually quite good because you can search by keyword (e.g., washer and dryer), price, and pet policy. However, most posts link to apartments listed by apartment brokers. On the one hand, working with a broker in Chicago is free; on the other, you get what you pay for.

Enter the brokers.

Our first appointment over the weekend is with Bob. We arrive at Bob's office at 9:55 for a 10:00 a.m. appointment. Unfortunately, Bob never shows up and some guy in flip-flops, apparently the owner of the brokerage—and is it wrong of me to say I really don't want to see the toes of anyone with whom I do business, particularly those of the prehensile variety?—tells us he's going to fire Bob for bailing on us.

Sorry, Bob!

Instead this guy named Jose steps in and shows us a number of inappropriate places (too small, too dark, too damn many roaches), asking important questions, like "Are you sure you want to keep your dogs?" and noting such selling points as "The exterminator comes once a month." Um . . . thanks, but I'm pretty sure I don't want to live somewhere an exterminator *needs* to visit on a monthly basis, regardless of how lovely the lighting fixtures may be.

We finally find a place we like and it meets the bulk of our needs—it's new construction with the most gorgeous dark cherrywood floors. There are stainless appliances in the clean, dry kitchen and the unit duplexes up three stories. There's a great loft I can write in, three bedrooms, and the living room is two stories high. Yes, it's got a view of the expressway, but that's why you buy curtains. (Which is also why we can afford it.) Plus, there's a twenty-five-by-fifty private roof deck with an unobstructed skyline view and I kind of lose my mind thinking of all the stuff I could grow up there. (Traffic exhaust is good for plants, right?) However, we aren't 100 percent sure of the neighborhood,[20] so we tell Jose we'll think about it, knowing we have an appointment with the biggest brokerage on Sunday, and biggest equals best, right?

Ha.

The dirtiest person I've ever seen who actually holds a job is our leasing rep at the big brokerage. This gal hasn't had a proper bath since George H. W. Bush's reign and was last acquainted with her razor during the Nixon administration . . . which was about the same time she declared jihad on using soap and wearing a bra. I'm not kidding—I could actually see

---

[20] It's south of the Loop and only about three miles from where we live now. However, Chicago is divided into North Side and South Side. Pretty much no one has ever made the longitudinal switch, so we're hesitant to be the first.

large streaks of dirt? Mud? On her forearms and shoulders. To make matters worse, she squires us about in the Stankmobile. Lest you think I'm exaggerating, allow me to paint you an accurate picture. Imagine every cigarette in the world. Then imagine one person smoking all of them. In this car. With the windows rolled up. For fifteen years. And even though Fletch and I both have to shower when we finish with this appointment, it wouldn't have been so bad had the rep actually shown us anything decent. (And I'm not being an elitist here—as a person whose dog craps in her house every night, it's not like my standards are terribly high. When we say to please not show us anything without a yard or a deck, *do not* take us to five deckless, yardless places in a row.)

Unfortunately, Stinkarella's apartments are the high point of the day.

Seeing the caliber of apartments out there, Fletch and I panic. We like the place south of the Loop, so we drive down to check out the 'hood in the dark. And you know what? It's actually fine and now I kind of get why the Southsiders think the Northsiders are a pack of snobs. We call Jose and say we'll take it, toasting each other with our root beers when we come to this decision while eating club sandwiches at Goose Island Brewery.

The next day Jose calls in a panic and says our FICO score isn't great. Um, no kidding. That's why we told him twenty-four hours earlier, "Our FICO score isn't great. We're looking to rent for another year or two so we can improve it and then buy our own place. However, we can provide excellent landlord references and W-2s and is that okay?" to which he replied, "No problem!"

Arrgh.

We manage to pass the credit hurdle only to find out the landlord wants the lease to start immediately, and not September 1, like we'd requested. In addition, he wants a *$7,000* deposit because of the dogs. Apparently he's concerned they might remove a load-bearing wall or perhaps install an illegal hot tub, as naughty dogs are wont to do. Whatever happened to the good old days of college when if you showed up, the place was yours? Jesus, it's probably easier to get a job with the FBI than it is to secure an apartment in this city.

We tell Jose to pound sand and start over.

Fletch is in our living room, holding the cordless phone to his ear. "Hold on, let me check with my wife—Jen, how about a noon appointment with the apartment brokers on Sunday?"

We haven't found anything yet, the rain's coming down harder in the kitchen, Tracy has yet to be carted off to proper rehab, and I'm starting to feel desperate. "Sounds good."

Fletch tells the caller, "Okay, noon it is. See you Sunday."

Five minutes pass as we both quietly work on our laptops. The icon blinks telling me I have mail, so I log on. "Hey, Fletch, I got an e-mail from you."

"Uh-huh, I know."

I open the e-mail and scan its contents. "Whoa, is this a *meeting request* to look at apartments on Sunday?"

"Yes."

"Are you trying to be funny?"

"No. I used the Yahoo Scheduler. Now you can add this

to your Yahoo Calendar so you can manage your personal affairs."

"But I don't *have* a Yahoo Calendar and I was sitting ten feet away from you when you made the call. And as eager as I am to move out of Melrose freakin' Place, chances are good I won't forget this appointment."

"Au contraire. You *do* have a Yahoo Calendar. I set it up for you."

I'm getting agitated. "You're missing the point—I don't *need* a Yahoo Calendar to manage my personal affairs, nor do I want to receive meeting requests from you. Here's a quick rule of thumb: no meeting requests to anyone you've seen naked, okay?"

He is resolute. "It's very handy."

"That may be, but when you e-mail your wife to schedule an appointment, you set an ugly precedent. What's next, sending me a request to clean the bathroom on the third floor?"

"Now that you mention it . . ."

"Sweetie, I love you, but I promise that I will smother you in your sleep if you ever assign me a chore via e-mail."

Five more minutes go by while we both quietly work on our computers, and then Fletch asks me, "So, are you going to respond to that request?"

"Fletch? This? Right here? Is exactly why you used to get beat up in junior high school."

✉

The broker on Sunday manages to show us something good. It's a gorgeous house with lots of bedrooms and skylights and a gourmet kitchen with a full basement. We fall in love on the spot. Naturally the broker neglects to tell us the place is a thousand dollars over the strict budget parameters we'd established with him.

Dude, you're *so* fired.

A few zillion calls and appointments later, we finally find the perfect place—spacious, lots of outside area, tons of amenities, dog-friendly, plenty of privacy, and with its polished concrete floors we can have a pony without any fear of damage! We've got to find something, like, *today* because we've given our landlord notice and he's already found another sucker who wants our place. In addition, Holly's not yet back from her trip and this morning Tracy offered Fletch a hummer and the gay boys and fat girls are starting to collect pitchforks and torches.

We've got to go *now*.

As we stand outside the building while the broker fiddles with the lock, we look at each other and agree as long as there are no dead bodies on the floor, we'll take it. All we have to do is see it to be sure.

Do I even need to mention the lock is broken and we can't get in?

Uncle.

We give up.

I hope the dogs like living in a van.

from the desk of Miss Jennifer A. Lancaster

An open letter to the dogs,

Although I don't blame you for your behavior with the squirrel, I am holding you accountable for your actions Saturday night.

Let's be clear about one thing—your daddy and I don't have a lot of people who like us. So when we're able to convince a few of our handful of friends to come over for a barbecue, we expect you to be on your best behavior.

"Best Behavior" does *not* include the following:

- Head-butting Angie so hard that you split her lip.
- Using your collective hundred and sixty pounds to pin Carol down on the couch while you lick her stupid (especially offensive considering your penchant for "salad tossing").
- Plowing into the screen with such force that you sent *the entire door* crashing into Jen, which then almost knocked her over the side of the porch.

Again, we don't have that many friends and we'll have even fewer should you accidentally kill them in your zeal to shower them with affection.

Best,

Mumma

P.S. I shall be sending your daddy a note under a separate cover detailing my issue with him delaying dinner by almost three hours when he set his shorts on fire.

P.P.S. Perhaps he'll listen to me the next time I say he's using too much lighter fluid. And regardless of your behavior, at least you two didn't set your *pants* on fire, which is more than I can say for your daddy.

To: angie_at_home, carol_at_home, wendy_at_home,
jen_at_work
From: jen@jenlancaster.com
Subject: *i got all my sisters with me*

Good morning,

Oh, yes, they're at it again.

Setting: My kitchen, Saturday morning, on the phone.

Dad: Hello?

Me: Hey, Dad, what's happening?

Dad: Not much. I'm getting ready to take your brother
Bruno for a walk. *(FYI, Bruno is their dog. This has led to many
protracted family tree discussions with my parents that if Bruno
is my brother, is the dog then an uncle to my brother's children
and my dogs, because I am their mother, or are all the dogs
cousins somehow?) (I wish I could claim that alcohol was a factor
in these conversations.)*

Me: I hoped to see you guys this weekend, but I don't
want you coming up until I get paid. Wouldn't it be nice if
we could actually take *you* to dinner? That way you and
Mom wouldn't have to arm wrestle over whose turn it
was. *(After forty-two years of marriage, my parents still
attempt to trick each other into picking up the tab. My dad is*

notorious for ducking out of store lines right before it's time to pay, thus sticking my mother with the obligation, while my mom is famous for forgetting to grab her credit card when she changes purses.)

Dad: Good. If she's not paying, let's go somewhere she doesn't like. How about Gene & Georgetti? I'll never forget the time we were there and Dan Rostenkowski joined us at our table. But we can't go next weekend. It's the NFL draft and I need to be here for it.

Me: If they're looking for seventy-year-old men with bad knees, I'm sure you'll go in the first round. Hey, where's Mom? I want to say hi. Is she there?

Dad: Nope. She already left for your brother's house. By the way, she's not speaking to me again.

Me: Now what? *(The key to my parents' successful forty-two-year marriage is that they've spent twenty of these years giving each other the silent treatment over major offenses like Dad using real butter on the vegetables or Mom letting Todd have all of Dad's $15 socks.)*

Dad: We got into a fight over who'd be more important historically—Pope John Paul or Winston Churchill. She said the Pope was a great humanitarian and I said without Churchill we'd all be speaking German.

Me: If we put video cameras in your house, people would pay to watch you guys.

Dad: Okay, then. Next time your mother speaks to me, I'll tell her you called. Have a good weekend.

Me: Bye, Dad.

After I hung up the phone I couldn't stop snickering about how silly my parents are. How could I have been spawned from such patently ridiculous people? Of course, three hours later I stopped talking to Fletch (and had to sit on my clenched fists) when he *wrongly* claimed the Sex Pistols were the Monkees of punk rock.

On the bright side, at least I can safely say there's no chance that I'm adopted.

TTFN,

Jen

Maisy and Me: Life and Love with the World's Most Spoiled Dog

I'm dreaming about the salty tang of a bag of Nacho Cheese Doritos. There's a plate of them in front of me, crisp and golden with just the right amount of spice, and I want them desperately but I'm having trouble getting to them. They're so close to me that I can smell them, yet they're out of my reach for some reason. I feel myself pitching forward, stretching and angling, and just about the time I'm near enough to take my first bite, I wake up when Maisy kicks me in the mouth with a corn-chip-scented foot. I groan and try to shove her onto Fletch's side of the bed, but when Maisy sleeps she turns from pit bull into a wet carpet, making her as heavy and difficult to move as depleted plutonium.

This sleeping in the bed with us business isn't new. A couple of years ago when we went from our penthouse in Bucktown to the mean streets of Sucktown[1] we had to disassemble

---

[1] Also known as the "West Town" area of the city, or, when we lived there, the West Si-ee-de.

the dogs' crates on moving day. Exhausted from ascending stairs and descending a lifestyle, we didn't put their crates back together, instead allowing the dogs to roam free during the night for the first time. Because Loki is a good boy, he immediately settled into a nest of pillows across the room and slept quietly. Maisy, on the other hand—and despite having been crate-trained for almost a year—peed on every new rug in the house, then ate and subsequently threw up half a pizza box before demanding entry into our bed and diving under the covers.

And she's been there ever since.

For days we tried to coax her back into her crate, or, barring that, a dog bed, but she wasn't having any of it. We later read that once a bully finds something she likes, such as sitting on the couch, she will spend the rest of her life attempting to replicate that action. No matter how strong your will is, hers? Is stronger. Now she sleeps in the bed, under the covers, spooned with Fletch, and yes, it's more than a little disconcerting when I lean over in the dark to kiss him good night, only to connect with a cold, wet muzzle.

In addition to needing to move for myriad neighbor-related reasons, we've got to find a new place so we can have a room large enough to accommodate a king-sized bed. I'm tired of losing the Battle of the Bully and the Queen Bed and sleeping in the office. As a van by the river simply won't do, we continue with our Hunt for Lease October, much to my chagrin. (If there's such a thing as heaven and hell, I'm pretty sure I'll be spending eternity riding in the backseat of some broker's smoky Ford Taurus, looking at an endless loop of apartments filled with Harvest Gold appliances, tiny closets, and no fewer than five flights of stairs.)

We have yet another brokerage appointment today so I grudgingly get out of bed when the alarm sounds. I throw on my bra and a pair of slippers and go downstairs to start morning duties. First, I dump out the drip bucket in the kitchen. We've discovered that the occasional sprinkles of ceiling water are in fact condensation from the air conditioner, which, while not exactly sanitary, is a damn site better than the sewage from before.

I open a couple of tins of Friskies to stop the cats from yowling. The way these creatures carry on, you'd think they were starving despite their 24/7 access to a tower of dry kibble. The truth is they're all so fat I have to assist them onto the counter, where they circle around the plate of wet food like spokes on a wheel. I lift them all and they begin to gorge, energizing themselves for a long day of sharpening their claws on the chenille couch and trying to trip me on the stairs.

Next up I start the coffee, because if I don't I'll get similar histrionics from Fletch. I wash out the dogs' dishes and give them clean, cold water and I pour in dry food, topped with a can of Science Diet. I made the mistake of giving Maisy some at my parents' house once. God forbid we don't have it in the house now, because I cannot take a day of her sitting in front of her bowl, grunting and yipping until I serve her *exactly* what she wants. Before I call everyone down for breakfast, I open all the curtains in the living room, checking the patio for Winky.

Winky, thusly named because of his permanent squint, is a twee little reddish-brown[2] squirrel so darling and cute I'd

---

[2] Even without the wonky eye, we'd recognize him because he's the only one in our neighborhood who doesn't come in standard squirrel-issue gray.

want to make him soup or perhaps carry him in my pocket if I didn't hate him with every fiber of my being. Ounce for ounce he's more evil than bin Laden, and I actively pray for his demise. You wouldn't think four pounds of puffy tail could inspire such passion, but that's where you'd be wrong. Every day he sits just on the other side of our glass door, waiting for seeds to magically fall out of our bird feeder. In so doing, he causes the dogs to lose their minds. They've already yanked down a set of curtains and torn $400 worth of custom miniblinds[3] trying to claw through the glass to get at him, while he lounges just out of reach, so relaxed it's as though he were hanging out in a Parisian café reading *Le Monde* with his orange pressé and croissant. Other than the house actually catching fire, there's nothing more distracting while trying to write than two dogs barking their heads off, running up and down three flights, and hurling themselves at windows.

Unfortunately, whenever I try to chase Winky away, one of the neighbors manages to walk out at the exact time I'm brandishing a broom, shouting, "Oh, I will *give* you something to gobble. Eat straw, you little bastard!" That said, it's not as if they didn't already hate me after I went all Sean Penn on them during the Tracy debacle, so at this point I guess it doesn't much matter.[4]

I flip on the news to watch Shepherd Smith report live from New Orleans about the post–Hurricane Katrina devastation, but before I can even take my favorite Cisco-logo mug

---

[3] Good-bye, security deposit!

[4] I wanted to help get Tracy to rehab; they wanted me to help get Holly evicted. Guess which path I chose?

out of the cabinet, the dogs have inhaled their breakfast and want to go outside. *Now.*

As I hunt for poop bags and truss them up in heavy canvas leashes and stainless pinch collars, I think again of how much I'd like a house with a yard. Right now taking the guys for a spin around the block in the outfit I slept in isn't so bad because it's still summer. But there's nothing worse than getting out of a warm bed at six a.m. and putting on layers of sweatpants and sweaters, followed by a coat, scarf, gloves, hat, and boots in order to walk the dogs in the icy darkness, only to be yanked clean off my feet the second they spot another animal, be it dog, cat, rat, or, God forbid, squirrel.

Some people fantasize about threesomes or winning the lottery—in my daydream, I see myself in flannel pajamas and thick socks, standing in a bright doorway, mug of coffee in hand, while Maisy and Loki gambol predawn through freshly fallen snow. I love the idea of a private, fenced yard where the dogs can run and play and not get all distracted by the smells of the thousand other creatures that were there before them. I bet not even a ride in the car to Dairy Queen for cups of soft-serve would make them happier than their own little doggie park. The great irony here is we have a gated patio, but the condo Nazis dish out fines to anyone letting their dogs relieve themselves on their own private property. Sure, I don't like walking the dogs, but not $100 worth.

Leashes firmly attached to my arm, the dogs and I explode out the door, as usual. Unfortunately, in the ten seconds it's taken them to eat, Winky has returned and the dogs dislocate my shoulder lunging at him. He squawks his demonic little squirrel laugh and scampers up a tree to taunt them from a safe distance.

Since the beasts are now in a lather, they aren't content just to take their usual lap around the block. Oh no, they want full-on "walkies," which sucks because I'm still in my V-neck and cutoff jammie pants with the dancing hamburger, hot dog, and French fry print. Although I'm okay with the hateful neighbors seeing me in what I sleep in, roaming the entire 'hood, where I have to pass people waiting for the public transportation that will take them to their jobs, is another story.

As we walk, I hobble because I hurt my back at the grocery store earlier this week when I slipped by the front door. Were I to choose to take action, I'd probably have a lucrative lawsuit on my hands since the incident was caught on the security camera. Unfortunately, before exiting the car I donned a produce bag from the fruit market to protect my hair from the rain. Fletch declared, "You appear to be wearing a giant condom on your head." I shot back, "Yeah, but my hair will be dry and you *wish* you had this kind of self-esteem." And then I'm sure the folks in the Jewel's security office laughed their asses off as the chick with the giant prophylactic skidded on the broken bottle of Italian dressing and flew ass-over-teakettle, landing in a near-perfect split.

I fear that someday while eating pork chops in front of the television, we'll see this video on the Fox special *When Fat Girls Fall Down.*

I continue walking hamstrung behind the canine Teds Kaczynski and Bundy all the way past the spot where I like to

pick wild sunflowers.[5] Normally this is a good, long consti-
tutional, yet these rotten dogs still aren't satisfied with our
circuitous route. Our endless perambulation continues and
all I can think of is how I would kill for a fenced yard right
now.

The dogs drag me over to a little wooded area that banks
up from the expressway. With its dense pine trees, green
grass, and mountains of garbage, it looks like a lovely place
for a picnic were one perhaps a crack dealer, prostitute, or of
the homeless persuasion. As we proceed, the dogs are practically crossing their legs knowing the walk is over the second
they relieve themselves. Under one of the pine trees, I notice
an abandoned magazine, so I pick up what turns out to be the
January 1991 issue of *Honcho*—a gay porn magazine. *Hmm,* I
think, *I guess my neighbors had a picnic here.*

I open it and begin to thumb through the pages. I'm
standing in this grassy spot until the dogs just *go* already, so I
figure I should have something to look at. As I scan photo after photo, I realize I'm always using "gay porn" as a punch
line in my writing, yet until this very moment, I've never actually *seen* any. And . . . wow. All I can say is that being in a gay
men's pornographic magazine requires careful shaving. A *lot*
of careful shaving.

I briefly debate taking the magazine home and stuffing it in
Fletch's computer bag, but then the dogs finally begin to
potty in tandem, drawing my attention elsewhere. Business
complete, I'm dragged back to the apartment, where Winky

---

[5] Jen's Budget Homemaking Tip #475: Why purchase flowers when you can
steal them from a vacant lot?

sits in the center of our brick patio, perfectly positioned so when the dogs spot him they dislocate my *other* shoulder.

"Okay, how about, um, see any movie starring Lindsay Lohan?" I ask.

"Yes." Fletch nods. "Yes, I'd rather see any Lindsay Lohan flick, particularly if she's starring in it with a Volkswagen Beetle. Your turn—and keep in mind death is not an option—how about discuss your feeelings[6] with your bat-shit crazy mother?"

"She's not *really* bat-shit crazy, Fletch. Her mental fitness surpasses us all."[7]

"Yeah? Then how come she's afraid of towel bars?"

"I don't know that they *scare* her, per se; I think it's just that she hates them. Or, maybe her fear is of dirty towels, and if there are no towel bars, you're never in danger of using one that's been soiled, right? Although I'm pretty sure she does fear closet doors. You notice the last time we were there, she'd succeeded in getting rid of all the ones upstairs?"

"I did. This compulsion may be symptomatic, but I'm not sure of what."

"Regardless, I'd probably rather discuss my feeelings."

"All right, I've got one. Debate merits of Ayn Rand's Objectivism philosophy with Anna Nicole Smith or continue to look for a new apartment?"

We're supposed to leave in the next few minutes to go see

---

[6] The extra *e* is for "emotion."
[7] I love you, Mommy. Please don't cut me out of the will.

288 · *Jen Lancaster*

yet another broker, but we haven't worked up the will to leave the house. This process is not only taking forever, but it's getting increasingly frustrating. A couple of days ago we saw a place with mauve kitchen appliances, including a mauve Sub-Zero fridge, mauve granite, mauve vanities, and a mauve toilet, sink, and tub.[8] The whole joint was lousy with faux-Tiffany glasswork and track lighting and we couldn't get out of there fast enough. I mentioned to the broker this apartment would be the perfect place for Michael Milken to whip off his suspenders and listen to Oingo Boingo on his reel-to-reel, talking on his boot-sized cellular phone, before heading out to a fern bar to drink gin with Patrick Bateman and Gordon Gekko. Then I laughed myself into an asthma attack. In a completely unrelated story, that broker called us yesterday to say she was leaving the country for an undetermined amount of time and was sorry she couldn't work with us anymore.

Today, we're starting over with *yet another* broker (our seventh or eighth—they've all blurred together) and we're having a difficult time mustering the enthusiasm to see the latest in a string of $24,000/year crack dens.

"Ha!" I laugh. "Can you imagine it? Anna Nicole would be all, '*Me and Sugar Pie wholeheartedly disagree with the notion the ideal political-economic system is laissez-faire capitalism. And, um, TRIMSPA, baby!*' But yes, I would rather have this conversation with her than look at another goddamned place. How about you? Would you rather go now or pick shards of glass out of the dogs once they finally fly through the window to disembowel Winky?"

---

[8] I love me some pink, but mauve is not and never will be the new pink.

"Ooh, good one. But once they kill the squirrel and go to the vet, that's it, the situation's over. I'm going to say 'glass' because the apartment hunt has no tangible end in sight."

"I agree. Okay, then, would you rather go on another appointment or spend the night at the Superdome?" Fletch gives me a disgusted look. "Too soon?" I ask.

"Yeah. Way too soon."

"Oh, sorry. Well, would you rather ride around in the back of yet another broker's filthy Ford or listen to any sort of music that compares and contrasts the finer qualities of your milkshake?"

"The shake. Definitely the shake."

"Hey, speaking of, you know what would be a cool song? If William Shakespeare came out with a new version of the Baja Boys' 'Who Let the Dogs Out?' He'd call it 'Who Hath Released the Hounds?'" I begin to sing.

"Who hath released the hounds? (woof woof woof woof)
"Who hath released the hounds? (woof woof woof woof)"

Fletch looks thoughtful for a moment. "You know, I'd probably rather look at apartments than hear that song ever again. So it's decided. We're going to honor our appointment. Grab your purse, we've got to go."

We're standing in front of a nondescript single-family house with a FOR SALE sign in its tiny front yard. "Um, you know we're looking for a rental, right?" I ask.

"Yes, yes, don't worry," Tina, our newest broker, replies. "They've got the house listed because it's been on the rental market so long. No one wants it and if they don't rent it right now, they're going to have to sell it."

"Ooh, *Loser House*! Encouraging! I love it already!" I snark.

"Honestly, I wasn't even going to bring you guys, but we were going right by it and the keys have been in my ashtray for a while. Tell you what, we'll take a quick peek and then I promise to take you somewhere better, okay?" the broker pleads. Apparently our reputation precedes us.

"Well, what are you waiting for? Loser House awaits." Tina works the double locks and opens the elaborate Victorian front door into a hallway. The first thing we see is a set of stairs listing distinctly to the right.

"Ha!" I bark. "Loser House is on a slant. Niiice."

But as we get past the front hallway, I notice the place has gorgeous new walnut hardwood floors. They're a deep, rich brown, almost chocolate, with a light sheen. And then we walk through the living room with fully restored millwork and crown molding at least six inches wide. The smooth plaster walls are covered with what has to be a designer paint job. "Hey, this is—this is not so bad," I say slowly.

"Yes, according to my notes, the past owner was an interior designer. I guess she gutted the house and restored everything she could, and replicated those bits she couldn't. That's why the stairs slant—they're original—and so is the hand-tooled banister."

Hmm.

We pass the first bathroom, about the size of a small coat closet. Everything has been made to scale and the counter is a four-inch-wide strip of mossy green and sparkly gray granite with a teeny metal soup bowl sink tucked in the corner. "Okay, this is kind of cute," I admit.

We pass into the kitchen, which is no less than eighteen by fifteen feet, wainscoted with cream-colored bead board, and filled with GE Profile appliances, adjustable lighting, and forty-seven cabinets.

Forty. Seven.

Wow.

I wonder how many wineglasses I can store in here?

We go down to the basement, which runs the length of Loser House. There are glass block windows, a full-sized washer and dryer, and an entire workbench with built-in shelves, drawers, and cabinets, which would allow the man of the house to store his tools in style. Plus, there's a little nook at the front of it where someone could have a place to set up the stupid old futon he refuses to get rid of and hang his horrible seventies lighted Schlitz sign and enough space in the back that whoever lived here could finally give up the family's storage unit.

We leave the basement, cross through the gourmet kitchen, and climb the slanted stairs. They list to the right, but they're sturdy, and up close I see the detail of the original lathed woodwork in the newel posts. The master bedroom is big enough for a king-sized bed and there's a small dressing room to the side. All the brand-new, double-paned, flip-out windows are covered with expensive wooden blinds and they're already adorned with expensive decorative iron rods, so the only window treatment needed would be curtains. The walls appear to be covered with caramel-colored suede, but when we touch it we see that it's layers of paper, almost like torn grocery bags, giving it three-dimensional detail.

There's a tiled bath off this bedroom with dual shower-heads. I try the water pressure and it's powerful enough to knock the polish off my nails. Down the hall is a second bed-room, done in shades of mint and yellow with the most per-fect little mint-yellow bath off of it, housing an entire wall of the same cabinets found downstairs. I pretty much want to lick the whole room.

Fletch and I look at each other. This is *way* nicer than we expected, at a price we can afford, in a neighborhood that's walking distance to Target. "So, like, did anyone die here?" I ask. At this point, death is not a deal breaker, I'm just curious.

"I find it interesting that's your first question. But, no, no one died here," Tina replies.

"Then what's wrong with it?" Fletch wants to know.

"Nothing. It's just not a good roommate house," she ex-plains. "Most of our clients are friends looking to share a place. We don't get a lot of couples wanting to rent upscale apartments,[9] so that's why it's been empty. I think this place just needs the right people."

"And this is just a house—there's no condo or block asso-ciation we'd have to deal with?" I ask. "No one's going to pass capricious rules about my dogs not whizzing in the yard?"

"Not a chance."

"Oh, wait," Fletch says. "Yard—is there a yard?" The

---

[9] Because they're busy *buying* them, but she's too polite to mention this.

blinds were drawn in the kitchen and we didn't even look out back.

We walk down the stairs and through the glorious kitchen. But when we open the door, we don't go directly into a yard. First, we have to pass through a charming little den with a brick wall, vaulted ceilings, and built-in shelves.

And there it is.

Through the wraparound windows we see a yard, a glorious, magnificent, *don't ever have to walk the dogs again in inclement weather* yard. We spill out the door and onto its beautifully cemented flagstone patio. Empty flower beds are bricked off and the whole thing's surrounded by a new wooden fence that's six feet tall. There's a section at the end already covered in pea gravel, which would make an ideal potty spot. The only access to the street is through the private garage, so I could allow the dogs to stay out there as long as they wanted and never worry about their safety. I look back at the doorway, imagining myself on a cold winter morning, holding coffee, watching through broad panes of glass as two joyous dogs kick up snow in their wake. They'll think they died and went to doggie heaven.

In unison, Fletch and I blurt, "We'll take it!"

We go back to Tina's office, sign the lease, write a check, and are instantly given our new set of keys to (Definitely Not) Loser House.

Well, *that* was easy.

For the past few weeks, we've done nothing but box up smaller items and run them over to our new place. Prior to that, between temping, tramping through every open apartment in this city, dealing with condo complex foolishness, and trying to soothe the dogs, who know something's up and lose their minds every time we step out the door, I haven't had a minute of free time in the past month.

Our movers are coming this afternoon and everything I need to do here is done. The next few hours are the only ones I'll have to relax for a couple of weeks, as we'll be busy unpacking and cleaning. I plan on enjoying every minute of them by lounging around in front of *Fox News* while sipping Costco's spectacularly good Ethiopian-blend coffee.[10]

I get up and kiss the dog, whose head is resting gently on my pillow. As soon as I vacate my spot, the other climbs onto the bed. Both are exhausted from their two-week-long freakout and aren't yet ready to get up. They have no idea they're about to go on their last walk before discovering the joy of their new yard.

Fletch is still asleep, too, so I head down the stairs for opening duty. We brought the cats to the new place yesterday and they're thrilled at all the big patches of sunlight that flood the new house. This place has a northern exposure, and in the two years we've been here the cats haven't been able to bask in a single sunbeam, which always made me feel guilty.

I open the curtains and our living room brightens with the indirect light. Naturally, Winky is there standing on the broken remains of my birdhouse. Somehow he managed to cata-

---

[10]Jen's Budget Homemaking Tip #567: Costco kicks ass. The only reason they're not part of the new Holy Trinity of shopping is Fletch yells at me every time I buy their cheesecake in bulk.

pult himself up the brick wall and chew through its ropes. He's out there feasting on his spoils and I just know he's smirking at me. I have had it with this evil creature and throw open the door, swinging the first thing I can get my hands on—a tube of wrapping paper embossed with the phrase "Peace on Earth" and a bunch of penguins holding hands.[11]

Swearing, spitting, and swinging, I chase him to the edge of the complex while shouting, "Die, motherfucker, die!" and he dashes up a telephone pole. (You know what? Animal rights don't apply to those who break my birdhouses.[12])

Victorious, I strut back into the house with my paper battle-ax, but not before waving at one of the fat girls who glowers at me while getting into her car. Frown all you want, missy. For I? Am Audi 5000.

I flip on *Fox News* and walk over to my Cuisinart Automatic Grind & Brew. I pour in filtered water and carefully measure the smoky, nutty beans into the little basket. Never have I earned a cup of coffee more in my life. It's a tad cool today and my extremities are chilly from having been outside chasing squirrels through fresh dew. I long for the feeling of cold fingers wrapped around a warm ceramic mug. I flip the switch, expecting to hear the blades spring to life, but instead I hear a loud pop, followed quickly by the hum of all my household electronics dying in unison.

Wait, what?

No.

Noooo!

---

[11] Holding flippers?

[12] Or who are delicious. And, on some occasions, stylish.

Not again! I swear we're not deadbeats anymore! I'm (almost) sure we paid our electric bill! I frantically search through the stack of packed boxes, looking for the one with financial information. I finally locate my register and see the check was written, so I grab the phone, ready to tell ComEd, "Bitches, my bill is *paid*." But when I pick up my phone, it's not working because it's cordless. I know we've got an analog model that would work, but it's buried in one of the bottom boxes and I can't get to it.

At this point I notice all my contemptible neighbors are gathered outside, and for once I'm thrilled to see them because it means it's a neighborhood thing and not a *Jen didn't pay the bill* thing. I head out for information and learn we're in the middle of a brown-out, meaning there's a slight electrical feed running. Unfortunately, it's not enough to run my coffeemaker, but it *is* enough to power my wireless router.

I settle in with my laptop and a bowl of vanilla yogurt and granola. I may not be watching TV, but that's okay. I can still enjoy this precious downtime. As I scan the headlines on FoxNews.com, I get a physical longing for coffee. I yearn for a frothy concoction of milk and espresso and maybe a quick sprinkle of cinnamon. I practically ache for the delicate layers of spice and sweet fruit and the subtlest hint of caramel as the caffeinated goodness jump-starts my nervous system. Coffee is so essential to my morning that failure is simply not an option. I give the Cuisinart another whirl, but it sits there mute. Ever resourceful, I grab my keys and decide to treat myself with Starbucks.

I back out of my space, pull up to the gate, and hit the remote to open it . . . and nothing happens. Damn it! Electric gate! I punch the button again and again, but no luck. I get out of the car to inspect the gate's mechanics, looking for the fail-safe. I scrutinize every inch of it, getting grease all over my hands, but find no key, switch, or button that allows me to open it manually. Then I walk over to the mouth of the gate and give it a Herculean tug, but I can't budge it an inch.

I pull back into my assigned spot. I look down at my legs and realize God must have given them to me for a purpose other than simply having an excuse to get pedicures. I decide to hoof it the six blocks to the coffee shop. I march over to the gate and enter my code, fingers flying across the keypad, expectantly waiting for the lock-releasing buzz that opens the steel cage standing between me and my ultimate prize.

But the buzz does not come.

I'm trapped. *Trapped!* And with no possibility of garnering the sweet elixir of life, my raison d'être, the source from which all that is holy and righteous flows! I'm on my knees crying, *"It's not fair! It's not fair!"* when a gentleman in a ComEd vest catches sight of me. From the other side of the fence, in reassuring tones, he gently says, "Ma'am, he didn't feel a thing."

Huh?

"The squirrel," he said, holding up a hideously blackened yet distinctly still reddish-brown-furred carcass, "when he chewed through the wire, his death was instantaneous."

"Yes, the squirrel. I'm, um, devastated. Of course," I say.

"Yeah, anyway," he replies, "your power's back on."

And suddenly there's naught but a vapor trail between the man holding a barbecued Winky and my coffeemaker.

As I sit here with my third cup and reflect on this morning's happenings, I realize in fact that I'm a big ass.

Because I'm really glad that pesky squirrel is dead.

"They're going to go bananas!" I exclaim. Everything I hold most precious is in this car—my husband, my dogs, my Cuisinart. Fletch is driving us to the new house before doubling back to meet the movers. He could have caught a ride with them and had me drive over myself, but he wants to be there when the dogs see their yard for the first time.

"I bet Loki spins in circles and Maisy rocket-dogs back and forth like she used to when we'd take her to the beach," Fletch predicts.

"How great is it going to be for them to go outside every time they want?" Upon hearing "outside," the dogs, who are already bouncing all over the backseat, begin to yip and howl.

We get to the house and park out front. We figure the dogs should go in through the front door the first time, kind of like being carried over a threshold as a newlywed.[13] We open the door and find all the cats lying Jonestown-like in giant pools of sunlight. Bones, the spokesman for the cats' union, looks at the dogs and then us, as if to say, "Oh, you brought *them* here, did you? Fine. But so you know, this means we're going to have to keep wrecking the couch."

We let the dogs off the leash and they tear off, dashing up and down the stairs for a good ten minutes. We stand in the

---

[13] I did try to hop on Fletch's back once we got our own keys and he walked hunched over for the next three days.

living room, watching streaks of black and tan fur fly by, building the anticipation until the moment when they finally see their yard. We call them to the den, and when they settle down enough to come, they sit and wait for us to put on their leashes. "Not today, guys," I tell them. I open the back door and the dogs explode out into the yard. Loki runs around in laps, inspecting every nook and cranny of the property. He woofs and prances in between peeing on every single vertical surface. Then he notices the gravel area and squats to do his business, and I swear he's smiling.

Maisy, on the other hand, takes a few tentative steps on the flagstone before running back up the deck's stairs. "What's wrong with her?" Fletch asks.

"I don't know—maybe she's just nervous?" I try to coax her out into the yard, squeezing her favorite toy—a squeaky pink rhinoceros—which normally pushes her into overdrive. I throw it in the direction of the gravel and she makes no attempt to go get it. "Maisy? Baby dog? What's the matter?" I fetch her rhino and toss it again, getting the same reaction, while Loki practically tap-dances with joy. "Maybe she needs a drink?" I grab their bowl, fill it with water, and place it on the patio. She doesn't go near it. We spend the next half hour trying to get the dog enthused about her new yard, but she just sits on the landing, shoved up against the door, looking at me with big, soft, black-rimmed eyes and pouting her bottom lip. Fletch has to get back to the old house, so he leaves, and I bring Maisy inside with me, as Loki refuses to leave the yard.

When I bring my box of toiletries up to what will be my bathroom, I notice Maisy's already gone to the bathroom in the guest room. Poor thing's probably just nervous, I think. I take her outside again to do her business and she simply stands on the stairs and looks at me again.

When I go into the bedroom to unload a wardrobe box, I catch her midstream, and I drag her outside, where she refuses to finish. Again I chalk it up to nerves. At some point, she has to come around, right? As soon as she calms down, I know she'll love her new yard. After all, having spent most of the summer trying to find the perfect place for us and the dogs, there's no way our efforts will have been made in vain. I mean, really, what kind of dog doesn't love her own backyard?

Apparently, *my* kind of dog doesn't love her own backyard.

After almost three months, we're finally to the point where she'll dash out, pee on the patio, and return the second she finishes. She patently refuses to loiter outdoors, even if we're in the yard with her. And she'll occasionally consent to make a big potty outside rather than on my pink plaid rug[14] in the guest room. I consider this progress.

It snows for the first time today. I'm sitting on the love seat in the den drinking coffee as fat flakes drift slowly down from gray skies. Maisy spends her requisite eight seconds outdoors and comes immediately back inside. She curls herself into a small bean next to me, tail thumping, head resting on my lap as we watch Loki snap at snowflakes.

....

14 Now baby soft and completely faded after a hundred washings.

She wags harder when she sees our neighbor Dan get into his Jeep. He's the only person we've met here so far, and we've talked to him maybe a handful of times since he gave us a bottle of wine over the fence on our first day here. We've waved at a few of the other neighbors on the rare occasion we're out front, but that's about it. Funny how much less you know about people—good, bad, or indifferent—when you don't live in a big, glass, U-shaped fishbowl. I scratch Maisy's head and she stretches, giving me a big whiff of corn chip. She sighs contentedly.

So she hates her yard.

But she loves her house.

And that's good enough for me.

To: angie_at_home, carol_at_home, wendy_at_home, jen_at_work
From: jen@jenlancaster.com
Subject: *deep thoughts with jen handy*

Today I realized something while researching a flight for my boss—

www.aa.com is the Web site for American Airlines.

www.aa.org is the Web site for Alcoholics Anonymous.

I wonder how many people out there seeking salvation just said "fuck it" and booked a trip to Vegas instead?

To: angie_at_home, carol_at_home, wendy_at_home, jen_at_work
From: jen@jenlancaster.com
Subject: *more paid overtime, that's for sure*

Hola,

I woke up this morning and the first thing to pop into my head wasn't my usual, *"Coffee?"* or *"Who needs to go outside?"* or *"How many more trees can I get chopped down today?"*

Instead, I thought, *"I bet the Old Testament would have turned out a lot differently if they had OSHA back then."*

Ciao, bellas,

Jen

No Molestar—The Attack of the Sock-Monkey Pajamas

I'm busy in the Fortress of Solitude creating an antidote for kryptonite when the phone rings.

Well, that's not entirely true—I'm busy in the Fortress of Solitude writing the Great American Novel when the phone rings.

Okay, when the phone rings I'm actually in the Fortress of Solitude crafting virtual celebrity paper-doll makeovers at Stardoll.com.

All right, *fine.* If I'm being completely honest, I'm not in the Fortress of Solitude at all. I'm in my mint green office/ guest room/general garbage-I-can't-yet-throw-away-catchall room. However, I totally *would* be in the Fortress of Solitude if I could just find an apartment carved into the rock face of an Arctic mountain, but there seems to be a dearth of them here in Chicago.

Still, my home's an ad hoc Fortress of Solitude if you think about it. Casa Jen serves the exact same purpose as Superman's pad—it's where I get away from the noise and chaos of urban life and it's the only real place I can relax and work on special projects. Granted, it's not *quite* a secret sanctum far from civilization, what with it being around the corner from Burger King, and instead of glacial ice the floors are a nice glossy maple.[1] Also, our place has a garage and I'm guessing Superman's fortress doesn't, because who needs a car when you can fly? This is likely for the best because his X-ray vision would screw up his depth perception and he'd always be accidentally ramming his SUV into the garage wall until Lois Lane had a mini-meltdown and finally had to hang a tennis ball on a string from the rafters to stop him. Then they'd have an argument about his garage-ramming being genetic, because Superman's mom always used to hit *their* attached garage's wall when he was a kid back before his planet exploded. And since the family room's sofa shared a wall with the garage, the impact would knock pictures off the wall and throw Superman's brother Todd ass-over-teakettle from his prone position on the cushions every time she pulled in, while Superman's smarty-pantsed father would look up from his *Wall Street Journal* and dryly remark, "I think your mother's home," and—

Ahem.

The point is my home is a virtual Fortress of Solitude and that means I don't like to be disturbed by unwanted calls. I ignore the phone and get back to the very important business of

---

[1] But really, ice floors would be kind of a bitch to get clean because how would you mop them? You couldn't use hot water. It would be like trying to open a present of wrapping paper—when would you know to stop?

clothing Kirsten Dunst in punk-rock garb.[2] I glance at the phone's message light, see that it's not flashing, and return to my task.

Ten minutes later as I'm painting Kirsten's lips Goth black and rimming her eyes in red liner, the phone rings again. I continue to ignore it. I've never been the kind of girl to hurdle over dogs and ottomans to answer a ringing phone—if it's important, they'll leave a message. Plus, having recently recovered from a nasty bout with poverty, I'm still scarred from too many conversations with bill collectors. So that phone? Can ring away. Minutes later, I glance at the light to confirm its message-free status.

Far as I'm concerned, I'd rather not even own a phone. I prefer the opportunity to expostulate uninterrupted via e-mail. However, I occasionally do need to order a pizza and have since learned one must occasionally allow her friends to get a word in edgewise, so the phone's a necessary evil.

I've moved on to suit-up Scarlett Johansson in homeless-chic when the phone rings again. Concerned that Fletch may be having another one of his "I can't remember what I like to eat for lunch" dilemmas, I wander over to check the caller ID log. Skimming through the listings, I notice fifteen of the last twenty incoming calls have been from someplace called "Rodale, Inc." I'm annoyed that Rodale, Inc., hasn't left a message, but heartened to know that my beloved isn't standing in

---

[2] Oh, Kirsten! You little minx! Sid Vicious is going to come back from the grave to claim you as his bride!

a food court somewhere clutching his empty tummy. I return to the computer.[3]

I'm at a critical juncture outfitting Katie Holmes in Harajuku garb when the phone rings yet again. Arrgh. How exactly am I supposed to concentrate mixing plaid skirts and striped tights with these constant interruptions? I look at the caller ID and realize there's only one way I can nip this noise in the bud. Resigned, I lift the receiver.

"Yeah, hello?" I snarl.[4]

"Hello, is Mr. Fletcher in?" asks some guy I don't know.

"Nope."

"Oh, well then, is this Mrs. Fletcher?" God, I hate that. I am *not* Mrs. Fletcher even though I'm married to Mr. Fletcher. However, I'm anxious to get back to Katie, so I don't read Some Guy the riot act about how *many* women choose to keep their last names because we aren't chattel, for Christ's sake, and thus do not need to be branded with someone else's moniker like so many heads of cattle. (Although Fletch really isn't like this and totally didn't care what I did with my last name. The truth is that I was way too lazy to deal with the DMV and Social Security. Also, I particularly like how my given last name looks in calligraphy—pretty! Swirly![5])

I sigh. "Yes."

Some Guy begins reading from a script. "I'm calling from

---

[3] Yes, Scarlett, my dear—it's five coats, four sweaters, and every purse on the page for you!

[4] What? You think Superman wouldn't snarl at an unwelcome guest?

[5] But, still, Girl Power and all that.

Men's Health. Your husband is a subscriber and I wanted to know if he's enjoying the magazine."

Because I can't *not* mess with a telemarketer,[6] I reply, "Yes, absolutely. After Jesus and America, it's the most important thing in his life right now."

Temporarily thrown off script, he remarks, "Wow, really?"

"Um, no. But he does read it on the mug (Fletch's own version of the Fortress of Solitude), so he commits a good half hour to it each day. I guess that's something, right?"

I hear the rustle of paper as Some Guy tries to get back on message. "The reason I'm calling you today, Mrs. Fletcher, is to tell your husband about a free gift. Before we go any further, though, I have to ask you if you mind if I record this call."

"Why? Are we going to have an entire conversation about him enjoying the magazine in the bathroom? Because I've already shared with you the extent of my knowledge of his feelings toward said magazine. His washroom habits are not something to which I'm privy. We believe in boundaries around here, so I'm not sure what else we have to discuss. Also, he made a roast from a recipe in your stupid magazine and ended up ruining eleven dollars' worth of pork loin. Are you calling to offer me eleven dollars? Or maybe more pork?"

Some Guy stammers and I can hear him thumbing through pages. While he hems and haws on the other end, I try to imagine what Superman would do if he were me. Seems like he was only a jerk when the situation merited, so I wonder

---

[6] I've mentioned I'm a jerk, yes?

if I shouldn't cut the telemarketer a break. He's just trying to do his job, after all.

"Oh, Jesus, it's fine, all right? Record away. Add streaming video if you like, but I must warn you I'm wearing flannel sock-monkey pajamas. They're super-cute, though. The sock monkeys are driving little maroon convertibles, baking apple pies, and going bowling. Funny, though, they're not wearing bowling shoes. I wonder why that is? Since their feet are made out of socks, you'd think they'd slip all over the polished wood. That's a bowling alley begging for a lawsuit. Then there's one little guy who's in a hammock drinking a piña colada out of a coconut, which seems weird because you'd think he'd be more into banana daiquiris."[7]

After ten seconds of stunned silence, Some Guy continues, "Mrs. Fletcher, your husband is one of our best customers and—"

I interrupt him with a snort. "Sir, I know for a fact the *Men's Health* invoice sat unpaid in Fletch's in-box for almost four months, so if he's one of your best customers, I'd hate to know what your worst are like."

Admirably, Some Guy stays on point. "Yes, he is one of our best customers and because of this we'd like to send him a healthy eating book as a free gift."

A long awkward pause follows.

"And?" I finally ask.

"And I wanted to tell him he's receiving it."

---

[7] Another set of the sock monkeys are hand in hand—one's wearing a floral hat and the other's carrying flowers. I believe they are a same-sex couple, but don't find sapphic monkey love to be an appropriate topic of conversation with a virtual stranger, so I don't mention them.

More pausing.

"And?"

"Because he's one of our best customers."

"Yeah, you mentioned that. And?"

"Well, he gets to read the book free for twenty-one days, and if he likes it, he can keep this and we'll bill his credit card. Shall I go ahead and send it?"

See? This is why I'm allowed to be a little rude, particularly because we're on the federal Do Not Call list. I knew the "give me your credit card number" part was coming. So I reply, "Absolutely not."

"Mrs. Fletcher, I don't think you understand. The book is free and I'll—"

"Wrong. No charge for three weeks does not equal free. Plus, you're already well aware of our track record of not returning things in a timely fashion. I guarantee that if you send this to us, we'll forget to get it back in time and then we'll be stuck with a book we didn't want in the first place. Then we'll likely ignore the invoice, it will go to collections, and suddenly this stupid 'free' fifteen-dollar book will be a $276 ding on our credit record, my phone will ring all day with more unwanted calls, and then poor Lindsay Lohan will have to go naked![8] Sorry, not interested, but thanks for calling."

I hear fingers flying across pages. He bleats, "Wait! I will include a postage-paid envelope and he'll simply have to—"

"Thanks, but no."

"—drop it in the mail before the twenty-one days and—"

---

[8] And hasn't the poor dear had enough problems lately without adding a public indecency charge?

"I said no, but thanks again."

Three strikes and you're out, pal. Push me again and even Superman would agree it's time to fight.

"Well, Mrs. Fletcher, maybe you should let your husband decide, so I'll just go ahead and—"

Oh. No. He. Didn't.

"Listen, *you*, Mr. Script-Reading, Non-Flannel-Sock-Monkey-Pajama-Acknowledging Guy, let me be as clear as possible here. *Do. Not. Send. The. Book. Okay?* Testing, testing, one, two, three, do not send the book. Were you able to get that bit on tape? If so, play it back and get to the part where I tell you not to send the book. Ooh, play it right now and I can tell you 'no' in stereo! Better yet, how 'bout I 'splain in pidgin Spanish? Book-o no send-o because pork-chop-o ruin-o. *Sí? Sí*, book-o no send."

"But—"

"Listen, I've gotta scoot. Lindsay Lohan is *not* going to dress herself in desert camouflage capri pants, okay?"

Spirit broken, Some Guy gives it one halfhearted, last-ditch effort. "If your husband decides differently, he can call me at 800—"

"I've got your number fifteen times on my caller ID already. Thanks and have a lovely day!"

I take the phone off the hook and stick it in a drawer. Then I return to my computer to look for a site where I can dress up paper-doll Superheroes. Superman's Fortress of Solitude's got to be cold and I bet the guy could use a toasty-warm pair of sock-monkey pajamas.

To: angie_at_home, carol_at_home, wendy_at_home,
jen_at_work
From: jen@jenlancaster.com
Subject: *good news!*

Hey, all,

Excellent news—my mother has retired from her job so she
can come with me on book tour, which as of yet my publisher
has no plans to send me on.

However, if they do ship me off, she and my father are totally
coming, thus assuring I will be policing up wet towels and
glasses full of partial dentures in hotel rooms across the conti-
nent. (I may have mentioned that traveling with my parents is
like herding cats. Cats who drink scotch.)

Yay, me!

Jen

To: angie_at_home, carol_at_home, wendy_at_home, jen_at_work
From: jen@jenlancaster.com
Subject: *smashed*

Greetings from the couch,

If the past week is any indication of the coming month, my liver will be gone entirely by New Year's Day. As is now, it's already shriveled to the size, shape, and consistency of a lump of coal due to my heroic intake of liquor so far this holiday drinking season. The worst of it was Saturday at the open-bar birthday party when I told the waitress to bring me "anything pink" and thus discovered cherry margaritas.

Cherry margaritas.

I'd expostulate about how good they were, but apparently I im-bibed so much that I've completely lost the ability to put coher-ent thoughts on a page.

(Think I'm kidding? It's taken me an *hour* to write four tiny para-graphs.)

(And then I didn't even use the word "expostulate" correctly.)

(Of course, Fletch drank so much he can no longer recognize the letter *W*, but that's a story for another day.)

Speaking of writing, way before the book ever sold I envisioned the following scene:

Setting: Me, standing on the New York Times' *book reviewer's lawn, newspaper and pile of empty beer bottles at my side. I commence hurling.*

"Oh, yeah? Well, maybe I think *you're* pedantic and magniloquent, too!"

smash

"And as soon as I look up those words, you're *really* in trouble!"

smash

"Complete disregard for the traditional rules of grammar and excessive use of profanity?"

smash

"Oh, I will show you!"

smash

"A complete disregard!"

smash

"For traditional rules!"

smash

"Of grammar!"

smash

"Motherfucker!"

smashity-smash

Anyway, I just learned the first review of *Bitter* comes out December 15. I've heard the publication is brutal, so I'm already terrified, particularly because it's a memoir. That's *my life* detailed in those pages, so if they hate the book, that translates to them hating *me*.

Fortunately, I've got a *lot* of empty bottles around here.

And now there's some Alka-Seltzer with my name on it,

Jen

The Holiday Drinking Season

For me the best day of the year and the kickoff to the whole holiday season is November 5. Known as Guy Fawkes Day[1] in the United Kingdom, it's marked by villages building bonfires to burn Guy Fawkes in effigy and everyone eating a variety of toffee-based treats and watching fireworks displays. It's a huge annual celebration, second only to the *other* celebration that occurs simultaneously across the pond—my birthday. Unfortunately, today's October 31, which means not only do I have to wait five more days before I can start rejoicing again about my own birth, but I also have to get through my least favorite holiday first.

Fletch and I are on our way into the house from the garage when our neighbor Dan walks out his back door, dressed in a stethoscope and surgical scrubs, complete with bloodstains.

---

[1] Guy Fawkes was a traitor to the crown and tried to burn down Parliament.

Since he works in information technology, I assume it's a costume or else *someone* at IBM had a terrible afternoon.

"Jen, Fletch, hello!" Dan calls. "Big night, huh? You guys ready for it?"

"Yeah," I halfheartedly reply.

"What do you think?" He points at himself and does a little twirl. "Got the blood from my friend who's a butcher so I'd look realistic. Nice, huh?"

"I admire your authenticity," says Fletch.

Dan adjusts his surgical mask. "So, what are you guys going to dress as for Halloween?"

I field this one. "We're going to be dressed as two fat people hiding inside a dark house not giving out candy."

"Ha! You guys are a riot—have fun tonight!" He loads a case of beer into his Jeep and pulls away, blissfully unaware that I'm totally serious. As a matter of fact, the bag I'm carrying contains a box of garbage bags and thick masking tape that I plan to use to cover all the windows as soon as we get inside. If we had any money, we'd do what other grown-ups do—go out to dinner during trick-or-treat hours. Unfortunately, we're low on cash; Fletch doesn't get paid until the fifth, and what money he has had *better* be earmarked for something pretty.

To say I hate Halloween would be an understatement, although I'll admit I loved it as a child. Thirty years after the fact, I can still recall who gave out the full-sized candy bars[2] and who passed out apples, which were subsequently thrown back at their houses the second they shut their doors. Yes, I

---

[2] Thank you, Mrs. Sweeney!

318 · Jen Lancaster

admit that was bratty, but have you *any idea* how long it takes to do Ace Frehley's makeup properly? And then find a way to make your boots silver without spray paint because your mom says you can probably wear them another winter?[3] And rat your hair so much that even Johnson's No More Tangles can't get all the knots out and you have to use scissors? Surely that deserves a Milky Way! I'd have preferred if people had simply gone to the movies than waste my time with a stupid piece of fruit. The kid universe does not continue to spin on its axis in anticipation of being given the kind of "treat" that can already be found in a big wooden bowl in the middle of the kitchen table, and—

Ahem.

Anyway, enjoy Halloween as an adult? Not so much. It's a holiday that serves no purpose in my opinion. Personally, I like my pumpkins uncarved and my doorbell unrung. And if I'm lucky enough to have a big bag of candy? The last thing I want to do is share it. The whole concept annoys me and smacks of extortion and general thuggery—"Trick or Treat. Give me something good to eat, *or I will mess your shit up.*" Is this a lesson we want to teach our children? Plus, I was hurling apples thirty years ago and I was a sweet little girl from the suburbs. So opening the door for those scary city kids today? Who would *so* cut me given the chance? Nope, not happening.

Most of all, I would rather quaff a cat litter colada than have to wear a costume. I despise seeing adults duded up for Halloween, especially when they're supposed to be working

---

3 Aluminum foil, BTW.

professional jobs; regardless of what you might think, I assure you, it is not cute, charming, or kitschy. For example, every year I seem to have to do banking on October 31. And every freaking year I wind up conducting my transaction with a teller in a gorilla suit.

And really?

Nothing builds confidence in one's financial institution more than handing over one's paycheck to a creature not wearing pants, especially at my crappy bank, which is not only located in a grocery store but is entirely staffed by gang-bangers.

I envision going into my bank after I get my first book royalty check, and I expect to have this conversation . . .

"Hi. I have a sizable[4] check here and I'm not sure what to do with it. Since you're my banker, I'm hoping you can advise me on how to utilize these funds to the best advantage," I'll say.

"Chure, man," he'll reply.

"Should I invest in a money-market fund? Pay off debts? Use it as a down payment on a home to build equity? Do a bit of each?"

"Dunno. Lemme see da check first." He'll hold out a giant, furry paw and will walk my check over to the manager, who apparently chose not to wear a costume. Although, when your neck is covered in gang tats, who needs additional adornment?

"Well, what do you think?" I'll ask them both.

In unison, "Man, we think you should buy some rims!"

Fletch unlocks our back door and the dogs rocket off their

---

[4] Please, God.

respective ends of the couch and hurtle in to greet us. They station themselves in the front window and bark each time a blade of grass waves or a leaf falls off a tree. The activity exhausts them, their looming presence in the windows scares off would-be intruders, and our walls are thick and no one can hear them, so we've yet to come up with a compelling reason to discourage this behavior because tired dogs equal dogs less likely to eat delicious shoes. I go to the front door and get the mail, shrieking and dropping to my belly to army-crawl back to the kitchen, when I spot a little girl in a Princess Jasmine costume walk by with her mother.

Fletch, by the way, does not share my fear and hatred of Halloween. He rolls his eyes and sorts through the envelopes I've just delivered. He asks, "So you were scared by a registered trademark of the Walt Disney Corporation?"

"How was I supposed to know they were getting into a car? They could have been coming here. And then what, huh?"

"Then you would have answered the door, told her you liked her costume, and given her one of the mini Snickers bars we bought specifically for those kids who show up here before we finish 'securing the perimeter.'"

As a graduate of the School of Snappy Retorts and Clever Rejoinders, I respond by telling him, "Shut up."

"If being home without the protection of our garbage-bag shutters is going to elevate your base level of crazy, why don't you run to the bank and deposit this while I put them up?" He hands me a rebate check from a recent hardware purchase.

"Thank you. I will do just that." I grab my raincoat and keys and drive over to the grocery store–bank, bumping into no fewer than three Napoleon Dynamites[5] on my way from the parking lot. I stand in line behind someone in disco clothing with an enormous Afro and platform shoes, and can't for the life of me tell if it's a costume.[6] I shuffle through the line, and when a normal girl in regular clothes calls me to her window, I let out a sigh of relief.

"Oh, thank God," I say. "It's always my luck that—" But before I can finish, the girl is called away by another employee. A moment later, a different banker comes up to my window.

Of course he's dressed in a gorilla suit.

I tell him I have a deposit and he holds out a giant, furry paw.

Happy fucking Halloween.

We've managed to avoid the deluge of trick-or-treaters, Fletch by working on his laptop in the back of the house, and me by watching TV with lights off and headphones on in the front. At eleven p.m., I think it's probably safe to tear down the plastic, so I tackle the first floor and Fletch takes care of the second. When we're done we get ready for bed. After I've washed my face and put on my nightgown, I move the dogs off my side of the bed and lie down. When I look up I notice

---

[5] Here's the thing. I love Target; I've made that abundantly clear. But when Target begins to sell "Vote for Pedro" shirts, any hip indie cred you may have once garnered from wearing one is *gone*.

[6] It's a tiny bit badass, and I find myself wishing this is that person's own unique style.

one of our ornate, very heavy, and exceptionally stabby-looking curtain rods has come loose.

"Fletch? Fletch! Come here!" He strolls out of the bathroom holding a book, walking at a pace that makes me glad I wasn't choking.

"You rang, madam?"

"Yes! Look at that—the curtain rod is barely hanging on by a screw. It's about to come out of the wall."

"How about that." He gets into bed and opens his book.

"I bet it came loose when we were either hanging or removing those plastic bags."

"Probably."

I watch him as his eyes travel down the page, making no movement to get up. "Well?" I ask.

"Well, what?"

"Aren't you going to fix it?"

"No, I'm not going to fix it. It's midnight. I'll get to it tomorrow."

"But it looks like it will fall *right now*."

He flips a page. "It'll be fine."

"No, I don't think it will. Look how loose it is." I demonstrate by yanking on it so that the sharply curlicued end dips even more precariously down toward my pillow.

"I wouldn't worry about it."

"*Of course* I'm going to worry about it. That's how I roll. I worry. About everything. Do I need to remind you of my head-in-the-toilet phobia?"

"I forgot about that."

"Well, what if this thing falls down during the night? It might stab me in the eye!"

He yawns and stretches. The bad thing about being a drama queen is when something potentially big finally does happen, no one takes you seriously. "It won't fall."

"But what if it does? I'll be blinded! I can't be blind. How would I put on eye makeup? And how would I get around? Last week I saw a blind guy get off the bus and his pointy-stick-dealie didn't alert him to the solid sheet of Plexiglas one foot up because you know those bus shelters are open at the bottom and *splat!* He totally bit it! And I laughed! I mean, not until I helped him maneuver around it. But the second he was out of earshot I practically wet my pants. Christ, one second he's tooling along all blind but happy and the next, *wham!* His face got all smushed up against the plastic and then he bounced off. A week later and it's still funny!" I stand and begin to pace, and the dogs, frightened by the tone of my voice, slink off to cower in the guest bathroom.

I catch my breath and continue. "Shit, I'm not good at navigating public transportation fully sighted—there's *no way* I could do it as a blind person. And if some random commuter laughed at my disability like I did Mr. Smashy O'Plexiglas, I'd swing my pointy white stick at the sound of their voice like they were a piñata! Then I'd get arrested and I *cannot be blind and in jail!* And even if the rod only stabbed me in one eye, I couldn't wear an eye patch because not only would it totally ruin my birthday but it would also mess up my hair."

I stand on top of the mattress, hands on my hips, glowering down at Fletch. He turns another page. "You present a compelling argument."

"So you'll fix it?"

"Yes."

I smirk. "Good."

"Tomorrow." He flips off the light on his nightstand.

"Arrggh! Why are you so willing to dick around with my vision? How is this a chance you're okay with taking? I mean, if I go blind because you're too lazy to go downstairs and get the stuff to fix this—which would take all of five minutes, by the way—how will you live with yourself? I think this pointy bastard's coming down tonight and you know how often I'm right. What if I'm right *right now* and I get blinded because you couldn't lift a finger to take the slightest effort to prevent it? So, what would you do then, huh? What? Tell me, fat boy, *What would you do?*" I begin to nudge him with my foot.

Fletch sits back up and turns his light on again and I can see him processing the various scenarios. He scratches his head and finally he says, "That is a dilemma, but I guess . . . I guess . . . I guess I'd owe you a Coke."

"Fine!" I shout, taking my pillow and putting it down at the other end of the bed. I figure I can probably live with being stabbed in the toe, and don't think for a minute I wouldn't make him carry me around. "You know what? I'd better get the best birthday present *ever* after this."

He rubs my calf. "No worries. You'll get what you deserve."

🎁

I receive a carpet shampooer for my birthday.

But the joke's on him, because it's exactly what I wanted.

Not content to celebrate the big day in one state, I go to my parents' house in Indiana for the weekend. As a gesture to Fletch, I don't force him to come with me this time. He loves my family, but sometimes they're a bit of a handful. I mean, I didn't get this way on my own, you know? Plus my parents are moving closer to my brother's family soon, so I want to get another visit or two in at the old homestead before the house sells.

Fresh from reading *The Da Vinci Code*, my parents and I spend a great deal of time chatting about Sir Isaac Newton. Big Daddy marvels how the bulk of Newton's accomplishments took place over an eighteen-month span. Can you imagine? Shoot, I've gone eighteen months without returning a library book. We wonder if minds that great exist today, and if so, would they have been able to break away from their BlackBerrys and IMs and TiVos long enough to come up with the concept of gravity and the advancement of heliocentrism. Speaking from purely personal experience with said devices, I'd say no. I mean, TiVo? I can record *Lost* and *Veronica Mars* at the same time. *We are on the other side of the looking-glass here, people.*

We also talk about this "family planning" clinic I always pass when I take Fletch to work. A lot of times when I drive by, I see a bunch of Catholic clergy lined up next to the door. We discuss the efficacy of this strategy, wondering if in fact their presence stops women from seeking birth control, and thus spurs more unwanted pregnancies. We don't come up with any answers (which really wasn't our goal anyway); rather, my point here is it's kind of nice to have been spawned from people who can use "efficacy" in a sentence.

Our conversation wraps up with an examination of modern literature versus the classics. My mother has recently become addicted to Jane Austen and talks about how dark the

Brontë sisters are in comparison. My father prattles on about the genius of Arthur Conan Doyle, and even though our tastes in reading material vary greatly, we all agree Thomas Hardy (brilliant though he may be) bores us silly with his three-page descriptions of brocaded upholstery.

Please keep the above in mind as I detail what happens next.

"Jen, come here, I need your help," my mother calls down the stairs, where I'm having coffee with my dad.

"What's up, Mom?" I join my mother in the guest room, which she calls the Heritage Room because (a) it's filled with family photos, and (b) she can be incredibly queer like that. Fortunately, I did finally convince her to pack away Sandy, the previous inhabitant of this room. Sandy was the doll my mom made me in fourth grade. She was life-sized and wore my Brownie uniform and was one of the best Christmas presents I ever got. Unfortunately, Fletch found her flat-out creepy and never slept well in the room because he was afraid Sandy was going to come to life and strangle him with her long, cotton-stuffed panty-hose arms.

"I'd like you to help me move this piece of furniture downstairs. The neighborhood is having a garage sale and I want to sell it." She points to the one thing in their house I desperately want. (Many a time I've been tempted to put a "Jen" sticker on it, like in that episode of *Frasier* when he thinks he's dying and Niles claims all his stuff.)[7] Anyway, this

---

[7] Note to my brother, Todd: I also have dibs on the Union Jack–draped Royal Doulton bulldogs in the china cabinet. (You can have the big TV—I don't want that monstrosity in my house.)

gorgeous Shaker-style buffet would be perfect in my house, and it's decided that I'm going to take it because my parents can be that kind of cool.

While readying the piece for the big trip down the stairs, we determine the cabinet doors need to be taped shut. "Mom? These are going to fly open when we put it on an angle. Can you please find some tape so we can keep them closed?"

My mother returns promptly. "Um, are you trying to be funny? Because I'm pretty sure Scotch tape isn't going to work on two heavy maple doors." However, when she returns with duct tape, we realize it really makes no difference because *someone* has just polished the entire thing and it is slick with lemon oil.

Oh, yes, I think you know where this is going.

A different yet equally clueless member of the family helps me maneuver this piece to the staircase. (At this point I'm going anonymous about who's who due to my desire to get those damn bulldogs.) In a nod to said member's love of all things Sir Isaac Newton, this person thinks we'd be better flipping it over and allowing gravity to propel it down the stairs, instead of the more controlled method of carrying it down step, pause, step, pause. I'm to stand in front and navigate and he's going to follow, supporting his half of the weight in back as we do a controlled freefall.

About halfway down the stairs, someone loses his grip and suddenly my body is the only thing standing between the wall and two hundred pounds of freshly oiled maple, careening toward the landing at approximately the speed of light.

All I can think is, *Dear God, please don't let me be hurt to the extent that I must be rushed to the same local hospital where they accidentally treated me for* hepatitis *when I was fifteen years old.*[8]

Fortunately, the buffet strikes me in the back with such force that I'm thrown down the remaining seven stairs. As I float through the air in slow motion, I think, *The realtor is going to be here in ten minutes and maybe the house will have a better chance of selling if there's not a Shaker-style buffet sticking halfway out of the wall, thus preventing my parents from moving closer to their beloved grandchildren.* And because I am a good daughter[9] I'm able to reposition and hurl myself back in front of it to protect the wall at the end of the stairway and to keep the piece from smashing into a lot of greasy wood chips.

I find myself up against the sea grass wallpaper, two hundred pounds of fine—albeit slightly oily—Shaker furniture pinning me in place, when Captain Obvious finds it germane to mention in his lifelong Boston accent, "Hey, Jennifah? I think I may have lost my grip," while Mrs. Captain Obvious muses, "I wonder if I shouldn't have polished it first?"

No. Shit.

Yet people still wonder why after being around my family, I always threaten to spend my *next* holiday in Hawaii.

---

[8] I had mono. Although I wonder who those quacks thought I'd been kissing, anyway—Tommy Lee?

[9] Despite overwhelming evidence to the contrary. Please see chapter 6 in *Bitter Is the New Black* for more details.

Thanksgiving comes—and goes—and Fletch and I have vowed to never speak of it again. Suffice it to say Hawaii looks pretty damn good right about now.

Fletch, the dogs, and I drive home for Christmas and the trip is entirely without incident. Regardless of how much we watch the Weather Channel, we seem to have an uncanny ability to hit a big storm and the three-hour trip takes more like nine. But this time? Smooth sailing across dry, empty roads. We even manage to find a radio station we can agree on—although it's probably because we now have XM rather than any sort of Christmas miracle—so we don't spend the trip toggling between a Rammstein[10] CD and the soundtrack to *Cabaret* in the kind of musical compromise that satisfies no one.

Instead of the usual cartwheels and backflips the dogs normally enjoy while we're driving on a snowy, truck-filled expressway, they settle right down and nap from the second we leave the 60647 until the moment we arrive. (They do stir when we give them each a cheeseburger—they aren't machines, for God's sake.)

We spend the trip recounting yesterday's adventure. Since Fletch is off until after New Year's we decide we're going to do something fun every day. Although most of our time is taken up with holiday parties, yesterday we went to a place in the suburbs with artificial snow, little ski slopes, and an inner-tube run. Hungover as we were, we decided skiing would take too much effort, so we opted for sledding.

---

[10] German death metal, precisely as bad as you'd think.

The hill was quite steep but it didn't matter because a towrope pulled us up, so we avoided having to climb. The first run we did alone—it was fast and fun, but kind of tame. Next, Fletch and I decided to see what it was like to ride down together, so we held on to each other's snow tubes.

There's a physics principle at work here and I'm not sure what it is. All I know is that four hundred pounds of Republican careen down an ice-covered incline about ten times faster than if each party went separately. We flew down the hill at Mach 10, pulling the same g-force as a space shuttle launch. It was as though we'd coated our tubes with nonnutritive cereal varnish,[11] because we were going so fast we sailed off the hill, across the highway, and into the Wal-Mart parking lot.

Okay, that's not exactly true.

But all the stupid little kids who didn't get out of our way learned an interesting lesson about force equaling mass times acceleration.

We're still laughing about the day as we pull into my parents' driveway. "You know," I tell Fletch, "I *should* feel guilty about toppling them like so many bowling pins . . . yet here I am."

"You were supposed to be steering because I was backward. I didn't see that one kid until he went flying over our heads."

"I couldn't steer; I was too busy covering my eyes."

"We've got to go there again before I head back to work."

"Definitely." We bring the dogs in the house, hug my par-

---

[11] Best. Holiday movie. Ever.

ents, and load in bag after bag of presents. It's the first time we've been able to go all-out for the holidays in a long while, so we've been really generous to thank everyone for their support over the past few years. On my last trip in from the car, I slip on the one patch of ice anywhere in Indiana,[12] but otherwise our time passes without incident.

We spend three days entertaining each other and marvel at how well the holiday is going. The fire department doesn't have to come,[13] no one winds up passed out under the dining room table after eating all the vodka-laden fruit from the champagne punch for breakfast,[14] we have running water,[15] the oven works,[16] and Dad doesn't knock the grill into the pool.[17] We end up having exactly the kind of good, old-fashioned, functional-family holiday you see in greeting cards and it's borderline glorious. The food's great, the company's even better, and Mother Nature gets into the spirit of things and gives us our White Christmas after all. I can't imagine how I ever thought Hawaii would be better than this.

It's the night before we leave and we're all gathered by the fire having hot chocolate and cookies and watching *Family Guy*. Quagmire, the show's resident sex fiend, makes a comment about a "reach-around" with a spider monkey and we all snicker.

Except my mother, that is.

----

[12] Naturally, located in my parents' driveway.
[13] Christmas '82.
[14] Fourth of July '86.
[15] Christmas '97.
[16] Thanksgiving '98.
[17] Labor Day '99.

"What's a reach-around?" she asks.

Fletch, Dad, and I sit there silently, unwilling to meet each other's eyes, and trying not to laugh because that will only encourage my mother. I screw up and look at Fletch and we both start snorting.

Uh-oh. The floodgates have just opened.

She sits up on the couch. "No, really, what's a reach-around?"

We giggle uncomfortably, saying nothing.

Mom starts to get frustrated. If there's a joke, damn it, she wants to know why it's funny. "Someone tell me what a reach-around is right now. Fletch, what is it? Have you had one? Did you like it?"

"I am *not* having this conversation with my mother-in-law. Now if you'll excuse me, I'm going to wash my brain out with beer," says Fletch before disappearing into the garage.

"Ron, what's a reach-around?"

"Martinis!" he exclaims. "Who wants a martini? Yeah, I'm going to go make martinis. I'm going to go make them right now." My father sprints out of the family room with the kind of quickness you'd never expect from a man with seventy-one-year-old knees.

She turns to me, determined. "Jen? What is it?"

"Mom, does the fact your question just cleared the room tell you anything? Like, maybe we're all incredibly embarrassed and would prefer this line of questioning to stop immediately?"

"Oh, please." She brushes off their leaving with a flip of her wrist. "You came out of my body. The least you can do is explain what a reach-around is."

"Look it up on UrbanDictionary.com if you're so curious because I am not telling you. You know how modest I am; I couldn't explain it to you if my life depended on it."

She crosses her arms and taps her foot impatiently. "For heaven's sake, Jennifer, you're what—thirty-eight years old? Grow up and just tell me. Did I have a reach-around when I gave birth to you?"

"No." I squeeze my eyes closed and shake my head.

She gestures toward her dog, Bruno, who immediately slinks out of the room to join our two already hiding under the dining room table. Dad and Fletch are still missing. They may be under there as well. "Does he do a reach-around?"

"No."

"Why not?"

"No thumbs. Can we *please* change the subject?"

"Did your Dad get a reach-around when he was in the marines?"

I shudder. "I'm leaving to watch TV in the den now." I grab my cocoa and dump it in the sink, deciding to exchange it for wine.

While I attempt to scuttle out of the room, Mom points to her chest and asks, "Are these my reach-arounds?" She then gestures lower. "What about this?"

"Gah!" I stop pouring in lieu of grabbing the entire bottle.

"Why won't you answer me?"

"Because you are making the baby Jesus cry right now."

She finally gets the hint and reach-arounds are not mentioned again in mixed company, *thank God.* Eventually the guys find their way back to the family room, but Dad changes the channel to *It's a Wonderful Life,* secure in the knowledge that Jimmy Stewart will never, ever mention a Cleveland Steamer.

Today I wake to a mélange of delicious aromas and the sound of carols echoing though the house. My brother and his family are on their way so my mother's starting another round of cooking. Because of a miscommunication about kennel arrangements[18] we're not overlapping our holiday visits this year. I'm sorry not to see Todd's wife and children, although I can't help but notice there's a lot less arguing when we're apart. (Although I'll admit it was fun being together last year, even though I slept in the morning of the tsunami and awoke to a house full of Asian weather-pattern experts.)

I throw on my slippers, pull a sweatshirt over my sock-monkey pajamas,[19] and come down for coffee. My mother is the only other person up—I imagine the boys are sleeping it off right now—and she putters around the kitchen making a variety of tempting breakfast treats.

"Hey, Mom. Something smells delicious."

"You're up early! Good morning!" My mom kisses me on the forehead and hands me a cup of French roast.

"Anything I can do to help?"

"Um . . ." Her eyes scan the cooking projects scattered throughout the kitchen. "Yes, yes, actually. There is one thing."

"What's that? You need me to cook the bacon?"

---

18 Our dogs *hate* my brother's dog and we avoid incidents by keeping them separated.

19 Big Daddy likes to keep the house at a bracing forty-two degrees. The one Christmas the heat went out, we didn't even notice for a couple of days.

"Got it already, thanks."

"Want me to make mimosas?"

"Aren't you driving back today?"

"Oh, yeah, scratch that. I guess I can spend one morning without booze. So what do you need? Want me to slice the English muffins? Or feed the dogs?"

She pours herself a mug of tea and sits down at the breakfast bar next to me. She places her hand over mine, giving me a couple of pats and a wide smile. "No, no, it's all taken care of." Aw, it's good to be home.

"Then what do you need?"

She clutches my wrist and holds me in place. "I need you to tell me what a reach-around is."

-☼-

A couple of points to be made here:

First, I completely blame my mother for inspiring my subsequently heroic holiday liquor intake.

Second, she still doesn't know what a reach-around is.

Third, Fletch and I are definitely going to Hawaii next Christmas.

Alone.

To: angie_at_home, carol_at_home, wendy_at_home,
jen_at_work
From: jen@jenlancaster.com
Subject: *d-day*

Hey, all,

Do you have any idea how surreal it is to walk into a bookstore
and be greeted by your own book?

Last night I needed to refer to a certain book in order to complete a new proposal. So after running other glamorous errands
such as buying kitty litter and grout cleaner, we popped into the
Barnes & Noble at Webster Place. Although I knew there was a
possibility my book would already be for sale, I didn't expect to
run into an entire display of it before I even set foot into the
second set of double doors . . .

. . . yet there it was.

Mesmerized, Fletch and I gawped at the stack until we drew
curious stares from the other patrons. We finally bustled
through the doors, took five steps into the store, and bam!
There it was again on the nonfiction table, nestled in with all
the other new releases. I ran my hands over it to make sure it
was real, fingers tracing the blue foil of the dress on the cover.
I kept opening it to the last page to look at my photograph,
but had someone else's face been there instead, I wouldn't
have been surprised. It didn't feel real. I mean, how could the

past three years of my life be distilled onto thirty-five square inches of a bookstore table?

I looked at *Bitter* among the sea of other books and honestly felt like an impostor. How on earth did *my* book end up on the table with a bunch of *real* authors? Shoot, fifteen minutes previous I was buying cans of Chicken with Stars soup to bring for lunch at my temp job. How the hell did I wind up by Elie Wiesel? For God's sake, Wiesel wrote about surviving a litany of terrors in a Nazi death camp with dignity and honor, whereas I cried like a little bitch about not getting my hair colored. (So in case you're wondering, yes, it's possible to be humbled, embarrassed, and exhilarated all at the same time.)

We worked our way through the store and found the book in two other places—in the memoir section and on a paperback favorites table on the second level. In each instance, we stood and stared and stared. It was such a strange feeling watching people pick up and look at my book. I was dying to solicit their first impression and yet I didn't want to know if they thought it sounded kind of dumb. Somehow I thought beating a patron with a Harry Potter book would not bode well for my reputation within B&N. So, conflicted, I finally stepped away from the table.

As we made our way over to the café, we encountered the biggest surprise—a giant poster with my name, face, and book jacket on it. Being the suave, urbane sophisticate I am, I, um, certainly didn't shriek, "Holy cats, that's *me*!!" Nor, um, did I then stand next to it for a good ten minutes to see if anyone recognized me. (Just because I felt like a big, fat impostor didn't mean my natural propensity for vanity suddenly vanished.)

Since this is the store where I'm doing the reading this weekend, I figured I should chat with someone to find out any additional details. With a grin I couldn't hide, I talked to the person at the customer service desk and asked if there was anything specific I needed to know. She politely relayed the information I needed to know and . . . that was it.

I'm not sure what I was expecting when I spoke with the clerk—accolades? Admiration? Recognition? Perhaps a choir of angels trumpeting in the background? But there was none forthcoming. I may as well have been asking where the ladies' room was for all of her matter-of-factness.

After I thought about it, I realized being an author in a bookstore is a lot like being a bride—on *your* day, you feel like you're the only person to have ever gotten married and it's the be-all and end-all of your existence. But the truth is, for professionals involved in the wedding industry, they see brides every day and it's no longer a big deal. Same thing must hold for booksellers. How can they be surprised when they see an author? Books are their whole business.

Anyway, we eventually stopped wandering around in a haze and came home. And although I left the house as a writer and came home an author, I found that nothing had changed. The cats still snuck onto the counter in our absence, and Maisy left yet another steaming "present" in the hallway. With the exception of fresh doody, everything was exactly the same.

So I guess I'd say seeing *Bitter* in the stores was bittersweet—exciting to see the culmination of my life's dream, but sobering to realize that my dream's there . . . nestled between thousands and thousands of others.

See you Saturday,

Jen

from the desk of Miss Jennifer A. Lancaster

Dear Zontick LLC,

Currently you're auctioning autographed copies of my book on both Amazon and Barnes & Noble for almost $65.00 per copy.

The thing is, it seems like autographing a bunch of books would be something I'd remember, don't you think? Sure, there were a couple of copies left over after the signing event on Saturday, but they were here in Chicago. What's the likelihood of all of these few books ending up in NJ? Especially within a day of the signing?

More important, who in their right mind would pay $65.00 for my autograph?

Does a market for this exist??

If so, please give me a call—I've got a ton of unpaid bills, a drawer full of Sharpies, and a shitload of free time. We should talk.

Best,

Jen Lancaster

To: angie_at_home, carol_at_home, wendy_at_home, jen_at_work
From: jen@jenlancaster.com
Subject: *scat, rat or rat scat—your choice*

Yo,

This is the kind of day a gal *might* get a fat head with the local-media-double-barrel mentions in the *Chicago Sun-Times* and *Chicago Tribune* (and a second shout-out in Sunday's *Washington Post*).

Of course, I won't because I spent the morning in the backyard picking up *rat poop*.

You know, it's humbling enough to clean up dog mess, cat boxes, and Fletch's occasional WC misfires. (With his lack of depth perception, I honestly don't understand how he keeps from walking into walls.) But seriously, *rodent doody?* That's a new low and a surefire way to keep me from drinking my own Kool-Aid about the good press.

In other news, I suddenly feel like boiling my hands again.

Later,

the jenster

The Marquis de Sade
in Mary-Kate Clothing

hen I wake up this morning, I find myself sweating extra-virgin olive oil and cookie dough.

Wait, I should probably explain.

My book is coming out in a few months, and it's the first time since the dot-com crash that Fletch and I have had real reason to celebrate. And what better way to rejoice than eating, drinking, and being merry? So, despite my newfound commitment to physical fitness, the past sixteen days have been a blur of twinkle lights, holiday parties, and daring levels of overconsumption.

I ate some variety of cake daily for the better part of December—topped with delectable varieties of mousseline buttercream, chocolate ganache, coconut pecan, and cream cheese. I swallowed my own weight in miniature Key lime cheesecakes and oversized peanut butter balls. On Christmas Eve, I constructed a gingerbread house with fun-sized Hershey bar shingles and M&M masonry and laughed like I'd been possessed by Hansel himself as I ate it down to its cardboard foundation, only pausing to lick the powdered confectionary snow.

If it was sugar-coated, deep-fried, or con queso it found its way into my mouth, as did each horseradish-filled shrimp cocktail, cracked Dungeness crab leg, and drawn-butter-drenched lobster tail that crossed my path. I devoured everything served on a chip or at the end of a toothpick—oceans of guacamole, mountains of Swedish meatballs, a Grand Canyon full of cheese. I could create four food groups based solely on the kinds of sausages I inhaled. I partook of sweetly tangy bacon-wrapped figs, succulent honey-baked ham, spicy garlic mustard pork medallions—pretty much if it came from a pig, I called it dinner. Sure, I had a few vegetables, but only those swimming in beurre blanc or Hollandaise sauce. (Seriously, how do you *not* feel festive when you're double-fisting teriyaki-glazed spare ribs?)

I downed turkey legs during *A Christmas Story*, roasted cinnamon almonds while watching *Scrooged*, and inhaled an entire section of a six-foot sub during the *Married with Children–It's a Bundyful Life* special where Sam Kinison plays the foulmouthed angel.

And I can't forget to mention the other half of my holiday diet: the liquor. I imbibed vats of champagne, tankards of martinis, gallons of Bailey's Irish Cream, and snifter after snifter of cognac washing down every single bite of the buffet. I didn't miss a party, appetizer, or cocktail for sixteen whole days. And you know what? It was fantastic!

However, when I catch a glimpse of myself in the mirror this morning, I realize I look and feel (and let's be honest—probably smell) *exactly* like Marlon Brando. My glorious prime-rib-and-wine-soaked Holiday Eating and Drinking Orgy has taken its toll.

The formerly cute ex–sorority girl reflecting back at me is haggard, puffy, and utterly blown out. Her hair is twisted into unbrushable origami from too much sticky product and too many complicated up-dos; the artfully applied sparkle powder is flat and metallic, making the purple shadows under her eyes even deeper from too many nights heavy on food and laughter and short on sleep. The dehydration from swilling whole punch bowls of rum-tastic eggnog highlights every line on her face. Her joints ache from dashing from party to party in jeweled, ridiculously heeled shoes. The delicate skin on her lower lip is burned from a clove—not the cigarette, but the actual spice, hidden in the ham she shoved in her craw directly from the oven. Most disturbing is the way her flesh oozes over the straps of her once-loose cotton nightgown in lumpy blips and blobs. She's now soft in all the areas where she used to be hard.

She is—or rather, I am—a portrait of excess.

And in desperate need of a shower.

And a salad.

And a StairMaster.

And I will totally seek out those things.

As soon as I locate my liver and my "indoor voice."[1]

Oh, wait—the room just got all spin-y. Must lie down first.

---

[1] Last seen strolling hand in hand down Trader Joe's wine aisle, shouting, "Hell, yes, we need more fucking Merlot!"

I tend to go back and forth on my weight. Most of the time I'm okay with it, partially because of a narcissistic personality disorder, but mostly because Chicago isn't what you would call a "skinny" city. There's a reason the old *Saturday Night Live* "Superfan" skits rang true. You know, the guys who were always downing brats and beers between angioplasties? Shoot, take a stroll through the stands at Soldier Field and the men look a lot more like John Goodman than George Clooney. Part of the issue is there's no overt social pressure to exercise all the time here like there is in LA or Miami. And if people are dieting here, it's Atkins, and only because they're looking to add more beef and bacon to their daily intake. Matter of fact, Chicago was recently voted the Fattest City in America.[2] Yay, us!

Honestly, I don't look much different from other Chicagoans, so my recent thoughts of losing weight stemmed from health concerns, not vanity. However, when I find out a celebrity magazine plans to do a feature on my first book, I'm terrified at the thought of my photo near Jessica Simpson's. Take a picture of me in a crowd at Wrigley Field and I'd be wholly unremarkable. But next to La Simpson? I'm pretty sure I'd look like the parade-balloon version of her, especially after the deliciously disastrous Holiday Drinking Season.[3] And

---

[2] I'd like to think my discovery of the dessert aisle at Whole Foods helped propel us, sweaty and jiggling, over the finish line to beat other porky places like Houston and Kansas City.

[3] I imagine a bunch of people in Macy's smocks, scratching their heads wondering what happened to my towropes.

that? Is a reality check my fat ass simply cannot cash, so back off to the gym I go, full of good intentions and spandex pants.

I work out at a place called West Loop Gym, and ever since the *Biggest Loser* audition, holidays notwithstanding, I've been really good about going regularly. However, I'd considered joining the chichi East Bank Club, although it's actually more of an urban country club.[4] At a staggering 450,000 square feet, the facility is amazing—their cardio room alone is 20,000 square feet! But the issue is they have so many non-exercise-based amenities that I'd dig—a 60,000-square-foot sundeck, outdoor pools, wireless lounges, dining rooms with gourmet meals, spa and salon services—that I figured the place was a bit too "cowbell," so I chose not to join.

Okay, that's a lie.

In a rare instance of putting his foot down and actually meaning it, Fletch wouldn't pay for me to join. He said I'd go to work out and instead come home with a tan and a manicure. He claimed with my lack of self-discipline, I'd be the first person who got fatter because of her membership. I'd have argued with him . . . except he was right. So, the West Loop Gym it was.

Regardless, I'm glad—I kind of love this place; it's exactly what I need. The owners converted an old warehouse and kept the decor kind of minimal; there's no cheesy neon or checkerboard like in some gyms, just lots of preserved old brick and wood-beamed vaulted ceilings. The floor is made of some weird rubber, and when you walk you get a bit of a bounce in your step. The staff stresses "functional fitness"

---

[4] Oprah's a member!

and their philosophy is to do the kind of exercises that will make you strong for your day-to-day life—like by strengthening your abdominals so if you slip on a patch of ice, your core muscles will help you right yourself without injury.

With their emphasis on personal training, the gym's kept membership small, limiting themselves to about five hundred clients. This way, everyone gets one-on-one attention. Granted, they don't have a cedar sauna, but again, if I can sit motionless and read a book, it doesn't count as exercise. Besides, WLG does have a dedicated staff who routinely patrol the floor, happy to answer any technique or nutrition questions—basically, they make me feel as important as Oprah and you can't put a price on that.[5]

Not only does each employee know my name when I come in, I also never have to wait for a piece of equipment. Sometimes when I come here during the day I'm the only person in the cardio area. I like to pretend I'm Candy Spelling and this room is actually part of my house.

For the longest time, I was one of those dummies who were embarrassed about being big and working out in a public place. I wanted to tone up before joining a gym because I was afraid the other patrons would laugh at me. Now that I'm here, I realize it's just the opposite—I'm shocked at how kind and supportive the other members are. The more I chug away on the treadmill, the more people meet my eye and smile. So, a note to all the other big kids out there: If you're fat, you're a lot less likely to get mocked at the gym than if you're holding a Gotta Have It–sized cake-batter cone at Cold Stone Creamery. Think about it.

....

[5] I mean, past the $59/month I pay in dues.

348 · *Jen Lancaster*

Anyway, today's the day I get back in the saddle. I pull into the parking spot closest to the door and enter. I say hi to the nice girl[6] behind the desk.

"Jen!" she exclaims. "We missed you! Where've you been?"

Okay, sometimes belonging to a small gym has a downside. If you don't show up for a couple of days? They notice. And they mention it. For your own good. "You do *not* want to know. Suffice it to say I've been busy consuming the whole year's calorie count in the past couple of weeks."

Nice Girl laughs and pats her perfectly flat stomach. "Yeah, I hear you. I put on five pounds over the holiday."

"Ha!" I bark. "Amateur! I put on fifteen and at this point my underpants are cutting off my circulation." Oh, no. Did I say that out loud? Judging from the look on her face, I did.

"Hmm, perhaps I shouldn't keep you then?"

"Yeah, I've got some sweating to do. Going to change now—see you in a bit."

I change into a dove-gray pair of calf-length spandex pants, a fuchsia Champion T-shirt, and my cushy Nikes accented with the pink swoosh. I yank my hair back in my madras plaid do-rag and remove my watch.

The pearls, naturally, stay on.

I grab a towel and hit the cardio area. I decide I'm not going to go full force because I don't want to, you know, *die.* I select a treadmill with the best view of all four plasma TVs and I start to move, slowly, but gradually more surely. Ellen,

---

6 You'd think because they know my name, I'd know theirs . . . yet here we are.

CNN, and a couple of sports channels are my only companions in the cardio room. My heart thumps pretty hard, but it feels good.

My workout progresses nicely. I spend half an hour on the treadmill and do ten minutes on the elliptical machine. I get my heart rate into the fat-burning zone and break a decent sweat. Yay, me! I do a ten-minute cooldown on the bikes, deciding to skip the weight training for another day. Satisfied, I return to the locker room to change.

I'm congratulating myself for a job well done when the unthinkable happens.

I bend over to remove my sneakers and my pants explode. Let's milk it, shall we?

My.

Pants.

Explode.

Kaboom.

I struggle to remove what's left of the dove-gray material and hold it up for examination. The back side appears to have been taken out by a Scud missile. Or possibly the aftereffects of inhaling six pounds of creamy, nutty, imported Gouda at Shayla's pre–New Year's Eve New Year's bash. I shake my head and say to myself out loud, *"The camel's back? Just broke."*

I throw on my street clothes and march up to the reception desk. I hate myself for what I'm about to request, but it has to be done. It is time.

"Jen! Happy New Year!" Mike, a friendly kid with massive shoulders, is now working the desk. "I didn't see you come in. Hope you had a great holiday! So, how are you?" Not only does he know our names, but he knows all about us—like about Fletch's job,[7] our dogs, the new house, etc. He always asks how my writing's going, but I have no time for his pleasantries today because *I Am Resolved.*

"Resolved," I tell him.

He bends his head and holds a finger to his right ear while turning down the gym's sound system. "I'm sorry, Jen. I didn't quite catch what you said."

Louder, I repeat, "I said I'm *Resolved.* It pains me to do this but I need to"—I grit my teeth and straighten my spine—"schedule ongoing sessions with one of your personal trainers."

"That's great!" He's really enthusiastic about people getting fit and it would be adorable if it didn't make me want to kill-self-comma-others. He cheers and attempts to give me a high five, but I'm having no part of it. I'll suck it up and work out with a trainer, but damn it, I will *not* celebrate that fact. I hate that my lack of willpower over the buffet table has brought me to the point I need to pay someone to get me back on track. "Any specific goals you'd like to achieve?"

I hold up the spandex tatters. "Yes. I'd like to never explode out of my pants again."

He pauses for a moment, looking thoughtful. "So . . . weight loss?"

"Obviously. And thank you for not laughing. Now I won't have to gut you like a trout."

"Lemme take down your info for Tim." He writes my day-

---

[7] Shoot, *I'm* not even sure what he does for a living.

time phone number on a Post-it note for the owner. "Have you got a preference of who you want to work with?"

Without hesitation I tell him, "I want someone mean."

"Come again?"

"Mean. M-E-A-N. As in the opposite of nice."

"Okaaayy."

"Mike, please write this down. Tell Tim I can't train with someone who's going to offer me cheery *'You can do it!'* platitudes. I'm not motivated by positive reinforcement. I *need* mean. I require yelling. I want boot camp. Think drill sergeant. Better yet, think *Nazi* drill sergeant. And if he can holler at me about my deplorable eating habits, too? Even better."

Mike looks thoroughly confused. "So—"

I interrupt because I'm on a roll and I've got to get this out before I lose my nerve. "In order for me to be successful, I must have someone breathing down my neck, screaming at me that I'm worthless and weak if I can't give him *'one more effing squat!'*[8] He needs to shout at me until the tendons stick out on his neck. Because if my trainer doesn't do this, I won't give one hundred percent. And I need to give one hundred percent or else I'll be a fatty at my book events and that means Jessica Simpson wins."

"Um—"

"Seriously, I wrote and sold my book not because of the people who told me I could. Rather, I wanted to show up

---

[8] Actually, I'd prefer if he didn't swear. I find profanity unpleasant. Heh, kidding!

everyone who told me I couldn't. Make me mad enough and I'll be unstoppable."

"Wait—"

"Really? If I could hate my trainer? That would be ideal. I'd prefer to despise that person with the fire of ten thousand suns. So when I walk—nay, crawl—out of here at the end of my workouts, I want to lull myself to sleep by picturing my very talented and inspirational trainer getting hit by a bus. A bus that I am driving." I pause to take a breath, having not done so in the past five minutes. "Hey, are you getting all this down?"

"Well—"

"Anyway, there's a whole bunch of publicity already lined up for this spring and when *OK!* magazine writes up my book, I'd rather they not have the option to reference my gigantic ass. And thus, I need a trainer, because this getting thin business? Is obviously not happening on my own. So, can you guys set me up? Find me a trainer who fits my parameters so I can in turn fit my pants? Can you make it happen?" By the time I finish this diatribe, I'm in full-on, I-Am-Woman-Hear-Me-Roar mode, legs akimbo and hands on my hips. I defy this kid to tell me no.

Mike opens his mouth to speak a couple of times before sound actually comes out. "Um, well . . . yes. We can make this happen. That's what we do."

"Outstanding!"

"Except I don't know how to say all of that on a Post-it note."

"Oh."

"How about I just write 'Jen Lancaster—ass kick,' and have Tim call you?"

I smile and nod. "That'll work."

✉

When I reviewed the wall of framed trainer photographs yesterday, I assumed I'd be assigned to Steve, a former Mr. Arizona. He's definitely the most buff trainer on staff—his neck alone is the size of a California redwood! Sure, I prefer my neck less of a tree trunk rather than more, but I imagine he'll know how to do that and I'm confident he'd be the best guy to navigate the tricky waters of my quest for physical fitness.

I park right next to the door again and enter, swiping my membership card at the check-in desk. After stowing my bag and coat, I exit the locker room, expecting to find Steve, who'll be eager to kick my soon-to-be-smaller ass, but there's no sign of him. Where is he? I wonder. A slip of a girl in one of my gym's logo sweatshirts is milling around the desk, so I decide to ask her.

"Hi, I'm looking—" But before I can finish my sentence, she holds out a tiny mitt and delicately shakes my hand.

"Hi! You must be Jen! I'm Polly and we'll be training together today!" I take in Polly's slender neck and bandy arms. She's got an *itty bitty, would look like a sheet of paper if she turned sideways* torso and toothpick-variety legs. She's built less like the brick shithouse I was expecting and more like a ten-year-old Olympic figure skater. I don't fear her so much as I want to babysit her. I groan inwardly. *Oh, great*, I think, *I asked for the Marquis de Sade and instead I got an Olsen twin.*

I follow Polly[9] to the juice bar to go through a health assessment. After a quick discussion of my medical history[10] she asks about my fitness goals. Naturally I answer, "To not look tubby in the national media." We move on to discuss diet, and touch briefly on the Holiday Eating and Drinking Orgy. I watch her squirm when I mention the sheer caloric input, but even without her reaction I have a hard time taking her seriously. Shoot, this little gal probably hasn't had anything but lemon water and air-popped corn in all of her fourteen years on this earth, so how can I expect her to appreciate the virtues of a buttercream cupcake?

I follow along behind her to a mirrored training room, where we warm up doing stretches with small weights. I first have to watch her whip and twirl dumbbells around as though they're made of Styrofoam. *Fantabulous*, I think while rolling my eyes, *her effortless execution of these stupid exercises further disappoints me because I came here to exercise, not dance.*

Before I continue, I should mention that thirty-eight years' worth of red meat and gin have formed such a layer of blubber on my brain that it's incapable of comprehending anything not at face value. A mind not swimming in cholesterol and noncomedogenic wrinkle cream might have deduced that just because a trainer is wee doesn't mean she can't and won't *completely kick my fat ass.*

I huff and wheeze through the warm-up, and at the end of ten minutes my heart hammers and I've already sweated out every snickerdoodle I've ever consumed. *An anomaly,* my stu-

---

9 Who I'm already mentally referring to as "Mary-Kate."
10 Surprisingly good for a fat chick, yay, me!

pid, lardy brain tells me. *Surely the real workout won't be so hard—that bit was just to get the blood flowing. Little Mary-Kate's probably exhausted, too. I bet she suggests we blow off the session, grab our enormous hobo bags, and get skim lattes at Starbucks! She'll drive so we can smoke in the car and then we'll go buy big plastic jewelry to wear with our shawls before we post a bunch of smack about Ashley on all the fan sites!*

We walk[11] to a larger training room that is filled with a bunch of innocuous-looking items. There are no heavy objects or scary machines, only harmless stuff like little traffic cones, jump ropes, and big, bouncy balls that remind me of my favorite childhood toy, the Hoppity Hop. *Whee!*, the gray matter in my head cheers. *Hoppity Hops! Happ-ity, hopp-ity fun!* "Hey, Mary— I mean Polly, when can we do stuff on those?" I ask, gesturing to the wall of brightly colored orbs.

"We'll get there," she replies.

I lurch through four circuits of exercises, each specifically designed to show how the past six months, during which I've been almost a daily visitor to this gym, have had absolutely no effect on my endurance, balance, or strength.[12]

I'm cowed, whipped, and dripping Alfredo sauce from each of my pores, and Mary-Kate chirps, "Okay! You asked for it! It's ball time!" Two things to note here: (a) my corpulent cerebral cortex gasping with glee because it is *incapable of learning*, and (b) that "perky" is the new "sadomasochistic."

Mary-Kate chooses a large pink ball and sits on it. She lies back and shows me how to do a crunch, legs out and bent at

---

[11] Rather, one of us walks—the other limps.
[12] Which is *so not fair*.

the knee, butt balanced on the ball, and arms crossed in front like an Egyptian mummy. With deft fluidity, she demonstrates how *very, very* easy it is to rise to a forty-five-degree angle. She cuts through the air again and again with ballerina-like grace until she's sure I grasp the exercise's proper form.[13]

"Your turn," she sings, rolling the ball toward me. I arrange myself on it per her instructions. *Pfft,* boasts my chunky cerebellum, *ball not hard! Ball fun! Bouncy! Woo!*

And then I try to sit up.

Ha.

"I think it's broken," I tell her.

With a wintry smile she replies, "Hmm. I'm waiting."

I grunt and strain and tighten and clench and . . . nothing happens. I don't even move a millimeter. I'm in the exact same position.

Mary-Kate tosses her hair and tilts her head to the side and tells me through narrowed lips, "Push it."

I muster all the strength I have and haul and heave and . . . nada.

Her voice drops an octave. "Are you even trying? I said *push it.*"

Huh. That almost sounded like she, like she . . . growled at me.

I try again.

I am wholly unsuccessful.

She clears her throat with a delicate little cough. "I said

---

[13] Bitch has yet to perspire and she's bundled in multiple layers of fleece. I, on the other hand, have stripped off so many items I'm down to sweaty granny panties.

push it. Now! Go! Go! Go! Do you want people to think you're
the girl who swallowed Jessica Simpson? No? Then do it, do it,
do it!!"

Her sudden personality turn terrifies me. Why, she's not
Mary-Kate, she's Sybil! And she's screaming her wee little
schizophrenic head off at me!

With all the fight and pride I have left in me, I strain and
pull until it feels like vomit is going to shoot out of every one
of my orifices. I bear down with all my might, clenching said
orifices closed in case I accidentally give birth to an eight-
pound rib roast. Finally, I manage to lift myself up for a mi-
crosecond before collapsing again. "I did it! I did it!" I hoot,
face shiny with the glow that only comes from conquering
true adversity.

"That's great," she replies. "But you're not getting up until you do it eleven more times."

The session dissolves in a blur of sweat and tears, although I end up blacking most of it out as a coping mecha-
nism. Through the scrim of perspiration and pain, I swear I
see her whip out a cat-o'-nine-tails and smack it against her
bare palm. Fearing the alternative, I struggle through the
litany of torture until she finally allows me to crawl back to my
car. When I arrive home, I'm so sore I can't even make it up
the stairs. Fletch finds me a short time later, clinging to a banister and muttering what I think sounds like, *"Michelle Tan-
ner hurted me."* He fireman-carries me up to the tub, where I
spend the rest of the day in a hot bath chewing ibuprofen and
slathering myself liberally with Bengay.[14] I swear to myself I

---

[14] I also cried for glasses of wine, but they were more recreational than medicinal.

will never, ever see that devil woman again. And for good measure, I won't even go near people named Ashley.

I awake today to pain in places I didn't know could hurt. My armpits ache and my butt feels like two clenched fists, which is nothing compared to all the stabbing in my legs and abs. I could prattle on about all the places that are sore but it's quicker to describe those parts that aren't throbbing: my fingers, eyelids, and teeth.

I settle on the couch for a day of TiVo and nursing my wounds when Mary Ann, my publicist, calls. She tells me yet *another* celebrity magazine has committed to a spread on me and the book. My celebration is short-lived as I quickly calculate the odds of my photo appearing beside Nicole Richie's in a tragically hilarious before-and-after manner. My vanity trumps my sloth, and I huff and cry my way back up the stairs to don my exercise clothes.

I'm whimpering my way through five miles on the treadmill when Mary-Kate strolls by.

"Hey, how are you doing today? Did I work you hard enough?" she asks, the hint of an evil glint in her big, lashy doe eyes.

"To properly reply to that question, I'd need to punch you. Unfortunately, I can't lift my arms."[15]

She laughs but I'm telling the truth. I didn't apply makeup and I threw on another do-rag rather than have to hold my incredibly heavy blow dryer and round brush. Then she poses

---

[15]Or, for that matter, lift my leg high enough to kick her in the ass.

the most difficult question I've ever been asked. "So, Jen, see you next week?"

My mental Rolodex spins though all the things I would rather do than spend one more second in this pint-sized sado-masochist's presence. I think of paper-covered tables and ice-cold stirrups . . . of arguing with deranged passengers on the number 56 bus . . . of Hair Cutterys and dull scissors . . . of seeing strangers' bungholes . . . and finally, of Jessica Simpson in Daisy Duke shorts *standing right next to me.*

I wipe the sweat from my forehead and wipe my hand on my shorts. And then I look this hateful woman straight in the eye and say, "I'll be there."

To: angie_at_home, carol_at_home, wendy_at_home,
jen_at_work
From: jen@jenlancaster.com
Subject: *just so we're clear*

Aarrggh.

Apparently listing "No pedophiles or stalkers" on the "Who I'd
Like to Meet" portion of my stupid, publicist-required MySpace
profile isn't enough. I think I need to amend it to include "No
fucking weirdos."

A couple of days ago I received the following e-mail:

"Would u consider having me be ur slave?"

Um . . . no.

Although, really? It's mainly because I loathe when people use
ridiculous text message abbreviations in an attempt to express
their thoughts. For example, why would you write "LOL" when
there are so many better ways to say "funny," e.g., amusing,
blithe, capricious, riotous, risible, waggish, whimsical, etc.? Personally, I want to know the kind of guy or gal who describes a
situation as "droll" or "gelastic." But those who opt for the
LOL? I kind of want to punch them in the jimmies.

However, the more I thought about it, the more I
reconsidered—maybe having some help around the house

would be nice. I've been meaning to spend additional quality time with my TiVo—I mean, Fletch—and perhaps an extra pair of hands could be helpful. There's always laundry to fold, and having a domestic would likely prevent him and me from arm wrestling over whose turn it was to take out the trash. Plus slave equals free in my book, so the price was certainly right. But I had to make sure we could keep our slave happy because I wouldn't want someone surly moping about the house, stomping off to his bedroom all the time while complaining about the litany of assigned chores. (FYI, this is also why we aren't having kids.)

So, I responded to the query with, *"I guess it depends. How do you feel about picking up rat poop and killing fire ants?"*

My potential slave politely declined.

Damn.

Today I received this little missive from a gentleman named John:

"What would you do to make me buy your book?"

I thought long and hard until I came up with the perfect response.

"Write well?"

To which he replied:

"No, I'm going to need to be convinced. Would you consider flashing me your tits? ;)"

Okay, seriously? I am old, fat, Republican, and quickly losing the battle with gravity. Believe me, he does *not* want a piece of this.

And what exactly about me leads someone to believe I've got a cache of nekkid photos I'm willing to share with the class? My penchant for pearls and the collected works of Ann Coulter? My love of knee-concealing capri pants? The fact that Mormons think I need to loosen the hell up already?

And even if I did have said boobie shots—*which I don't*—the last person I'd send them to was some weirdo who ended his request with a smiley face.

No.

No, no, no.

No freaking way.

Just so we're clear.

Jen

To: angie_at_home, carol_at_home, wendy_at_home, jen_at_work
From: jen@jenlancaster.com
Subject: *i suppose a salad would be far too pedestrian*

Ladies,

Brace yourselves.

For I have horrible news.

Fletch has taken it upon himself *to start cooking again.*

By using multiple burners and the oven, he raised the temperature in here from a manageable seventy-six to an unpleasant eighty-six last night. (We have central AC, but it's no match for hundred-degree temperatures *and* Fletch's cooking.)

So, what did he prepare that was worth ten degrees and a portion of my sanity?

BLT pasta.

Mmm-hmm, that's right.

Bacon, lettuce, and tomato pasta.

And what's better on a scorching day than a big bowl of hot lettuce and sweaty tomatoes coated in a thin sheen of bacon grease?

While discussing our dinner plans for tonight, he mentioned he might use the leftover lettuce to whip up some soup . . . which neatly answers the question whether there's anything *less* appealing than hot lettuce pasta on a sweltering summer day.

Send help.

Or pizza.

Jen

To: angie_at_home, carol_at_home, wendy_at_home, jen_at_work
From: jen@jenlancaster.com
Subject: *gladys kravitz rides again*

'S up, girls?

With my recent no-tree-left-behind pogrom, it's abundantly clear I'm a yard Nazi. Every year I treat my planting like I'm participating in the Sheffield Garden Walk. Gardening for me is less of a Zen activity and more of a way to thrash my neighbors in a competition they didn't know they'd entered.

That being said, there's no way anyone's yard will be up to my satisfaction. I know this. I accept this. This is my cross to bear. The fact the old, weird hippies next door refuse to do anything so patrician as fix their windows with glass instead of garbage bags or mow their "grass" is essentially none of my business. (BTW, I used to feel sorry for them because I thought they were poor. I've since learned they feed their dogs the $40/bag *vegan* kibble from Whole Foods. Shit, I can't afford *people* kibble at Whole Foods.) If they choose to be slovenly, it's their privilege to do so. And if I don't like it, I have a fence to hide their three-foot-tall weed patch.

However, when my hose sprays under their fence and the water causes the entire community of mice nesting in their unmown yard to *surge at me in a sea of wet gray fur,* I have a legitimate gripe.

(Yes, I did have to go upstairs and lie down after all the screaming.)

Once my voice recovered, I called the city and used as few four-letter words as possible under the circumstances to lodge a complaint. I calmly explained that if my dogs eat one of the rabid mice living so comfortably in the neighbors' overgrown backyard, we're going to have a real problem after I beat the old hippies with my shovel. The city said something about poisoning the alley again and having Streets and Sanitation talk to the folks next door, but they couldn't really force my neighbors to do anything, and if they actively chose to harbor mice, so be it.

And then I may or may not have started yelling and spouting shovel-wielding threats.

Anyway, you'd think that would have ended the issue.

Enter today.

I woke up really early and decided to get a running start on the day. After vacuuming, mopping, polishing, scrubbing, and washing any fabric that comes in contact with pets, it wasn't even eleven a.m. yet. So, I decided I'd prune my plants and give them a healthy dose of Miracle-Gro. The dogs hung out in the yard with me until they'd had their fill of hose water. After putting them inside so they could immediately start making things smell like wet dog again, I headed back down my stairs to hit my terra-cotta planters.

I was in the process of deadheading my geraniums when I saw a big gray butt skulk under the stairs. My first thought was, *Damn it, how did my cat Jordan get out here?* She's always trying to let herself out, and I'm always extra-vigilant about not letting her. I walked over to the stairs and called to her.

What came out the other side was not Jordan.

It was a rat *the size of* Jordan.

Instead of screaming myself hoarse like when the mice washed into the yard, I completely froze. The rat looked at me, took a bite of delicious ivy, chewed it, and looked at me again, as if to say, *"Yeah, you know what? Fuck you,"* before leisurely slipping through a hole in the fence the size of a quarter. (Apparently the dogs, hose, and I had been disturbing him.)

So, not only have our repeated attempts to poison and drown the rats been unsuccessful, they've found a way to feed on our weakness and have morphed into some super-breed with the strength of ten rats and the attitude of a fourteen-year-old boy.

So now I'm obsessing about my neighbors, their decayed and infested yard, and the damage I could inflict with said spade.

For now the war is *on*.

Like *Donkey Kong.*

(Shut up, it almost rhymes.)

Off to polish my shovel,

Jen

Dear Alderman,

Today I received your campaign literature asking me for my vote in your bid to become a District Congressman in the State of Illinois.

Here's why you won't receive it.

According to your own brochure, you're the person who "wrote and passed the City Council ordinance calling for an end to the war." The first time I heard about this, I thought it was an *Onion* headline or Leno monologue. This leads me to wonder—if Chicago can call for the end of a war, would the reverse be true? Could *we* also declare war? If so, we should totally go kick Saint Louis's ass just because they've been asking for it, sitting down there all smug for so long. We'll paint the Arch yellow and claim it in the name of McDonald's!

Seriously, though, whether or not I support the war is not the issue. (And actually, I admire the principle that drove you to make such a declaration.) However, the issue here is that I'd greatly prefer the City Council to concentrate on issues confined to, you know, *the actual city*. Once you guys resolve the problems we have with drugs, gangs, poverty, homelessness, and internal governmental corruption, then sure, feel free to branch out—you'll have earned that right. Until then, let's try to concentrate on Cook County, okey-dokey?

In regard to issues currently within your control, I've been calling your office for six months about getting a new city-issued garbage can. You've yet to resolve this. How exactly are you going to broker a lasting peace agreement in the Middle East like your brochure says when you can't even procure me another plastic receptacle? Also, you *are* going to have a war on your hands in your own district if the weird family next door shoots me one more dirty look. (I do thank you for responding to my four hundred requests to cut down the tree in their front yard, though. Now my living room is even sunnier!)

If you're as "tough on terror" as you are on the neighborhood rat situation, then we have a *big problem*. What started out as a "pack" of rats in my alley became a "hoard" and is now verging on "swarm." And I'm going to be one pissed-off resident if I catch bubonic plague in my own backyard.

Also, do you honestly believe including a photo of a SpaghettiO-covered baby with the caption *Who's going to clean up George Bush's mess?* to be the best way to persuade me about the horrors of war? If so, I urge you to fire your campaign manager, like, immediately. I have two words about effective campaign imagery for you, pal—"Daisy Girl." Please consult Lyndon B. Johnson's playbook if you're confused. You'll note his marked lack of SpaghettiOs usage. (You should probably avoid any "Hang in There, Kitty" imagery as well.)

Finally, can you please tell the rest of the aldermen to stop voting to ban pit bulls and foie gras within city limits? This is the kind of ridiculous shit that makes me want to pack up and live in a militia compound in the middle of Wyoming, which would suck because I'm sure there's no Trader Joe's or Target anywhere near there.

By the way, if I move, I'm leaving the rats here.

Best,

Jen Lancaster

P.S. You included a lot of photos of yourself in your brochure and all I can say is, a mustache *and* leather suspenders? No.

emember in the show *Bewitched*, Darrin was always having his boss, Mr. Tate, over for soirees and somehow each time the evening was ruined? Roasts were burned, drapes set on fire, and new clients accidentally turned into goats, each incident jeopardizing his job at McMahon and Tate. And even though it was never directly his wife Samantha's fault, Darrin always blamed her. I mean, she *was* a witch, and sometimes when you're a witch, witch-type stuff happens; it's unavoidable.

So, you'd think after shit continued to go down in the Stephens household, Darrin would instead decide to take everyone to a restaurant for dinner in order to avoid the unpleasantness. Or maybe he just wouldn't mix his business and personal life together, because if history taught him anything it was that the evening was going to break bad every freaking time and he'd spend the remaining twelve minutes trying to resolve the crisis before the credits rolled.

At some point Darrin should have, like, *learned* something, but he never did. So when you'd see him running around, totally losing his mind, you don't even empathize because you think, *You pomade-abusing ass-clapper—how did you not expect Uncle Arthur to show up in the ice bucket? Or Aunt Clara to tumble out of the fireplace?*

Come to think of it, many old sitcom wives messed stuff up for the head of the household. Lucy was always plotting ways to insert herself into the show, Lisa Douglas refused to acclimate to life on those vast green acres, and Jeannie lost her mind when Major Nelson gave her a credit card.

Given the fine examples blazed by the shows of yore, you'd *think* someone as smart as my husband, Fletcher, would have the good sense to never allow his boss to meet me.

Fortunately, Fletch realizes this.

Unfortunately, we're already on the way to his boss Paul's boat when he does.

"I don't get it," I say. "We're just hanging out on his boat? We're not going to go anywhere?" When we left our house, we waited on our corner for half an hour to hail a cab, but none passed us. Resigned, we waited another twenty minutes to board a bus to take to the Blue Line to take to a neighborhood where taxis are available.[1] Fletch suggested we just give up, but having already committed most of an hour, I said there was no way we were turning back. We're finally in a cab

---

[1] Although our neighborhood is safe, it's also not stylish, and is therefore ignored by the cab companies. I've already mentally composed twenty scathing letters to Mayor Daley about the situation.

on our way to Diversey Harbor when I begin to grill Fletch about boating specifics.

"Right. Paul had the boat out earlier, so it will just be docked now," Fletch replies.

"Then why are we going to his boat? Why don't we meet him in a bar or something?" I read that there's a Chicago phenomenon about its boaters simply hanging out on the docks all day, but it makes no sense to me. I mean, this is *Chicago*. People actually have outdoor space in their apartments and condos. You want to catch some air, go stand on the deck off your house, you know?

"Here—turn left down Cannon Drive, please," he instructs the driver, who pulls down the tree-lined street by the lake. "This is what we do on Fridays—after we take the boat out in the afternoon, we hang out on the dock in case any clients drop by."

"If anyone shows up do we start sailing?"

"Jen, it's a powerboat with three outboard motors. It's not called *sailing*, it's called *boating*. But, no, after getting in from the afternoon run Paul will have cocktails and then he stays docked."

"Didn't you tell me he lives in a huge house up by Wrigley Field? Why don't clients go there?"

"Because they like to be on the boat." Fletch pays the cabdriver and we grab the bags of ice we were tasked to bring. We walk down the path to the iron gate between the sidewalk and the docks and Fletch punches in the code to open it.

"Is the boat that great? I mean, are there bedrooms? Bathrooms? Is there a kitchen?"

"Jen, it's not a yacht, and you're using the wrong terms. There's a small galley and a head, but no separate stateroom."

"Pfft. If this thing isn't moving, it's pretty much a studio apartment in my book. By the way, how do I look?" I hold out my arms, modeling my boring preppy black cotton shorts and yellow polo shirt. I'd planned to show up dressed exactly like Danny Noonan, but (a) I couldn't find an ascot, and (b) wasn't sure anyone would get the *Caddyshack* reference.

Fletch stops and takes a long, hard look at me right before we get to his boss's slip. "Am I going to regret bringing you here?"

I kiss him on his freshly shaven cheek. "Would I ever intentionally embarrass you?"

"Intentionally? No." We arrive at Paul's boat and Fletch holds my arm and helps me in the boat. "We're here!" Paul is downstairs[2] and emerges to greet us. "Paul, please meet my wife, Jen. Jen, this is Paul." I'd planned on sucking up to his boss, telling him the boat was "yar," but since we're parked, I've no idea if the boat is trim, lively, or responsive because it's just floating in one spot. Basically, I know it's watertight and holds a lot of beer, so it may as well be a Coleman ice chest.[3]

"Hey, Paul. Nice boat, thanks for inviting me. Are we going out into the lake tonight?" I ask. I figure if I badger him, maybe I can change his mind.

"Nice to meet you, Jen." He shakes my hand. "Sorry, I've already had a couple of drinks, so we're going to stay docked."

I mull this over for a minute. Damn it, I did not just spend

---

[2] A.k.a. "belowdeck."
[3] Or Fletch, for that matter.

one and a half hours of my life in motion just to arrive here to sit still. "Oh, that's a shame. Hey, I've got an idea—next Friday, you should come over to our house and we can sit in my car in my garage."

He laughs and I bristle. I hate when people don't bite back, although judging from the beads of sweat that just appeared on Fletch's head, perhaps it's for the best.

We busy ourselves filling the ice chests conveniently located all over the back of the boat and crack open a few beers. After the initial awkwardness, our conversation begins to flow and I can see Fletch unclench. Paul turns up the stereo and we sit and talk, gently buffeted by the ripples in the water. The sensation is not wholly unpleasant, and I begin if not to understand the whole parked boat business then at least to appreciate it. The sky is bright blue and cloudless and I catch some rays before twilight comes.

A little while later, a couple of people wander down the long dock to join us. The guy, whose name I don't catch, is a potential client. The girl tells me her name, but as I've had four beers already, I promptly forget. These two are fresh from the Cubs game and have been drinking in the hot sun all day. We discuss the game[4] and exchange other pleasantries. They're both slurring, so conversation isn't as easy as it was before they arrived.

The darker it gets, the less these two talk to us and the more they talk to each other. With, um, their tongues. What had started out as an innocent kiss here and there has morphed

---

[4] Cubs win!

into a bit of a mash session. I find it terribly inappropriate and begin to slam drinks in response.

As a distraction, I ask about the boat's various features, so Paul points out the lights that change colors and flash in time to the music, the video display screen, and the boat's computerized navigation system. He gestures at the couple. "And right over there we've got the Maker Outer." We laugh uncomfortably.

Paul begins to busy himself behind the console steering panel, so I turn my back to the hot and heavy petting happening behind me, directing my attention solely on Fletch. They are getting louder and louder and I'm the kind of mortified only three more beers can assuage.[5]

I'm about to launch into an unsexy discussion about the city's smoking ban when I distinctly hear the guy part of the couple tell the girl, "I can't wait to kiss your boobies."[6]

Awkward!

Chug!

I wonder if I'm the only one disturbed by their display of affection when I notice that Paul's been quietly closing up the boat, even though it's hours before we'd all planned to leave. We stand—one of us rather unsteadily—so Paul can clip the coverings over our seats, and we help him police up the empty cans.

The couple detach themselves long enough to exit the boat. We're saying our good-byes when the girl says, "Hey, do you mind if we, um, just hang out here and finish our drinks?"

---

[5] What is it about boats that brings out the bad touch in everyone?
[6] Boobies. Arrgh. What is this, fourth grade?

Paul thinks about it for a moment. "Well, you're welcome to stay on the dock, but I absolutely can't have you on board the boat for liability reasons, okay?" He continues to talk in fine print about his insurance policy until they agree, and the three of us start down the long path to the gate.

I raise my eyebrows at Fletch—is he kidding? The boat is still wide open—they could reboard in five seconds. All we did was cover the seats and the electronics, and something tells me these two aren't going to need access to the boat's sonar for what they have in mind.[7]

As I stagger to the gate, I turn and look back through the wan dock lighting to see them watching us. Half in the bag and full of bravado, I tell Paul, "Better bring some paper towels for tomorrow."

"Why's that?" he asks.

"Because those two are about to have sex on your boat."

He stops in his tracks and grimaces. "No. No, no. They wouldn't do that. I specifically told them they couldn't get back on."

"Two bucks says you find evidence tomorrow that they totally did."

He begins to fidget with his wedding ring. "They aren't going to do anything."

"Please allow me to quote what I heard ten minutes ago. 'I can't wait to kiss your boobies.' Does that sound like a friendly drink on an exposed dock, or does it sound like you're going to need to be swabbing your deck tomorrow? Two bucks says you're swabbing."

---

[7] Depths may be plumbed, but not on the lake's floor.

"Not happening."

"Afraid you're going to lose? Are you a big chicken about losing?" I start clucking and notice Fletch is giving me the stink-eye. "What? Don't glare at me. *I'm* not the one about to have sex on Paul's boat."

"They aren't going to do it."

"Just 'cause you say it's not true doesn't make it not true."

"Unless it's actually not true."

"Bock, bock, bock." I flap my imaginary wings and bob my neck.

"They aren't getting on my boat because I told them not to. Besides, I think he's married and not to the girl who's with him."

Fletch begins to throw me all sorts of high signs.

"You mean to tell me you believe he'd have no problem violating his marriage vows to his wife and possibly his Lord, and yet would respect your request to not climb aboard? Riiiight." I laugh. "Ow, who kicked me?" Fletch's eyes are the size of saucers. "What's your problem?" I return my attention to Paul. "Seriously. You. Me. A black light like they use on *20/20* when they do a hotel exposé. Two dollars."

Paul's lips are set in a thin white line.

I start to tell him, "I'm right, you know I'm right, and you know I know you know I'm right, yet you refuse to admit it because you're afraid of losing two—" when I find myself being yanked into a cab by the back of my collar.

"Thanks for everything, see you Monday!" Fletch calls as we pull away.

"What, wait, where are we going?" I ask.

"Master thinks it's time for Jeannie to get back in her bottle."

A week later, we're on our way to the boat again.

Yeah, I can't believe I was asked back, either.

When Paul called earlier to invite us, I specifically asked Fletch if he was sure I was supposed to come. Fletch said yes, although this is likely only because we were actually taking the boat out and no one would be able to hear me over the roar of the three outboard engines. Also, if I brought up the two-dollar business, I would be summarily tossed overboard without a life jacket.

When we arrive at the boat, I turn down cocktails, opting instead for a soda. A few of Fletch's coworkers are there, too, and I'm surprised and pleased at Fletch's skill and grace when acting as first mate. He and Paul easily detach the boat from the dock and soon we're headed for the underpass that separates the harbor from the lake.

It is the perfect night to be out on the water. Paul says we have maybe ten days like this a year when the lake turns to glass. There's not a single wave except those we create.

I always thought I was someone who preferred the gentle choreography of sailing to the obvious power of a motor boat. But something strange happens when Paul opens up the engines. As someone with a lifelong fear of motion, I figured I'd be screaming and looking for a seat belt and helmet. But the faster we go, the more exhilarated I am. The wind in my hair is empowering, not terrifying, and the noise coming out of my mouth is laughter.

We head out a couple of miles and the evening is so clear I can see the city all the way south to Indiana and north to where the suburbs begin. The sunset reflects pink and gold off all the skyscrapers and the horizon is iridescent in the fading light. We roar down the coastline, following the path of Lake Shore Drive, taking in all the sights that make this city so spectacular—the Hancock Center, Buckingham Fountain, Navy Pier, the Sears Tower, the Shedd Aquarium, the Adler Planetarium, and the Field Museum, among others maybe not quite so famous, but still special and unique.

As we roar past, I fall in love with my city all over again. Yes, it's crowded and expensive and full of people who annoy me, but at this shining moment, I've never seen anything more gorgeous. I realize Chicago's a great city not because it's glamorous, but because it's real. It's full of places where you can be fat and over thirty and still be allowed inside the velvet ropes. People come from all over the world to live here, and each of them fits right in without missing a step. The beauty of this city is not that it's *ex*clusive, but that it's *in*clusive. And I finally get that when Carl Sandburg calls Chicago the "hog butcher to the world," it's meant as a tribute, not a criticism.

We're out on the water for hours but it's such sensory overload that I don't even realize it's after ten p.m. when we pull back into the slip. I've been a perfectly behaved girl all night and Fletch's boss has finally let his guard down around me again.

As we exit and softly say our good-byes, I realize with the quiet and the audience, now's the perfect opportunity to shake Paul down for my two dollars.

But I don't.

Because I'm not always a big ass.

Dear Carrie Bradshaw,

To grasp the enormity of what I'm going to tell you, I've got to give you the background. Were you to come into my office right now, you'd see a garbage can overflowing with candy wrappers and Pringles tubes. I haven't been to the gym in a month and am but a Mars Bar away from Muumuu City, all because I've been too involved with writing another book.

My roots are an inch long, my manicure is completely trashed from digging in my garden, and my arms are raked with fresh claw marks from where one of my cats dug in for traction when the alarm clock scared him.

My left side is bruised because I slipped and fell at the grocery store since I'm the kind of dumbass who forgets you shouldn't wear slick flip-flops when it rains, no matter how nicely the plaid ties your pants and shirt together. (My Keebler Mint Crème cookies and pint of heavy cream survived the fall nicely, thank you.)

For the pièce de résistance, I had a small bump at the top of my cheekbone and I couldn't leave it alone. A little poke here, a little prod there, lather, rinse, repeat to the point that I've not only gouged a hole in my face, but have also given myself a black eye.

In short, I look like I just stepped off the set of *Fat Girl Fight Club*.

So naturally I heard from British *Cosmopolitan* today, wanting to set up a photo shoot to get a picture of me to go along with the article they commissioned from me last month.

When?

The very next day, of course.

The end result is almost exactly what happened to your character in the "They Shoot Single People, Don't They?" episode of *Sex and the City*—looking my very worst in the one place I really wanted to be pretty.

Touché, Miss Bradshaw.

You win this round.

Best,

Jen Lancaster

Acknowledgments

I'd like to acknowledge my husband, Fletch, for allowing me to make our private lives public and also for saying the kind of hilarious stuff I immediately claim as my own. I love you so much that I promise to eat whatever you cook next without complaint . . . or at least with slightly less bitching and moaning.

Many thanks go out to my lovely agent and friend, Kate Garrick, as she continues to make the impossible anything but. Without you I'd be trapped in a boardroom somewhere, listening to a jackass prattle on about mission statements. In short? You (and the rest of DeFiore) rock.

More thanks go out to Kara Cesare at NAL, who would totally win the Best Editor pageant for making me feel like I'm the only author in the world, never hesitating to discuss even the most inane of my concerns. Thanks for always getting it; you're the best!

For Mary Ann Zissimos of Penguin: YES, YOU WERE TOTALLY RIGHT. See? There it is in big letters, to live on in the Library of Congress for eternity. I can never thank you enough for your hard work. (FYI, you've ruined me for every other publicist.)

For the rest of the folks at Penguin, sincere thanks and much admiration to Kara Welsh for everything, the art department for the second phenomenal cover in a row, the sales team (I so owe each of you drinks), Lindsay Nouis (and Nindsay Louis, of course), and everyone else who worked so hard to make this a reality.

I must say a special thanks for the support of the booksellers, particularly Barnes & Noble and Borders, for taking a chance on a foulmouthed polar-bear-pajama-wearing nobody. I pledge to devote the rest of my life to forcing your café campers into actually buying books and snacks. (It's not an ad hoc library, damn it!)

Much love to my family and pets for endless hours of amusement (and material), and big thanks to MySpacers Benjamin Kissell, Don Purvis, Sean Faulk, and author Nicole Del Sesto for their invaluable feedback, to Patrick Dester for the subtitle that made me snort coffee, and to Linnea Beasley for, well, everything. It's simply not a party without you.

For Stacey Ballis, Jolene Siana, Martha Kimes, Caprice Crane, Jennifer Weiner, Lori Jakiela, Allison Winn Scotch, Jennifer Coburn, Robert Rave, Karyn Bosnak, Melanie Lynn Hauser, the city of Chicago, and all my neighbors—thanks for inspiring me on a daily basis.

Finally, a million thanks to all the fans out there! I may not be great about returning e-mail, but I promise I pore over every word you're kind enough to share with me. For each of